CULT SHOCK

Praise for
CULT SHOCK

"*Cult Shock* is a great apologetic resource to give you the confidence and knowledge to answer many cults with truth and logic."

—**Josh D. McDowell**, bestselling author/speaker

"This book shows where Christian apologetics hits the road. The authors deploy provocative and interesting arguments to engage those who come from alien—sometimes outlandish—theological frameworks. The result is a readable, educational book that is a valuable addition to every Christian's apologetics toolkit."

—**Dinesh D'Souza**, filmmaker, author, *What's So Great about Christianity*

"This father-son team provides a fresh, practical approach for sharing the good news and pointing people to the Light. Common objections to key Christian beliefs and how to respond with grace and truth are highlighted. The suggested conversations based on real-life encounters make this a must-read for those who have a passion for proclaiming the real Jesus."

—**Dr. Gary C. Woods**, EdD, Alliant International University,
Postgraduate Studies, Southern California Seminary;
MDiv, Southwestern Baptist Theological Seminary;
BS, Liberty University; Professor, Southern California Seminary

"Practical, not theoretical. Profoundly simple and yet deep. The attention to biblical detail is to be applauded and appreciated. In a day and age when many are forsaking truth for lies, this is well written for the believer's personal benefit as well as training for apologetics. This book gets a 10 out of 10!"

—**Mike Reed**, Senior Pastor, Calvary Chapel Oceanside

"I highly recommend *Cult Shock* as a resource for those who desire to be a better witness for Jesus. This book is a great tool in helping Christians defend and proclaim the Christian faith to those who have been misled."

—**Miles McPherson**, Head Pastor, Rock Church, San Diego,
author, *Do Something! Make Your Life Count and God
in the Mirror: Discovering Who You Were Created to Be*

"The Stenglers offer clear and concise points to address in love, particularly with Jehovah's Witnesses and Mormons. Their proof provides inspiration to dig deeper in understanding the claims of these and other false religions, to continue to grow in knowledge and faith in the truth of God's Word, and to live out Christ in confidence and boldness."

—**Jim Doyle**, Associate Pastor, North Coast Calvary Chapel, Carlsbad, California, author, *Study Guides for Books of the Bible*

"The Stenglers have done the body of Christ a great service in putting out this unique work that will effectively equip Christians in defending the faith and reaching those trapped in the cults of Mormonism and Jehovah's Witnesses. These cults are tenacious in their efforts to pull Christians into their false belief systems, and most believers are unable to respond reasonably, biblically, and theologically. *Cult Shock* is unique in that it not only provides biblical and theological answers to the cults' attack on core Christian doctrines, but it also gives practical ways of answering them. The book accomplishes this through providing witnessing techniques and possible scenarios of conversations a Christian would have with members of these cults. These sections of the book will serve to build the confidence in the average Christian when having to answer the lies, whether it's on their front doorstep or coming out of a grocery store. As a pastor, I love that *Cult Shock* is highly accessible to the wider body of Christians rather than being limited to only scholars and those well versed in the Scriptures. This book will also solidify some of the Christians' most important beliefs in understandable ways and all with a solid foundation in the Bible. I highly recommend this book to all those who profess to be followers of Jesus Christ."

—**Walter Colace**, Senior Pastor, Christ Community Church, El Centro, California

"In dealing with members of the Jehovah's Witnesses or Mormon faith, so often Christians find themselves not only unable to defend their faith but also unable to expose the falsehoods of these two religions. This book is a strong resource to help Christians be encouraged in their faith and to challenge those who believe these false doctrines. I highly recommend *Cult Shock*."

—**David Hoffman**, Senior Pastor, Foothills Christian Church, El Cajon, California

"Have you ever been at a loss for words when confronted by Mormons or Jehovah's Witnesses at your door? If so, *Cult Shock* is the book you need. It will expose the cultists' erroneous beliefs and give you the answers you need to lead them to the truth with confidence and competence. It will enable you to 'speak the truth in love' as you guide them to Him Who is the Truth."

—**Dr. George W. Hare**, DMin, Chancellor Emeritus,
Southern California Seminary

"With regard to the allure and snare of the cults, to be forewarned is to be forearmed. What are their distinguishing marks, recruiting techniques? And is there a rescue strategy? Jesus referred to cult leaders as 'wolves in sheep's clothing.' Mark Stengler Jr. and his dad do not want us to be shocked or unaware of their schemes. Engaging in meaningful dialogue with two of the most influential cults, the Mormons and Jehovah's Witnesses, they assess their truth claims to expose their deviations from biblical faith. Importantly, they examine the doctrines of the trinity and deity of Christ that reveal how these antichrists with 'another Gospel' deceive and devour naïve sheep. The best antidote for heresy is sound doctrine, which you will find in this useful book."

—**Dr. Chris Gnanakan**, DMin, PhD, DD,
Professor of Theology, Apologetics, and Global Studies,
Liberty University; Executive Director, Outreach to Asia Nations

"God bless the Stenglers for their love of the lost, their faithfulness to scripture, and their desire to equip the Church with this great resource."

—**Ray Comfort**, bestselling author; CEO of Living Waters Ministry

CULT SHOCK

THE BOOK JEHOVAH'S WITNESSES & MORMONS
DON'T WANT YOU TO READ

MARK STENGLER JR.
MARK STENGLER SR.

NASHVILLE

NEW YORK • MELBOURNE • VANCOUVER

CULT SHOCK
THE BOOK JEHOVAH'S WITNESSES &
MORMONS DON'T WANT YOU TO READ

© 2017 **MARK STENGLER JR. & MARK STENGLER SR.**

Published in New York, New York, by Morgan James Publishing. Morgan James is a trademark of Morgan James, LLC. www.MorganJamesPublishing.com

The Morgan James Speakers Group can bring authors to your live event. For more information or to book an event visit The Morgan James Speakers Group at www.TheMorganJamesSpeakersGroup.com.

Unless otherwise noted, Scripture quotations are from the New King James Version (NKJV). Copyright 1979, 1980, 1982 Thomas Nelson, Inc.

ISBN 978-1-68350-484-9 paperback
ISBN 978-1-68350-485-6 eBook
Library of Congress Control Number: 2017904968

Cover Design: Chris Thompson

In an effort to support local communities, raise awareness and funds, Morgan James Publishing donates a percentage of all book sales for the life of each book to Habitat for Humanity Peninsula and Greater Williamsburg.

Get involved today! Visit
www.MorganJamesBuilds.com

TABLE OF CONTENTS

DEFEND AND PROCLAIM THE TRUTH

Bible-believing Christians need to step up and provide reasons for the faith and hope that lie within us. We must illuminate the truth to fight against the heresy of cultural Christianity, false doctrines, and erroneous worldviews.

God has given us His Spirit so that we do not have to be fearful but rather trust in Him and His Word.

Let us unite together to share the joy and truth of our Lord and God Jesus Christ. We pray this book is helpful in your effective witness and evangelism to help others.

—**Mark Stengler Jr.**, Liberty University, Biblical Studies student, president of Please Tell Me the Truth Ministries

—**Dr. Mark Stengler**, naturopathic medical doctor, author, Master of Religious Studies, Southern California Seminary

www.pleasetellmethetruth.org

ACKNOWLEDGMENTS

I would like to thank the Triune God of Scripture for saving me and for the opportunity to spread His truth. I would also like to acknowledge my family, friends, and teachers who have supported me along the way.

—**Mark Stengler Jr.**

I would like to acknowledge all the dedicated evangelists, theologians, pastors, and apologists that defend and proclaim the one, true God.

—**Mark Stengler Sr.**

CHAPTER 1
THE REAL JESUS MATTERS

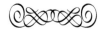

You've surely encountered this situation before: a knock rattles your door, and two or more people greet you with a smile and introduce themselves as Jehovah's Witnesses or as elders from the Church of Jesus Christ of Latter-day Saints, also called Mormons. What's your first thought? Take a second to really think about it. Are you indifferent or annoyed at the nuisance? Are you afraid?

Maybe you're just insecure because you don't know how to share your own faith, yet these people who are so misled have the gumption to peddle their "wisdom" on your doorstep. They have been deceived and are deceiving others. Do you know how to tell them the truth?

After reading this book, you will be prepared to give an answer with the hope that is within you and refute false doctrine *(1 Pet. 3:15)*. This knock on your door is actually a gift! It's your opportunity to proclaim the real Jesus and way of salvation so that these people may be set free from their bondage.

The number one question you should ask when it comes to different religions and cults is this: what is the truth? In our society, postmodernists claim there is no *real* truth, and relativists say truth is determined by culture. However, biblically speaking, truth is whatever conforms to the mind of God as revealed in Scripture.

And with that in mind, Jehovah's Witnesses, Mormons, and other religions have fabricated their own doctrine, and it does not match up with God's Word. Many have distorted who Jesus really is—and, consequently, do not have the truth residing in them (*John 14:6*).

Although everyone is entitled to their own opinions, everyone is not entitled to their own facts. But how do we know which group teaches the real Jesus? Truth is with the group that teaches the Jesus who is found in God's Word—the Bible. Jesus is the eternal second person of the Triune Godhead who has been preached by all orthodox Christians throughout history.

WHAT IS A CULT?

The term "cult" has different meanings. In terms of Christian theology, it refers to any group that denies or deviates from the biblical and orthodox teachings of historic Christianity and essential Christian doctrine.

In their *Handbook of Today's Religions*, Josh McDowell and Don Stewart argue that religious cults are growing because they seem to offer some answers to man's basic questions of existence, such as "Who am I? Why am I here? Where am I going?"[1] This kind of identity crisis creates emotional problems that make certain people particularly susceptible to cults. McDowell and Stewart write, "During such difficult moments, many cults give the unsuspecting a feeling of acceptance and direction."[2]

As well, they state, "Most cults tell their followers what to believe, how to behave, and what to think, and emphasize dependence upon the group or leader for their emotional stability."[3] But while the cults *seem* to offer solutions that are ready made, the *Handbook* says they're ultimately unsatisfying. We agree with

---

[1] Josh McDowell and Don Stewart, *Handbook of Today's Religions* (Nashville: Thomas Nelson, 1983), 17-18.

[2] Ibid.

[3] Ibid.

this because their answers do not align with what the Bible says and, therefore, they cannot receive abundant life from the true Jesus *(John 10:10)*.

This book focuses on two main religious organizations that have fabricated a faulty theology: Jehovah's Witnesses and Latter-day Saints. Each of these groups has its own view of Jesus that is not based on the inerrant Word of God—or on history. This book may also prove to be insightful for postmodernists, including cultural Christians who don't have a saving faith in Jesus Christ.

Many people believe Jesus was a good man and a great teacher but not divine. They view Jesus as a man of great virtue—no different than how they view the leaders in other religions. They also believe that multiple ways exist to attain salvation. In other words, you can travel multiple paths to reach the divine. However, the Bible *repeatedly* states there is only *one, true God*. Anyone or anything else worshipped is a false god.

Jesus states quite plainly in John 8:24 that to reject Him as God means eternal separation from Him forever. So much for the nonbeliever's argument that Jesus was *just* a good man or great teacher!

Additionally, Jehovah's Witnesses and Latter-day Saints commit two egregious errors in respect to the person and nature of Christ: they both claim that He is a god but not the one, true God. This is an obvious theological error. Anyone with even a *basic* understanding of Christianity could tell you the Bible teaches there is one God *(Isa. 44:6; James 2:19)*. For two thousand years, essential Christian doctrine has maintained that Jesus is the Eternal God who is the second person of the Trinity. He is uncreated and worthy of worship.

But the cults have committed a glaring philosophical error too. It boils down to this: if there is only one, true God, then any other god is a false god.

Just like the average nonbeliever, the Jehovah's Witnesses and Latter-day Saints have rejected the truth of biblical Christianity. At first, they'll tell you they are "Christians" and believe in the Bible as God's Word. But if you go deeper into their theological understanding and practices, you will quickly find that Jehovah's Witnesses and Mormons preach a *different* gospel. The doctrine they believe in contradicts the Word of God and the person of Jesus Christ. Thus, according to Galatians 1:8, they will be accursed if they do not repent.

Fortunately, God desires everyone to be saved and to know the truth (*1 Tim. 2:4*), so there's still hope for them. God has given Christians the task of proclaiming His Word to the lost. We are ambassadors of the Lord Jesus (*2 Cor. 5:20*), so we should jump at the opportunity to proclaim His truth to the cults.

We would ask any of those who adhere to these religious systems to examine our research and determine if it is true. But for those who are followers of God the Son, this book will teach you how to share who the real Jesus is and the way to salvation.

The goal of this book is to provide readers with a defense (apologetic) of the historic, Bible-based Christian faith as well as proactive tactics to evangelize to misled groups. It will also give reasonable and logical answers to commonly asked questions the cults raise about the Triune God and Christianity.

Additionally, *Cult Shock* is unique in that it contains Christian polemics. That is, the ability to argue against the beliefs and false claims of Jehovah's Witnesses and Mormons. It involves pointing out doctrinal errors and challenging their false belief systems. We see this concept in 2 Corinthians 10:3-5: "For though we walk in the flesh, we do not war according to the flesh. For the weapons of our warfare are not carnal but mighty in God for pulling down strongholds, casting down arguments and every high thing that exalts itself against the knowledge of God, bringing every thought into captivity to the obedience of Christ." Certainly, we find many examples of Jesus and the apostles Peter, John, and Paul using polemics. We too should incorporate polemics into our evangelistic endeavors.

To equip the believer to proclaim the real Jesus, we first provide a summary of the history and beliefs of the Jehovah's Witnesses and Mormons using primary sources. Next, we present a powerful chapter 4, titled "Is Jesus Really God?" The core issue that comes up with these groups revolves around the person of Jesus Christ. In reading the chapter, you'll learn how to demonstrate Jesus is God— even with the Bible translation that Jehovah's Witnesses use and despite the extra biblical literature used by the Mormons.

We have also written an excellent chapter on the Trinity, which the cults have grossly misconstrued and misunderstood. We'll help you correctly understand this important doctrine and show you how to explain it.

Throughout the book, you'll find tips on how to engage with the Jehovah's Witnesses or Mormons. First of all, to help you better understand them, we'll review their history and key doctrines; and in chapter 8, to help you evangelize effectively, we've provided examples of witness encounters based on real-life experiences. The last chapter deals with the importance of God's Word as the final authority on what is the truth.

Remember, false doctrines are dangerous. Jesus and his disciples repeatedly warn throughout Scripture of the eternal consequences of rejecting true doctrine and adhering to bogus teachings. The Bible has numerous verses warning about false teaching and its disastrous effect on those misled by it.

God commands us to tear down these falsehoods so the truth of God and His Word can shine. We are to defend God's Word with patience and truth. Jude 1:3 tells us "to contend earnestly for the faith which was once for all delivered to the saints." King David tells us in Psalm 119 that we must follow the Word of God, because it is true.

The Bible encourages its readers to test religious teaching and claims. The Apostle Paul urged the church at Thessalonica to test prophecies while clinging to the good and rejecting evil. Christians must take on the mentality of the Bereans *(Acts 17:11)* whenever one claims to be a teacher of the Word to decipher whether the truth is being proclaimed or not.

In his letter to the Corinthians, Paul warned about believing in something more than the Lord Jesus:

> But I fear, lest somehow, as the serpent deceived Eve by his craftiness, so your minds may be corrupted from the simplicity that is in Christ. For if he who comes preaches another Jesus whom we have not preached, or *if* you receive a different spirit which you have not received, or a different gospel which you have not accepted—you may well put up with it! *(2 Cor. 11:3-5)*

You may be feeling unconcerned or apathetic toward those who don't know the real Jesus and, therefore, will not receive abundant and eternal life. But we ask you to consider the following scenario:

Let's say you and three friends are trapped in a burning building with a choice of ten doors. No one knows where to go until a firefighter, who has assessed the situation, bursts through one of the doors and yells, "Quickly, come through this door! It is the only way to safety. All the others lead to other rooms on fire!"

You tell your friends to go with you to the fireman's door, but some of them just shrug and say, "I don't believe that fireman. I'm going to go to a different one." As your friends proceed to open the door leading to flames, you idly watch as their foolishness causes them to perish.

If you truly love your friends, you would *beg* them to turn to the only door that leads to safety. Similarly, Jesus is the only door to salvation. In John 10:9, Jesus states, "I am the door. If anyone enters by Me, he will be saved." This is true whether anyone believes it or not.

Therefore, the Jehovah's Witnesses, Latter-day Saints, and others who don't repent and put their faith in the real Jesus will be in serious trouble when Judgment Day comes. Do you care enough about these people to let them know they have been deceived by their respective organizations? Are you concerned for the people they mislead?

From the outset, you should understand that we are not attacking the members of these religious organizations personally. Instead, we are focused on the organizations and false teachers that have misled them and others. We care deeply about these people. Many of them are sincere and committed to their religion. But to reach them, we believe you must show them the truth and pray that the Holy Spirit will convict them. It is our desire that the unbeliever will develop a relationship with the Triune God of Scripture so he can be set free from the bondage of sin and death.

Note: For the rest of the book, we will mainly use the abbreviation JWs for Jehovah's Witnesses and LDS for Mormons.

CHAPTER 2
JEHOVAH'S WITNESSES' BELIEFS

From the outside looking in, Jehovah's Witnesses seem like just another Christian denomination. They'll tell you they believe in Jesus and in one God, whose personal name is Jehovah. They believe the Bible is the Word of God and is to be taken seriously. But there's more to the JWs than what they proclaim about themselves.

The organization was founded by Charles Taze Russell (1852-1916) in the nineteenth century. Cult expert Ron Rhodes writes in *The Challenge of the Cults and New Religions* that Russell was brought up in the Presbyterian church but later abandoned it because of its teachings on predestination and eternal punishment.

He became a Bible skeptic at age seventeen and studied other world religions. When he became acquainted with the Adventists, he took great interest in their prophetic "end times" views as well as in their teaching on annihilation (soul destruction) of the unbeliever instead of eternal separation from God (hell). Russell joined a Bible study in which he and his friends formulated theologies that rejected the Trinity and eternal punishment for the unbeliever. Additionally, they felt that eternal life was not a free gift, but rather something to be attained.

Adventist preacher Nelson H. Barbour heavily influenced Russell. Barbour convinced the twenty-three-year-old Russell that Christ had been invisibly present since 1874 and would fully establish His Kingdom on earth by the year 1914.[4] To spread the news of Christ's return in 1914, Russell published several writings on the subject. After that year had passed, it became clear that Russell's heretical prophecy had failed.

After Russell died in 1916, however, his legacy did not die with him. In fact, he left it to selected officials; and Joseph Rutherford, a lawyer who'd represented him in legal cases, took over the organization. Rutherford also abhorred the idea of hell, which is why JWs still believe in annihilationism and no eternal punishment for the unbeliever.[5]

The JWs have a worldwide governing body that, for most of their history, operated at their world headquarters in Brooklyn, New York. Recently, however, the Watch Tower moved to a new facility in Warwick, New York,[6] where it oversees the production and distribution of evangelistic materials and their one hundred thousand congregations worldwide.

The organization publishes two magazines in more than two hundred languages. The first is *The Watchtower*, which deals with world events and Bible prophecies. The second is *Awake!*, which provides recommendations for coping with everyday problems and tells of God's promise of a peaceful and secure new earth in the future. *The Watchtower* is the world's most circulated magazine with

---

4   Thomas Daniels, "Historical Idealism and Jehovah's Witnesses. A Critical Analysis of How They Resent Their History," accessed July 4, 2016, https://archive.org/stream/HistoricalIdealismAndJehovahsWitnesses/Historical_Idealism_and_Jehovahs_Witnesses#page/n0/mode/2up.

5   Ron Rhodes, *The Challenge of the Cults and New Religions* (Grand Rapids, MI: Zondervan, 2011), 78-81.

6   JW.org, "An Organization on the Move," accessed April 28, 2016, https://www.jw.org/en/publications/books/2014-yearbook/highlights/governing-body-news-world-headquarters-warwick/.

a monthly circulation of 45 million copies. *Awake* is the second most read at around 43.5 million.[7]

According to the organization, "True Christians serve as Jehovah's witnesses."[8] JWs claim their organization is like that of the early apostles and that their governing body has been the center of God's rule on earth (aka "theocracy").[9] Yet there is no historical record of early Christianity having a central organization controlling individual churches, literature distribution, or sermons.

Although JWs use the Bible, it is a corrupted version called the New World Translation (NWT). Their "New Testament" was first published in 1950, and subsequent versions have been produced since, including the most recent in 2013. [10] We know of no seminary, university with theological studies, Protestant or Catholic church, or any non-JW religious organization that uses this version. It is not accepted as a credible translation.

The late Dr. Bruce Metzger, professor emeritus of New Testament Language and Literature at Princeton Theological Seminary wrote, "The Jehovah's Witnesses have incorporated in their translation of the New Testament several quite erroneous renderings of the Greek."[11] Another leading Greek scholar, Dr. Julius Mantey, stated, "I have never read any New Testament so badly translated as the Kingdom Interlinear Translation of the Greek Scriptures."

Interestingly, the Watch Tower will not divulge who the translators of the NWT are. During testimony under oath, former vice president F.W. Franz "revealed that translations and interpretations came from God in such a way that they were invisibly communicated to the publicity department via 'angels of various ranks who control witnesses.'"[12]

7   Trendingtopmost.com, "Top 10 Most Read Magazines in The World," accessed March 12, 2017, http://www.trendingtopmost.com/worlds-popular-list-top-10/2017-2018-2019-2020-2021/entertainment/most-read-magazines-world-best-selling-famous-newspapers-cheapest-expensive/.

8   JW.org ,"Why Does God Have an Organization?," accessed April 4, 2016, https://www.jw.org/en/publications/books/good-news-from-god/jehovahs-witnesses-organization/.

9   The Watchtower, *Shepherds and Sheep in a Theocracy* (Brooklyn: Watch Tower Bible and Tract Society of New York, 1994), 16-17.

10   Avoidjw.org, "Bibles," accessed March 16, 2017, http://avoidjw.org/bibles/.

11   John Ankerberg and John Weldon. *Fast Facts on Jehovah's Witnesses* (Eugene, OR: Harvest House, 2003), 82.

12   Ibid, 78.

To say the NWT is controversial would be an understatement. It can be easily demonstrated that many verses referring to Jesus as Jehovah or God have been altered to suit Watch Tower theology. These will be pointed out in this book. Christian theologian Anthony Hoekema noted, about the NWT, that "[It] is by no means an objective rendering of the sacred text into modern English, but is a biased translation in which many of the peculiar teachings of the Watchtower Society are smuggled into the text of the Bible itself."[13]

A heavily promoted booklet produced by the Watch Tower called *What Does the Bible Really Teach?* claims that its version of the Bible is "historically accurate and reliable."[14] Yet the same book contradicts itself by also claiming that the personal name of God (supposedly "Jehovah") was removed from the Bible in ancient times.[15]

EVANGELISM TECHNIQUES

Similar to the LDS, JWs are known for their door-to-door evangelism. Although in recent times they have taken an additional strategy of setting up small JW carts that promote their website and offer free literature. Their key strategy is to have non-JWs take literature published by the Watch Tower. People are encouraged to read their literature and schedule a return visit. In addition, current world events are discussed to peak interest in their spiritual path.

JWs take the production and distribution of their magazines and Bibles very seriously. The Watch Tower claims that in 2012 they produced more than 1.3 billion magazines and eighty million books and Bibles.[16] The goal of the JWs is to have weekly home "Bible studies" with the interested party. These studies focus more on Watch Tower publications that promote JW theology than an actual Bible study.

JW publications promote non-orthodox views on the nature of God and the plan of salvation. They proclaim a different Jesus and attack the doctrine of

---

13   James P. Eckman, *The Truth about Worldviews: A Biblical Understanding of Worldview Alternatives* (Wheaton, IL: Crossway Books, 2004, 2016), 97.

14   Watch Tower and Tract Society of New York, Inc., *What Does the Bible Really Teach?* (Brooklyn: Watch Tower Bible and Tract Society of New York, 2005), 20.

15   Ibid., 195-197.

16   JW.org, "An Organization on the Move," accessed March 5, 2017, https://www.jw.org/en/jehovahs-witnesses/activities/publishing/global-printing/.

the Trinity and the credibility of mainstream churches. Also, *Awake* magazines, which discuss current world topics or social problems, are often given out as reading materials.

After an unbeliever attends the Bible studies, the next step is to have him attend a local congregation on a regular basis and be under the supervision of an elder. A convert is then expected to learn JW doctrine and become an active proselytizer for the Watchtower Society.

CHRISTIANS OR PUBLISHERS?

All of Jehovah's Witnesses are known as publishers. Publishers spend seventy hours each month in preaching work as regular pioneers. Those who devote one hundred thirty hours or more to ministry each month are known as special pioneers. Those who cannot pioneer full time serve as auxiliary pioneers.[17]

Congregations of Jehovah's Witnesses are based on geographical area of language spoken. They meet for religious services and studies at buildings known as Kingdom Halls. Members are required to report their proselytizing activity (including books and magazines distributed) during the month, which is reviewed by elders of their congregation. Each congregation then sends the final numbers to the Watchtower. Failure to submit one's reports can result in an investigation by elders and sanctioning. Critics charge this is as a component of cultic control by the Watchtower.

JEHOVAH *CANNOT* BE GOD'S PERSONAL NAME

As mentioned earlier, the Watch Tower booklet called *What Does the Bible Really Teach?* asserts the *New World Translation* is "historically accurate and reliable."[18] However, this is contradictory since they also claim the Bible has been corrupted because the name of God (Jehovah) was removed from the Old and New Testament in the past.[19]

---

17   JW.org, "What is a Pioneer," accessed March 12, 2017, https://www.jw.org/en/
      publications/books/jehovahs-will/jw-pioneer/.
18   Watch Tower and Tract Society of New York, Inc., *What Does the Bible Really Teach?*
      (Brooklyn: Watch Tower Bible and Tract Society of New York, 2005), 20.
19   Ibid., 195-197.

A foundational JW belief is that the personal and true name of God is Jehovah. For this reason, they call themselves Jehovah's Witnesses rather than Christians. They will use their NWT Bible and quote Old Testament (OT) verses (which were written for the Israelites) such as Exodus 3:15 to try and justify this to you.

So, are they correct? If the personal and true name of God is not Jehovah, then the JWs would lose one of their foundational beliefs. Consequently, they vigorously defend this belief. The truth is that it is impossible for Jehovah to be God's personal name. Why? The simple answer is this: "Jehovah" is a manmade term. Let us explain.

The Old Testament contains four consonants for the name of God. This is known as the "Tetragrammaton." The English equivalent is spelled "YHWH." Today, scholars believe the correct Hebrew form is Yahweh, pronounced in the English as Jahveh.[20] The most widely accepted meaning of the name is "the one who is, that is, the absolute and unchangeable one"[21] or "the one who brings things to pass, causes things to happen."[22]

The Jews regarded the name of God as so holy they were reluctant to pronounce it. Instead, they said "Adonai" (Lord) when reading the name of YHWH. This is seen in the Septuagint, the Greek translation of the Hebrew Scriptures by Jewish scribes in the third to second centuries BC, where the Greek word *kurios*, "lord," was substituted for the name Yahweh.[23]

According to the *Baker Encyclopedia of the Bible*, Jewish scholars, known as the Masoretes, took great care with Scripture:

[Masoretes] sought not only to determine the exact text handed down to them but to pass it on to future generations without change. To protect against copyists' errors and alterations, they filled the side margins with all sorts of data concerning how often and where various words and

---

20   Michael L. Brown, "Is Jehovah God's True Name," accessed March 5, 2017 at https://askdrbrown.org/library/jehovah-gods-true-name.

21   Walter A. Elwell and Barry J. Beitzel, *Baker Encyclopedia of the Bible* (Grand Rapids, MI: Baker Book House, 1988; published in electronic form by Logos Research Systems, 2016).

22   Brown.

23   Ibid.

phrases appearing in a given line of the text could be found elsewhere. The special contribution of the Masoretes was to provide the text with vowels and accent marks.[24]

These scribes were extremely careful about how they determined the "exact text" of God's Word, and they copied it "without change." Therefore, we have a clear understanding of how God's name should not be pronounced, namely it should not be pronounced Jehovah. Following the Jewish custom of not pronouncing the divine name, most Bible versions use the term "LORD" (to distinguish this from the Hebrew noun "Lord/lord"), while some will use the name "Yahweh."

In short, the term "Jehovah" is an anglicized version of the word "Yehowah," which is a result of the Masoretes adding vowels of the word "Adonai" to the tetragrammaton,[25] forming the term "Jehovah" or "Yahweh."[26]

Dr. Michael Brown, who holds a PhD in Near Eastern Languages and Literatures, writes about very important facts in regards to the name Jehovah. He notes the name is based on a mistaken reading of the biblical text by medieval Christian scholars. Although these scholars were educated in the Hebrew language, they were not aware of the Jewish tradition to write the vowels for the word "Adonai" with the consonants of the tetragrammaton. Jewish scribes did not indicate this in the manuscript margins since this was universally known to all literate Jews. As a result, they incorrectly read this hybrid word as "Yehowah," or "Jehovah" in English.[27]

Numerous Old Testament and New Testament passages that refer to Jesus as Yahweh (Jehovah) have been altered in the Watch Tower's corrupt New World Translation to avoid the obvious fact that Jesus is the incarnation of Yahweh. A few examples are Romans 10:13 and Revelation 1:8.

---

24   Elwell and Beitzel, *Baker Encyclopedia*, 1,415.
25   Samuel Macauley Jackson, ed., *The New Schaff-Herzog Encyclopedia of Religious Knowledge: Embracing Biblical, Historical, Doctrinal, and Practical Theology and Biblical, Theological, and Ecclesiastical Biography from the Earliest Times to the Present Day* (New York: Funk & Wagnalls, 1908–1914; published in electronic form by Logos Research Systems, 2016), 116–117.
26   Elwell and Beitzel, *Baker Encyclopedia*, 2,046–2,047.
27   Brown.

Since the anonymous New World Translation committee took the liberty of inserting the name Jehovah in the New Testament instead of Lord, one would expect to find the word Jehovah in the more than 5,550 Greek New Testament manuscripts. However, the truth is that there is not one Greek manuscript that contains the term "Jehovah."

To cover this up, JWs claim that superstitious scribes removed the name from the Bible. This is ironic because they also state that the Bible has been amazingly preserved throughout the centuries! There is no evidence to support the claim that the word "Jehovah" was *ever* in a Greek manuscript. As well, the name "Jehovah" did not exist in Israel!

The fact is, biblically speaking, the most personal name for God revealed in the New Testament is Jesus.

There's no doubt the Watch Tower is dishonest in its claims—and, as Christians, we must answer their arguments with the truth of Christ. We've found it useful to ask the JWs why the Watch Tower would claim Jehovah is God's personal name when it is manmade. Most JWs will be shocked by the question and not reply.

DO JEHOVAH'S WITNESSES THINK
THEY CAN WORK THEIR WAY TO HEAVEN?

Another foundational belief of JWs is that going to heaven requires hard work. Like most non-Christians, JWs believe that works are necessary for forgiveness and salvation. However, if you were to ask them what is required for salvation, most would quote John 17:3: "And this is eternal life, that they may know You, the only true God, and Jesus Christ whom you have sent." This is an answer the Watch Tower has trained JWs to use. Their organization has taught them that one must have a *knowledge* of God instead of a *relationship* with Him.

When pressed on the issue, most JWs concede that faith *plus* works is necessary for salvation. Numerous JW publications emphasize the requirement of works by their members for eternal salvation. In fact, per *The Watchtower* published in 1947, "to get one's name written in [the] Book of Life will depend on one's works."[28]

---

28   The Watchtower, "Judgment of Church and World," July 1947, 204.

Also, "Working Hard for the Reward of Eternal Life," an article in a 1972 edition of *The Watchtower*, states, "The man who does not shrink back from the hard work of being a Christian will come in line for the splendid and ultimate reward—eternal life."[29]

Additionally, a 1983 issue of *The Watchtower*[30] printed their four requirements for salvation:

1. Jesus Christ identified a first requirement when he said in prayer to his Father, "This means everlasting life, their *taking in knowledge* of you, the only true God, and of the one whom you sent forth, Jesus Christ" *(John 17:3)*. Knowledge of God and of Jesus Christ includes knowledge of God's purposes regarding the earth and of Christ's role as earth's new King. Will you take in such knowledge by studying the Bible?

2. Many have found the second requirement more difficult. It is to *obey God's laws*, yes, to conform one's life to the moral requirements set out in the Bible. This includes refraining from a debauched, immoral way of life *(1 Cor. 6:9-10; 1 Pet. 4:3-4)*.

3. A third requirement is that we *be associated with God's channel*, his organization. God has always used an organization. For example, only those in the ark in Noah's day survived the Flood, and only those associated with the Christian congregation in the first century had God's favor *(Acts 4:12)*. Similarly, Jehovah is using only one organization today to accomplish his will. To receive everlasting life in the earthly paradise, we must identify that organization and serve God as part of it.

4. The fourth requirement is connected with loyalty. God requires that prospective subjects of his Kingdom support his government by *loyally advocating his Kingdom rule to others*. Jesus Christ explained, "This good news of the kingdom will be preached in all the inhabited earth"

---

29   The Watchtower, *Working Hard for The Reward of Eternal Life* (Brooklyn: Watch Tower and Bible Tract Society of New York, 1972), 491-492.

30   The Watchtower, *You Can Live Forever in Paradise on Earth—But How?* (Brooklyn: Watch Tower and Bible Tract Society of New York, 1983), 12-13.

(Matt. 24:14). Will you meet this requirement by telling others about God's Kingdom?[31]

So you can see that more than just repentance and faith are required in the Watch Tower's requirements for salvation. Additionally, the official JW website states, "To gain salvation, you must exercise faith in Jesus and demonstrate that faith by obeying his commands."[32] However, it also states, "This does not mean that you can earn salvation. It is 'God's gift' based on his 'undeserved kindness,' or 'grace.'"[33]

It appears, then, that JW publications have contradicted what is described on their official website and what their other publications state in regards to salvation.

When you speak with JWs about the biblical teaching that salvation is by faith through grace, they will often claim that "exercising faith" is work. However, biblically speaking, "doing works" means following the commandments and performing actions to please God *(Gal. 3:10).*

In summary, the Watch Tower teaches that works are involved in salvation. Additionally, according to the JWs, only members of the JW organization are eligible for salvation. This, of course, is incredibly *un*biblical, as the Bible teaches that repentance and faith in Jesus Christ are the means of salvation provided by God's grace, regardless of your membership in any organization.

A DIFFERENT JESUS

Regarding Jesus Christ, every JW you meet will tell you that Jesus is the Savior and Son of God, but not God Almighty. This false doctrine would disqualify one from eternal salvation. Once again, they only reveal half of what they believe. In reality, JWs teach that Jesus, while in heaven, was the archangel Michael, but that Jehovah, after creating Him as Jesus Christ, made the physical universe through Him.[34]

---

31   Ibid.

32   JW.org, "What is Salvation? The Bible's Answer," accessed April 24, 2016, https://www. jw.org/en/bible-teachings/questions/what-is-salvation/.

33   Ibid.

34   JW.org, "Who Is Michael the Archangel?" accessed August 14, 2016, https://www.jw.org/ en/publications/books/bible-teach/who-is-michael-the-archangel-jesus/.

JWs teach that He lived a perfect life on earth, and after dying on a stake (not a cross), He was resurrected as a spirit and His body was destroyed. Few JWs will admit that Jesus is a transformed version of Michael the Archangel, mainly because there is no scriptural basis for it, and many people find it to be bizarre teaching. Additionally, they believe Jesus is "a god" not the one, *true* God.[35]

JWs have also been deceived into thinking the terms "firstborn" and "begotten" mean Jesus is a created being. They are like the Arians of the fourth century who believed Jesus was a lesser being. The JWs are similar to the Arians in that they believe in the heresy of subordinationism. They have a human understanding of the relationship between the Father and the Son, rather than a scriptural view. They believe the Son of God is not eternal like His Father and is, therefore, subordinate, or lesser, in His Being as He is not fully divine like the Father.[36] We will refute this heresy later in the book.

THE HOLY SPIRIT IS AN ACTIVE FORCE

Historical Christianity teaches that the Holy Spirit is the third member of the Trinity. However, JWs believe the Holy Spirit "is God's power in action, his active force."[37] We address this heresy in depth in chapter 5 on the doctrine of the Trinity.

THE DOCTRINE OF THE TRINITY IS EVIL

The Watch Tower has taught its members that the doctrine of the Trinity is pure evil. They make the claim that it is a fourth century invention. We refute this assertion with Scripture and historical references in chapter 5.

JESUS DIED ON A TORTURE STAKE—NOT THE CROSS

The Watch Tower claims that Jesus was not crucified on a cross but on a stake, an upright pole without a crossbeam. In addition, they teach the cross is unduly venerated by Christians. Interestingly, the cross symbol was on *The Watch Tower*

---

35   Eckman, *The Truth about Worldviews*, 101.

36   David Wilhite, *The Gospel According to Heretics* (Grand Rapids, MI: Baker Academic, 2015), 110.

37   JW.org, "What is the Holy Spirit?" accessed March 5, 2017, https://www.jw.org/en/bible-teachings/questions/what-is-the-holy-spirit/.

magazine cover up until October 1, 1931. They also used to teach that Jesus died on the cross.

The Romans used to execute criminals on a variety of different stake shapes. J. Warner Wallace cites evidence for four different shapes. The most likely, based on historical references and biblical textual evidence, is the traditional form Christians have historically observed with a vertical stake and horizontal cross beam.

Scripture makes it clear Jesus was crucified with a cross beam. This is evident because Matthew 27:37 states, "And they put up over His head the accusation written against Him: THIS IS JESUS THE KING OF THE JEWS." If Jesus was crucified on a torture stake, the sign would have been above his hands, not above his head. As well, John records in John 20:25 the plural term "nails" when referring to the crucifixion and Jesus's hands. [38]

Wallace, an adjunct professor of apologetics at Biola University, summarizes a number of early historians, such as Josephus, writing about crucifixion practices of Roman soldiers and their nailing Jews to crosses.[39] Also, he notes first century Roman philosopher, Seneca the Younger, who described different kinds of crosses, including the cross beam.[40] And early Christian apologist Justin Martyr (100-165 AD) described the cross of Jesus as being composed of two beams.[41]

HELL DOES NOT EXIST

The Watch Tower claims hell is a myth and God does not punish people in hell.[42] They also believe humans do not have a soul. When one dies, his life force, not soul, leaves. Therefore, one does not have a conscious existence following death.

---

38   J. Warner Wallace, "What Was The Shape Of Jesus' Cross?," accessed March 5, 2017 at http://coldcasechristianity.com/2014/what-was-the-shape-of-jesus-cross/.

39   Ibid.

40   Ibid.

41   Ibid.

42   JW.org, "Myth 2: The Wicked Suffer in Hell," accessed March 5, 2017, https://www.jw.org/en/publications/magazines/wp20091101/myth-the-wicked-suffer-in-hell/#?insight[search_id]=2fe86398-a7e6-43be-8453-32240462bb0a&insight[search_result_index]=2.

At the final judgment, everyone who has died will be resurrected, and non-JWs (as well as unworthy JWs) will be annihilated.[43] [44]

There are numerous Bible verses that refute these beliefs. For example, the soul must exist since Jesus refers to it in Luke 10:27 and Matthew 10:28. He also refers to hell in Matthew 10:28 and 25:46. Furthermore, we read in 2 Corinthians 5:8 that, at the moment of death, believers are immediately present with the Lord.

SECOND-CLASS CITIZENS

The JWs also have a strange view of the afterlife, which is unsupported by Scripture. In Watch Tower theology, two classes of saved people exist. The first group chosen by Jehovah are called the "Anointed Class," which is comprised of one hundred forty-four thousand faithful witnesses who are in heaven and will rule with Christ during His one-thousand-year reign (aka the "Millennium"). The JWs believe it is only this class that is born again. [45]

JW expert Ron Rhodes states that this "allegedly began with the 12 apostles and other Christians of the first century and was completely filled by the year 1935 (according to a 'revelation' Rutherford received)."[46]

Those who are not of this Anointed Class but are JWs do not have a heavenly destiny but will enjoy an eternal paradise on earth. This group, also known as "the other sheep," must *earn* salvation on earth and hope to survive the coming Great Tribulation and Armageddon.[47] The Watch Tower summarizes their "discovery" of these sheep:

> In 1923, Jehovah's servants discerned that "the sheep" of Jesus' parable found at Matthew 25:31-46 and the "other sheep" to which he referred as recorded at John 10:16 are people who would have the opportunity to live forever on earth. In 1931 those described at Ezekiel 9:1-11 as being

---

43   Jw.org. "Do You Have an Immortal Spirit?," Accessed March 16, 2017, http://wol.jw.org/en/wol/d/r1/lp-e/1102001150.

44   Jw.org, "What is the Lake of Fire? Is It the Same as Hell or Gehenna?," accessed March 16, 2017, https://www.jw.org/en/bible-teachings/questions/lake-of-fire/.

45   Rhodes, *The Challenge of the Cults*, 91-92.

46   Ibid.

47   Ibid.

marked in their foreheads were also seen to be those with the earthly hope. Then in 1935 it was learned that the great crowd form part of the other sheep class Jesus spoke about. Today, this favored great crowd numbers in the millions.[48]

The rest of mankind, including the righteous and unrighteous, will be resurrected during the Millennium. The unrighteous refers to "those who failed to meet God's standards but did not have the opportunity to learn and follow them." This would seem to indicate that all who consider themselves Christians would not be included. As well, those who are so wicked and vile they cannot be reformed will "suffer permanent destruction."[49]

The remaining Witnesses who merit Jehovah's favor through their works will spend eternity on the rejuvenated earth, not in heaven.[50] Nonbelievers will not suffer eternally in hell, a doctrine JWs consider a "teaching of demons."[51] Rather, they'll just cease to exist (aka "soul annihilation").

POLITICAL AND SOCIAL ISSUES

JWs differ from mainstream Christianity on a number of political and social issues too. These restrictions, sanctioned by the Watch Tower, can be damaging to their members as well as the rest of society. For example, the Watch Tower forbids its followers from receiving blood transfusions. They base this edict on a misapplication of Bible verses that prohibit the eating of blood. Come on! Transfusions are a medical procedure and have nothing to do with *eating* blood. The Watch Tower once forbade vaccines, too, but now it lets individuals decide whether to get them. In the past, JWs also forbade organ transplants, but now, they, too, are permitted.

JWs are also under strict political guidelines. They must refuse military service, and they cannot celebrate birthdays and holidays. Remarkably, they don't celebrate Easter, but they *do* celebrate the memorial of Jesus's death. JWs

48   JW.org, "Chapter Thirteen: A Great Crowd Before Jehovah's Throne," accessed January 29, 2017, http://wol.jw.org/en/wol/d/r1/lp-e/1102002073.

49   JW.org, "What Is the Resurrection?" accessed January 29, 2017, https://www.jw.org/en/bible-teachings/questions/what-is-the-resurrection/.

50   Eckman, *The Truth about Worldviews*, 102.

51   Ankerberg and Weldon, *Encyclopedia of Cults and New Religions*, 157.

are forbidden to salute the flag of any nation, recite the Pledge of Allegiance, sing a national anthem, or run for public office. Additionally, voting has been frowned upon in the past, although in recent years it appears to be left to one's conscience.

Last, as one would expect a cult to do, they frown upon higher education, such as university. According to the Pew Research Center, as compared to other US religious groups, "Jehovah's Witnesses tend to be less educated."[52] This, of course, is their concern: one would have more freedom in evaluating the truth claims of other religious organizations without the oversight of the Watch Tower.

DATES AND PROPHECIES

The Watch Tower has an infamous history of setting dates and prophesying events. The Watch Tower has an embarrassing history of *numerous* false prophecies, most of which center on the end of the world and Armageddon.

As mentioned earlier, founder Russell was greatly influenced by Nelson H. Barbour, a miner who believed he discovered the date of Christ's return, 1914.[53] Thereafter, Watch Tower literature warned about 1914, when the overthrow of human governments would occur.[54] To confirm the confidence of their date for concerned readers, the Watch Tower stated the following in the 1894 Zion's *Watchtower* publication:

Now, in view of recent labor troubles and threatened anarchy, our readers are writing to know if there may not be a mistake in the 1914 date. They say that they do not see how present conditions can hold out so long under the strain. We see no reason for changing the figures—nor could we change them if we would. They are, we believe, God's dates,

---

52   Michael Lipka, Pew Research Center, "A Closer Look at Jehovah's Witnesses Living in the U.S.," accessed January 29, 2017, http://www.pewresearch.org/fact-tank/2016/04/26/a-closer-look-at-jehovahs-witnesses-living-in-the-u-s/.

53   Thomas Daniels, "Historical Idealism and Jehovah's Witnesses," accessed July 4, 2016, https://archive.org/stream/HistoricalIdealismAndJehovahsWitnesses/Historical_Idealism_and_Jehovahs_Witnesses#page/n0/mode/2up, 3-4.

54   Zions' Watch Tower, *Millennial Dawn. Volume II. The Time Is at Hand* (Allegheny, PA: Tower Publishing, 1889), 101.

not ours. But bear in mind that the end of 1914 is not the date for the beginning, but for the end of the time of trouble.[55]

Many other unfulfilled prophecies were made throughout the years. In 1967 the Watch Tower erroneously prophesied human history was to end in 1975, with Christ returning to set up His Millennial Kingdom on earth.[56]

Interestingly, the Watch Tower publication *Is This Life All There Is?* hypocritically states the following:

It is obvious that the true God, who is himself "the God of truth" and who hates lies, will not look with favor on persons who cling to organizations that teach falsehood (Psalm 31:5; Proverbs 6:16-19; Revelation 21:8). And, really, would you want to be even associated with a religion that had not been honest with you?[57]

And for humor's sake, we have this 1991 Watchtower quote: "A religion that teaches lies cannot be true."[58] Indeed. For more insight on this problem, see chapter 9, "Jesus Is the Final Revelation."

SHUNNING

One of the saddest aspects of Jehovah's Witnesses practices is shunning. This is the ex- communication with family members (not including immediate family members still living in the same home), friends, and acquaintances who are unrepentant wrongdoers or those who no longer follow Watch Tower teachings.

Those shunned are avoided by all Witnesses in almost all circumstances. Members are told not even to say hello to the disfellowshipped individual. This

---

55   Zion's Watch Tower, *Can It Be Delayed Until 1914?* (Allegheny, PA: Tower Publishing, 1894), 227, accessed at https://archive.org/stream/1894ZionsWatchTower/1894_Watch_ Tower.

56   The Watchtower, "Where Are We According to God's Timetable," May 1, 1967, 262.

57   The Watchtower, *Is This Life All There Is?* (Brooklyn, NY: Watch Tower and Bible Tract Society of New York, 1974), 46.

58   The Watchtower, *Is Any Religion Good Enough?* (Brooklyn, NY: Watch Tower and Bible Tract Society of New York, December 1 1991), 7.

creates tremendous emotional suffering for the one who is shunned, as well as for the loved ones still active in the organization.

MAJOR DOCTRINAL SHIFTS

There have been major doctrinal shifts throughout the history of the JWs. For example, the organization used to teach that the worship of Christ was correct. In the March 1880 edition of *Zion's Watch Tower*, the magazine states, "Even in the flesh He was 'God manifest' and 'to worship *Christ* in any form cannot be wrong."[59]

Another example of changing doctrine is found in the August 15, 1941 edition of *The Watchtower* which reads, "[God] commands that all creatures in heaven and earth shall worship the Son as he worships the Father."[60] Then, a completely different doctrine is taught in the January 1, 1954, edition. *The Watchtower* writes, "no distinct worship is to be rendered to Jesus Christ now glorified in heaven."[61]

Furthermore, Watch Tower literature clearly shows how JWs shifted their stance on the validity of the cross. For example, the cross of Christ used to be on *The Watchtower* magazine. We have a photocopy of the October 1, 1931, issue with the cross proudly proclaimed on the front cover. We also have a photocopy of the October 15, 1931, issue when *The Watch Tower* stopped using the symbol on its cover.

There are many other examples of doctrinal changes we could provide. Nevertheless, the point is that God's proclaimed sole spokesperson has changed its essential doctrine, contrary to the Word of God.

ALLEGATIONS OF SEXUAL ABUSE

In recent years, the Watchtower Bible and Tract Society of New York has paid out millions of dollars because of sex abuse scandals. Many of these cases involve child molestation by church leaders that had been covered up by the JW governing

---

59   Zion's Watch Tower, *A Living Christ* (Allegheny, PA: Tower Publishing, 1880), 82-83.

60   The Watchtower, *Announcing Jehovah's Kingdom* (Brooklyn: Watch Tower and Bible Tract Society of New York, August 15 1941), 252.

61   The Watchtower, *Announcing Jehovah's Kingdom* (Brooklyn: Watch Tower and Bible Tract Society of New York, January 1, 1954), 31.

body. JW officials have a history of instructing local leaders to hide sexual abuse from law enforcement. They have defied court orders to turn over the names and whereabouts of alleged child sexual abusers.[62]

JW vs Biblical Christianity

Jehovah's Witness View	Christian View
GOD THE FATHER	
Almighty God	God the Father, part of Trinity
Omnipotent	Omnipotent
Not Omnipresent	Omnipresent
Omniscient	Omniscient
JESUS	
Created	Uncreated
One of many gods	The only true God, part of Trinity
Jesus is a mighty God	Jesus is Almighty God
Jehovah's agent in creation	Creator, along with other 2 Persons of the Trinity
Jesus is Michael the Archangel	Jesus is Almighty God
Constrained to one place at a time	Omnipresent
Limited power	Omnipotent
Not omniscient	Omniscient
Spiritually resurrected	Physically resurrected
HOLY SPIRIT	
God's active force	God, part of the Trinity
Not a person	Person
Created by Jehovah	Eternally God
Not Omnipresent	Omnipresent
Not Omniscient	Omniscient
Not Omnipotent	Omnipotent

---

62   Trey Bundy, The Center for Investigative Reporting "How Jehovah's Witnesses leaders hide child abuse secrets at all costs," accessed March 14, 2017, https://www.revealnews. org/article/how-jehovahs-witnesses-leaders-hide-child-abuse-secrets-at-all-costs/.

JW vs Biblical Christianity

Jehovah's Witness View	Christian View
MAN	
Sinner in need of salvation through repentance, faith, works, and an active member of the Jehovah's Witness organization.	Sinner in need of salvation through repentance and faith.
SATAN	
Created angel who rebelled against God and cast out of heaven.	Created angel who rebelled against God and cast out of heaven
AFTERLIFE	
When a person dies they are not conscious.	Those who lived before the time of Jesus who repented and put their faith in God and coming Messiah are in the presence of God in the heavenly realm. People from the time of Jesus and forward who repented and put their faith in Jesus are in the presence of God. Non-believers are conscious in a place separated from God.
Righteous and unrighteous will be resurrected. Unrighteous given 1000 years to learn about God and serve him on earth. The wicked are not resurrected and are annihilated. 144,000 people, mainly Jehovah's Witnesses that have died and are currently in heaven, will rule with Christ during His 1000-year reign.	With the Second Coming of Jesus all people(righteous and unrighteous) will be physically resurrected and reunited with their spirit. Believers will spend eternity with God and unbelievers eternally separated from God in hell.

SUMMARY POINTS FOR DIALOGUE WITH JWS

- Where in early Christianity (the first few centuries) did a central organization control sermons and literature distribution like the JW organization does today?
- Seminaries and institutions of higher learning do not use the JWs' New World Translation due to obvious mistranslations and corruptions.
- Jehovah cannot be God's personal name because it is manmade.
- The Watch Tower teaches four requirements for salvation. This contradicts the scriptural teaching that salvation is received by faith alone.

- Do you believe Jesus is a true God or false god since the Bible teaches there is only one God?
- The Watch Tower and JW leaders have a history of false prophecies that began with their founder, Charles Taze Russell.
- Why would God's organization make major doctrinal changes over time?

CHAPTER 3
MORMONISM IN A NUTSHELL

If you were unfamiliar with their history and doctrines, your first impression of Mormonism might be to consider the Church of Jesus Christ of Latter-day Saints as another denomination of Christianity. After all, this religious organization *claims* to:

- affirm a Trinity
- study the Bible
- believe Jesus is God
- believe Jesus atoned for our sins
- be a Christian organization

LDS may *seem* like Christians on the surface, but they have a completely different view of who God is and how one is saved. We will discuss this later in this chapter, but first, let us explore how this religion started.

Mormonism was founded by Joseph Smith Jr. He was born on December 23, 1805, in Sharon, Vermont, to a farming couple. Due to poverty, the family moved to a town called Palmyra in upstate New York.

To understand the Mormons, you've got to understand that the early 1800s were a time when America was *full* of religious revivals and new denominations, as well as new cults. Christianity experienced great schisms, and many denominations were formed. For example, there were people claiming to be the reincarnated Messiah. There were also numerous false prophets, such as William Miller, a preacher who falsely prophesied that Jesus would return and the world would end between 1843 to 1844.[63]

Smith grew up in a time of cultic frenzy. In short, practicing the occult was commonplace. [64] The Smith family (including Joseph Smith Jr.) had an interest in the occult. Dr. Michael Quinn, a historian of Mormonism with a PhD in history from Yale, notes that the Smith family was involved in astrology and practiced magic rituals.

It should be noted that Dr. Quinn (a former Brigham Young University professor) was ex-communicated from the LDS church in 1993 for publishing negative information about LDS history, including changes in their policy and doctrine.[65] In his book *Early Mormonism and the Magic World View*, Dr. Quinn writes of the Smith family, LDS, and magic:

> The following analysis of Mormonism and folk magic includes sources which have been available for more than a century. Their authenticity is beyond question. These sources give evidence of the Smith family's participation in treasure-digging; the possession and use of instruments and emblems of folk magic by Smith, his family members, and other early LDS leaders; the continued use of such implements for religious purposes in the LDS church for

---

63   Christianity Today, "William Miller," accessed March 18, 2017, http://www.christianitytoday.com/history/people/denominationalfounders/william-miller.html.
64   Michael Quinn, *Early Mormonism and the Magic World View* (Salt Lake City: Signature Books, 1998), 17.
65   PBS.org, "The Mormons. Interview D. Michael Quinn," accessed July 23, 2016, http://www.pbs.org/mormons/interviews/quinn.html.

many years; and the sincere belief of many Mormons in "the magic world view."[66]

Quinn also supplies references that Joseph Smith Sr. (the father) and Joseph Smith Jr. believed in witches and witchcraft. This continued while Joseph Jr. was president of the LDS church.[67] Additionally, the Three Witnesses to the Book of Mormon and some members of the first Quorum of the Twelve Apostles were also involved in folk magic.[68]

At age fourteen, Joseph Smith claimed he was concerned and confused over all the different religious parties at the time. He wanted to know which religious group was correct.[69]

NEW RELIGION BORN

On a spring day in 1820, Smith was reading James 1:5: "If any of you lacks wisdom, let him ask of God, who gives to all liberally and without reproach, and it will be given to him." He was struck by this passage and went to the woods near his home to pray.[70]

According to his 1838 account of this "First Vision," he was visited by two personages: God the Father and Jesus Christ. Smith asked them which religious sect he should join, and they told him that all were wrong, all creeds were an "abomination in his sight," and all religious leaders were corrupt.[71]

Later in 1823, while praying in his bedroom, an angel named Moroni visited Smith.[72] Supposedly, this angel had had a previous earthly life as a human who lived with an ancient people called the Nephites.[73] The Nephites

---

66   Quinn, *Early Mormonism*, xxi.

67   Ibid., 31.

68   Ibid., 240.

69   LDS.org, "Church History. The First Vision: A Narrative from Joseph Smith's Accounts," accessed January 29, 2017, https://history.lds.org/article/first-vision-accounts-synthesis?lang=eng.

70   Ibid.

71   LDS.org, "Joseph Smith-History," accessed January 29, 2017, https://www.lds.org/scriptures/pgp/js-h/1.5-20?lang=eng#4.

72   Ibid.

73   LDS.org, "Guide to the Scriptures," accessed March 19, 2017, https://www.lds.org/scriptures/gs/moroni-son-of-mormon?lang=eng.

were a Jewish tribe that escaped the Babylonian captivity at Jerusalem and sailed to the Western Hemisphere six hundred years before the time of Christ.[74]

Moroni was the son of the prophet Mormon. Both had lived fourteen hundred years earlier (circa AD 421).[75] While on earth, Moroni was said to be a prophet, military commander, and historian who lived in the Americas.[76] He and his father, it is said, wrote an abridged history on gold plates. These plates described two civilizations that came to the Americas.[77]

One group of Hebrews came from Jerusalem in 600 BC under the leadership of a prophet known as Lehi, a descendant of Joseph.[78] The other group, known as Jaredites, came from the Tower of Babel, much earlier.[79] The first group became separated into the Nephites and the Lamanites. All the groups were destroyed except for the Lamanites, who are the supposed ancestors of American Indians.[80]

The angel Moroni told Smith of a book written on gold plates that had the records of the people of ancient America deposited in the earth nearby.[81] Like others during his day, Joseph Smith used small stones known as seer stones to look for buried treasure and lost objects.[82] At age twenty-one, he found this ancient Nephite record, which was deposited in the earth in a stone box near

74   LDS.org, "Who and Where Are the Lamanites?," accessed March 19, 2017, https://www.lds.org/ensign/1975/12/who-and-where-are-the-lamanites?lang=eng.

75   LDS.org, "Moroni, Son of Mormon," accessed March 19, 2017, https://www.lds.org/scriptures/gs/moroni-son-of-mormon?lang=eng.

76   LDS.org, "Moroni and His Captains: Men of Peace in a Time of War," accessed March 19, 2017, https://www.lds.org/ensign/1977/09/moroni-and-his-captains-men-of-peace-in-a-time-of-war?lang=eng.

77   LDS.org, "A Brief Explanation about the Book of Mormon," accessed March 19, 2017, https://www.lds.org/scriptures/bofm/explanation?lang=eng.

78   LDS.org, "The First Book of Nephi," accessed March 19, 2017, https://www.lds.org/scriptures/bofm/1-ne/1?lang=eng.

79   BYU. Harold B. Lee Library, "Jaredites" accessed March 19, 2017, http://eom.byu.edu/index.php/Jaredites.

80   LDS.org, "Chapter 49: Mormon and His Teachings," accessed March 19, 2017, https://www.lds.org/manual/book-of-mormon-stories/chapter-49-mormon-and-his-teachings?lang=eng.

81   LDS.org, "Joseph Smith-History," accessed January 29, 2017, https://www.lds.org/scriptures/pgp/js-h/1.5-20?lang=eng#4.

82   LDS.org, "Joseph the Seer," accessed March 19, 2017, https://www.lds.org/ensign/2015/10/joseph-the-seer?lang=eng.

where he lived.[83] The box contained white or clear stones (seer stones) that were bound together with a metal rim in the form of eyeglasses, or spectacles, as well as the plates. He then used the spectacles (or seer stones, accounts differ on this) to translate the Book of Mormon.[84]

In all, Smith used the three seer stones to translate the golden plates that were written in so-called "reformed Egyptian."[85] [86] Smith would put the stones into a hat and then bury his face in the hat to receive revelation from God and dictate his translation.[87]

On April 29, 1829, a man named Martin Harris became convinced that Joseph had received a vision, and after receiving a vision himself, Harris helped fund Smith's endeavors.[88]

The one hundred sixteen pages Smith translated into English from an unknown language became known as the Book of Mormon.[89] The central theme of the Book of Mormon is the personal ministry or testament of Jesus Christ in the Americas among the Nephites soon after His Resurrection. It contains the alleged "complete" gospel and plan of salvation as well as the history of these civilizations.[90]

Oliver Cowdery, a schoolteacher and one of Smith's scribes, along with Smith, claimed that John the Baptist visited them while praying in the woods in May 15, 1829.[91] They were both ordained and received the Aaronic priesthood,

---

83   LDS.org, "Significant Events," accessed March 19, 2017, https://www.lds.org/churchhistory/presidents/controllers/potcController.jsp?leader=1&topic=events.

84   LDS.org, "Book of Mormon Translation," accessed March 19, 2017, https://www.lds.org/topics/book-of-mormon-translation?lang=eng&old=true.

85   LDS.org, "Book of Mormon Translation," accessed July 30, 2016, https://www.lds.org/topics/book-of-mormon-translation?lang=eng.

86   Quinn, *Early Mormonism*, 244.

87   LDS.org, "Book of Mormon Translation," accessed March 19, 2017, https://www.lds.org/topics/book-of-mormon-translation?lang=eng&old=true.

88   LDS.org, "The Contributions of Martin Harris," accessed March 19, 2017, https://history.lds.org/article/doctrine-and-covenants-martin-harris?lang=eng.

89   Josephsmithpapers.org, "History, circa Summer 1832," accessed June 21,2016, http://www.josephsmithpapers.org/paperSummary/history-circa-summer-1832?p=1#!/paperSummary/history-circa-summer-1832&p=4.

90   *The Book of Mormon, Introduction* (Salt Lake City: The Church of Jesus Christ of Latter-day Saints)

91   LDS.org, "Chapter 6: The Mission of John the Baptist," accessed March 19, 2017, https://www.lds.org/manual/teachings-joseph-smith/chapter-6?lang=eng.

also known in LDS theology as the lesser priesthood.[92] Later, they were upgraded to the greater priesthood, or Melchizedek priesthood, by the apostles Peter, James, and John.[93]

The Book of Mormon was published in Palmyra, New York, in 1830,[94] and the LDS (Mormon) faith officially began on April 6, 1830. The Saints moved to different areas of Missouri and were forced to constantly relocate due to hostility. They had originally planned to build a temple near Independence, Missouri; but before they could do so, they moved to Commerce, Illinois, which was renamed Nauvoo.[95] [96]

Tensions arose between Smith's followers and the city's residents as well as Mormon businessmen. Some of Smith's own leaders opposed his practice of polygamy. The local newspaper *Nauvoo Expositor* was operated by top LDS leaders who opposed Smith's new secret teachings, like polygamy.[97]

In retaliation, Smith a high-ranking church official and, along with the Nauvoo City Council, ordered the Expositor to be destroyed. As a result, Joseph and his brother Hyrum were put into jail at Carthage.[98]

A mob attacked the jail, and while in his cell, Smith fired on the crowd with his pistol.[99] On June 27, 1844, he was shot and killed. He is considered a martyr by the LDS.[100] Technically, a martyr is one who lays down one's life, not one who is killed in a shootout.

92   Ibid.

93   LDS.org, "The Restoration of the Aaronic and Melchizedek Priesthoods," accessed March 19, 2017, https://www.lds.org/ensign/1996/12/the-restoration-of-the-aaronic-and-melchizedek-priesthoods?lang=eng.

94   LDS.org, "Book of Mormon Historic Publication Site," accessed March 19, 2017, https://history.lds.org/article/historic-sites-new-york-book-of-mormon-publication-site-palmyra?lang=eng.

95   BYU. Harold B. Lee Library, "Missouri," accessed March 19, 2017, http://eom.byu.edu/index.php/Missouri.

96   BYU. Harold B. Lee Library, "Nauvoo," accessed March 19, 2017, http://eom.byu.edu/index.php/Nauvoo.

97   BYU. Harold B. Lee Library, "Nauvoo Expositor," accessed March 19, 2017, http://eom.byu.edu/index.php/Nauvoo_Expositor.

98   Ibid.

99   BYUStudies, "History of the Church: Volume 6, Chapter 34," accessed March 19, 2017, https://byustudies.byu.edu/content/volume-6-chapter-34.

100   LDS.org, "Carthage Jail," accessed March 19, 2017, https://history.lds.org/article/historic-sites-illinois-carthage-jail-carthage?lang=eng.

Under the leadership of Brigham Young, the Saints then moved to Iowa and later to Salt Lake City, Utah.

LDS missionaries often bring up the concern of the many Christian denominations. Reflecting the opinion of their founding prophet, Joseph Smith, they feel this is evidence that Christianity is apostate and needs to be restored by their church. We recommend that you inform them that there are as many as one hundred organizations claiming to be the true LDS church, who believe other Mormon organizations to be illegitimate.[101]

The second largest group, next to the official LDS church, is the Reorganized Church of Jesus Christ of Latter Day Saints, originally formed in 1860 by those from the original church who did not migrate to Utah. They have approximately two hundred fifty thousand members who reject certain practices and beliefs of the LDS church.[102]

The polygamists who live in Utah and the West are known as the Fundamentalists and are made up of at least thirteen groups. They consider themselves the "orthodox" part of the Utah church because they hold to the everlasting command of Doctrine and Covenants, section 132:61-63, which teaches men they can have many wives.[103] We'll delve into that later in this chapter.

While biblical Christianity is held together by core doctrines, regardless of denomination, LDS organizations are greatly divergent on essential beliefs.

PRIESTHOOD

The concept of the priesthood is important in the LDS organization. The priesthood is delegated to worthy male members of the church. This allows them to "act in God's name for the salvation of the human family."[104]

---

101   Religionfacts.com, "Branches of Mormonism," accessed July 26, 2016, http://www.
       religionfacts.com/mormonism/branches.

102   Ibid.

103   Blueletterbible.org, "Sects of Mormonism," accessed July 26, 2016, https://www.
       blueletterbible.org/study/cults/ramd/ramd25.cfm.

104   LDS.org, "Chapter 13: The Priesthood," *Gospel Principles*, accessed February 2, 2017,
       https://www.lds.org/manual/gospel-principles/chapter-13-the-priesthood?lang=eng.

Those with priesthood authority perform services such as baptism, confirmation, administration of the sacrament, and temple marriage.[105] There are two types of priesthood. The first is the Aaronic priesthood. A male is eligible for this at age twelve. They participate in priesthood ordinances and other acts of service. This prepares one for the greater priesthood, known as the Melchizedek priesthood. [106]

The Melchizedek priesthood includes the church leaders who guide the church and preaching of the gospel worldwide. [107] One must be at least eighteen years old to serve in it.[108]

From a New Testament perspective, these offices do not make sense. The book of Hebrews records that the Old Testament priesthood became obsolete and was changed *(Heb. 7:11-12)*. There is a new covenant *(Heb. 8:6-13)*, as Jesus Christ, our perfect High Priest, made atonement for sins once and for all. The priesthood became obsolete *(Heb. 9:13)*! True Christians can come before the throne of God directly through Jesus Christ—no earthly priesthood is required *(Heb. 10:19-21)*.

MORMON SCRIPTURE

There have been several differing accounts of Joseph Smith's First Vision, many of which can be read at the official LDS church website.[109] Smith himself dictated at least four accounts of his first vision, with differences in details.[110]

In the 1832 version, Smith claimed to only see a vision of Jesus Christ. A reading of the Scriptures provoked Smith to seek God, and he knew the churches around him were apostate before his vision.

---

105   Ibid.

106   LDS.org, "Aaronic Priesthood," accessed February 2, 2017, https://www.lds.org/topics/aaronic-priesthood?lang=eng&old=true.

107   LDS.org, "Melchizedek Priesthood," accessed February 2, 2017, https://www.lds.org/topics/melchizedek-priesthood?lang=eng&old=true.

108   Ibid.

109   LDs.org, "First Vision Accounts," accessed July 30, 2016, https://www.lds.org/topics/first-vision-accounts?lang=eng.

110   Ibid.

Compare this with the 1838-1839 version, in which Smith said he had a vision of *both* the Father and the Son, that a revival spurred him to seek God, and the two personages he saw told him that the churches were apostate. [111]

Most LDS are unaware of the thousands of changes made to the Book of Mormon from the time it was first published in 1830. Jerald and Sandra Tanner of Utah Lighthouse Ministry have documented at least 3,913 changes in the Book of Mormon since its first publication. [112] The Tanners completed this project by obtaining photocopies of an original 1830 edition of the Book of Mormon from the University of Utah Library. Then they compared it to the 1964 and 1981 editions.

The documented changes include words added and deleted as well as textual and spelling changes. This, of course, leads to major doctrinal changes. For example, the 1830 edition described Christ in 1 Nephi 13:40 as "the Lamb of God is the Eternal Father." The 1964 edition shows the same sentence stating, "The Lamb of God is the Son of the Eternal Father." [113]

Interestingly, it was LDS founder and prophet Joseph Smith who claimed a heavenly voice told him and witnesses that the translation of the Book of Mormon was "correct":

We heard a voice from out of the bright light above us, saying, "These plates have been revealed by the power of God, and they have been translated by the power of God. The translation of them which you have seen is correct, and I command you to bear record of what you now see and hear."

As well, Joseph Smith stated, "I told the brethren that the Book of Mormon was the most correct of any book on the earth."[114]

---

111   Ron Rhodes and Marian Bodine, *Reasoning from the Scriptures with the Mormons* (Eugene, OR: Harvest House Publishers, 1995), 20.

112   Jerald Tanner and Sandra Tanner, *3,913 Changes in the Book of Mormon* (Salt Lake City: Utah Lighthouse Ministry), 5.

113   Ibid., 32.

114   Tanner and Tanner, *3,913 Changes*, 2.

Most Mormons we have spoken to are unaware of the many changes to the Book of Mormon. In line with our documentation, Brigham Young University states there are many textual variants:

> A critical text of the Book of Mormon was published in 1984-1987 by the Foundation for Ancient Research and Mormon Studies. This is the first published text of the Book of Mormon to show the precise history of many textual variants. Although this textual study of the editions and manuscripts of the Book of Mormon is incomplete and preliminary, it is helpful for a general overview of the textual history of the Book of Mormon.[115]

OBVIOUS PLAGIARISM

Critics of the Book of Mormon have charged Joseph Smith with plagiarism. For example, more than eighteen chapters of Isaiah, the Ten Commandments, and several portions of the Old Testament are copied word for word into the Book of Mormon from the King James Version (KJV) of the Bible. There are also "a large number of New Testament verses and parts of verses strewn throughout the Book of Mormon."[116]

Mormon scholars admit that "more than fifty thousand phrases of three or more words, excluding definite and indefinite articles, are common to the Bible and the Book of Mormon.[117] Also, it is difficult to explain "large blocks of biblical text that are in many places exactly the same, word for word, as the King James versions of the same passages."[118]

No accounts exist to show that Smith used the Bible for his translation, and, in fact, accounts state specifically that he did not use any biblical text during his translation process.[119]

---

115   BYU. Harold B. Lee Library, "Book of Mormon Editions (1830-1981)," accessed March 19, 2017, http://eom.byu.edu/index.php/Book_of_Mormon_Editions_(1830-1981).

116   Jerald and Sandra Tanner, *Major Problems of Mormonism* (Salt Lake City: Utah Lighthouse Ministry, 1989), 153.

117   Daniel Belnap, BYU Religious Studies Center, "The King James Bible and the Book of Mormon," accessed February 5, 2017, https://rsc.byu.edu/archived/king-james-bible-and-restoration/10-king-james-bible-and-book-mormon.

118   Ibid.

119   Ibid.

The obvious problem is that the KJV Bible was not published until 1611. Keep in mind the historical claim by Smith that the Nephites were Israelites who came to the Americas around 600 BC. LDS leaders claim that the Nephites had copies of Old Testament Scripture written before then.[120]

If one assumed this were true (although there is no evidence for this migration account), how does one account for Smith receiving a divine revelation using language not common to his era? Why would God choose an outdated language form? As well, verses from the Old Testament writings of Malachi were included by Nephi. A major problem is that Malachi was penned more than a hundred years after the writing of Nephi.[121]

Mormon scholars would argue that although it is true KJV-style English was no longer normative in the 1800s, it was used in sermons to some degree.[122] This is not a compelling argument since the Book of Mormon is not a compilation of sermons.

Following are a few examples of parallels from the Book of Mormon and the KJV Bible:

BM: made white in the blood of the Lamb *(1 Nephi 12:11)*

KJV: made them white in the blood of the Lamb *(Rev. 7:14)*

BM: O wretched man that I am *(2 Nephi 4:17)*

KJV: O wretched man that I am *(Rom. 7:24)*

BM: endured the crosses of the world, and despised the shame *(2 Nephi 9:18)*

KJV: endured the cross, despising the shame *(Heb. 12:2)*

BM: to be carnally- minded is death, and to be spiritually- minded is life *(2 Nephi 9:39)*

KJV: to be carnally minded is death; but to be spiritually minded is life *(Rom. 8:6)*[123]

---

120   Tanner, *Major Problems*, 149.
121   Tanner, *Major Problems*, 149-150.
122   Belnap, "The King James Bible and the Book of Mormon."
123   Tanner, *Major Problems*, 153.

You decide if the similarities of these verses are a coincidence, and more examples could be given.

ADDITIONAL LDS SCRIPTURES

Besides the Book of Mormon, the Church of Jesus Christ of Latter-day Saints follows a cannon that consists of the King James Version Bible, Doctrine and Covenants, and the Pearl of Great Price.[124]

The Book of Mormon, as we already explained, is referred to by LDS as "another testament of Jesus Christ." Doctrine and Covenants is a collection of revelations Joseph Smith and other LDS leaders received as well as inspired declarations to establish and regulate the kingdom of God.[125] It is a book that describes LDS doctrine. The Pearl of Great Price contains selected works by Joseph Smith as well as his translations of parts of the Bible.[126]

The Pearl of Great Price contains two works unique to Mormonism. One is the Book of Moses, which contains Joseph Smith's edited version of the first several chapters of Genesis.[127] Smith claimed he was led by God to correct these chapters of the book of Genesis.[128]

The other work of Smith's is the Book of Abraham that contains a "translation" of ancient Egyptian artifacts that Smith's followers purchased from a traveling mummy exhibition in 1835. Modern experts say these papyri are Egyptian funerary (relating to a funeral or burial) texts that date to approximately 100 BC and not during Abraham's time.[129] Even though the LDS church believes the Book of Abraham is Scripture, their leadership states,

---

124 Rhodes, *The Challenge of the Cults*, 60-61.

125 LDS.org, "Introduction," accessed July 22, 2016, https://www.lds.org/scriptures/dc-testament/introduction?lang=eng.

126 LDS.org, "Introduction," accessed March 19, 2017, https://www.lds.org/scriptures/pgp/introduction.html?lang=eng.

127 LDS.org, "How We Got the Book of Moses," accessed January 29, 2017, https://www.lds.org/ensign/1986/01/how-we-got-the-book-of-moses?lang=eng.

128 LDS.org, "The Joseph Smith Translation: 'Plain and Precious Things Restored'", accessed March 19, 2017, https://www.lds.org/ensign/1997/08/the-joseph-smith-translation-plain-and-precious-things-restored?lang=eng.

129 J Warner Wallace,Coldcasechristianity.com, "How The Book of Abraham Exposes The False Nature of Mormonism," accessed July 27, 2016, http://coldcasechristianity.com/2014/how-the-book-of-abraham-exposes-the-false-nature-of-mormonism/.

"No eyewitness account of the translation survives, making it impossible to reconstruct the process."[130]

Although it was thought the papyri Smith translated were destroyed in the Great Chicago Fire in 1871, the papyrus fragments were rediscovered in the Metropolitan Museum of Art in New York City and transferred to the LDS church in 1967.[131] The Mormon Church validated these papyri as authentic, yet their official website states the following:

> The relationship between those fragments and the text we have today is largely a matter of conjecture . . . Neither the rules nor the translations in the grammar book correspond to those recognized by Egyptologists today.[132]

As noted by Wallace, LDS and non-LDS scholars agreed these papyrus scrolls were possessed by Joseph Smith and used to translate the Book of Abraham. He summarizes the situation:

> Modern examination of the papyri did not provide the confirmation Mormons were hoping for, but it did confirm something important. Mormons had accepted the *Book of Abraham* for decades, believing the Church's assertion Joseph Smith translated it by the power of God as he had claimed. This manner of translation, allegedly guided by God, was the same mechanism by which Joseph claimed to translate the *Book of Mormon*. The false translation of the *Book of Abraham*, therefore, casts serious doubt on the *Book of Mormon* as well, forever debilitating Joseph's claim he was a true, inspired prophet of God. Thousands of Mormons left the church as the result of this discovery, while thousands more are completely unaware of this important piece of evidence.[133]

---

130   LDS.org, "Translation and Historicity of the Book of Abraham." Accessed March 19, 2017, https://www.lds.org/topics/translation-and-historicity-of-the-book-of-abraham?lang=eng&old=true.

131   Ibid.

132   Ibid.

133   Warner Wallace, How The Book of Abraham Exposes the False Nature of Mormonism.

JOSEPH SMITH'S INSPIRED VERSION

Joseph Smith completed the translation of his own Bible version, known today as the Inspired Version or Joseph Smith's New Translation of the Bible. Of course, it could not be a translation in the normal sense of the word since Smith was not educated in Hebrew, Aramaic, or Greek.

Eric Johnson of Mormon Research Ministry makes the following point:

> About half of the Old Testament changes were made to the book Genesis while close to 80% of the New Testament changes were made to the four Gospels. Scattered changes were made throughout the rest of the Bible. One insertion made in Genesis chapter 50 added twelve new verses after verse 24a in the King James Version, including a conveniently placed prophecy about Smith![134]

LDS do not publish this version as they state the revision was not complete. Yet Johnson points out that Smith stated his translation was completed. He notes, "On July 2, 1833, *History of the Church* 1:368 reported, "We this day finished the translating of the Scriptures, for which we return gratitude to our Heavenly Father."[135]

ARCHAEOLOGY PROBLEMS

A powerful question we often pose to Mormons is, "Why doesn't archaeology support the Book of Mormon?" Dr. Mark once politely asked two young Mormon missionaries to provide their best piece of archaeological evidence for the Book of Mormon. They came back two weeks later with a printout of a cave drawing from South America with a stick figure pointing to the sun. This is more sad than humorous.

It is helpful to point out to LDS that there is no reputable archaeological support for the supposed migration of Israelites that populated the Americas with millions of people.

134 Eric Johnson, Mormon Research Ministry, "The Inspired Version: Why Isn't It Officially Used Today?" accessed February 5, 2017, http://www.mrm.org/smith-inspired-version.
135 Ibid.

No one knows where the cities mentioned in the Book of Mormon are located. According to Brigham Young University online, "Of the numerous proposed external Book of Mormon geographies, none has been positively and unambiguously confirmed by archaeology."[136]

Chapter 6 of the Book of Mormon records a battle between the Nephites and Lamanites at the Hill Cumorah that took place in approximately AD 385. It also records that *hundreds of thousands* were slain with the sword. Yet there is no evidence for the massive wars the Nephite and Lamanite people waged against each other, including no burial sites or weaponry.

Some Mormon apologists agree with past LDS apostles and apologists that the Hill Cumorah location is in the Palmyra, New York, region. Regarding the location where Moroni buried the plates, Brigham Young University has this to say:

Because the New York site does not readily fit the Book of Mormon description of Book of Mormon geography, some Latter-day Saints have looked for other possible explanations and locations, including Mesoamerica. Although some have identified possible sites that may seem to fit better (Palmer), there are no conclusive connections between the Book of Mormon text and any specific site that has been suggested.[137]

Today, you can visit the Latter-day Saints' Visitors' Center, which is open year-round at this location. A pageant is held there every summer, which includes a reenactment of the final battle that took place at Hill Cumorah. Unfortunately, there is no reputable archeological evidence to support the existence of these people groups or their wars in New York or any other part of the New World.

Another monumental challenge to the Book of Mormon claim that Native American Indians were principally the descendants of Hebrews is the absence of DNA evidence. To our knowledge, the evaluation of Native American DNA shows no obvious connection to Jewish descent as given in the Book of Mormon.

---

136   BYU. Harold B. Lee Library, "Book of Mormon Geography," accessed July 22, 2016, http://eom.byu.edu/index.php/Book_of_Mormon_Geography.

137   BYU. Harold B. Lee Library, "Cumorah," accessed July 30, 2016, http://eom.byu.edu/index.php/Cumorah.

The lack of evidence for a DNA connection is so compelling that few Mormon apologists with a background in genetics argue the point. In fact, many Mormon scientists now agree there is no DNA evidence for this claim. Instead, an increasing number of Mormon apologists propose alternative explanations that distance themselves from such strong claims.

Several LDS theories exist, which include, but are not limited to, the following:

- A small number of Jewish people migrated into a limited geographical area in the Americas so that no Jewish DNA is detectable.
- The science of DNA is constantly changing and may not be accurate.
- There was intermarriage with the migrating Jewish tribes, which makes Native Indian DNA difficult to detect.
- The Book of Mormon deals with a limited geography and covers only a small fraction of the New World.
- There could have been other migrations before and after Lehi came to the New World in 600 BC.
- It is unclear what the Hebrew DNA of Lehi and his family would look like.
- Previously inspired church leaders and apostles were mistaken that the Book of Mormon had a continental scope and should not be considered infallible.

Two main problems with these arguments arise. First, they contradict the historical teaching of numerous Mormon leaders, including several of their own "inspired" presidents and Mormon apostles. Joseph Smith himself wrote the following to a newspaper editor in 1833:

The Book of Mormon is a record of the forefathers of our western tribes of Indians . . . By it we learn that our western tribes of Indians are descendants from that Joseph that was sold into Egypt, and that the land of America is a promised land unto them.[138]

---

138   Kent P. Jackson, BYU Religious Studies Center, "Joseph Smith and the Historicity of the Book of Mormon," accessed February 3, 2016, https://rsc.byu.edu/archived/historicity-and-latter-day-saint-scriptures/5-joseph-smith-and-historicity-book-mormon.

And who would know better than Joseph Smith Jr., who received the revelation from God?

Second, it contradicts what is recorded in the Book of Mormon. In 1 Nephi 13, the introduction of the chapter notes what Nephi (son of Lehi) sees in his vision, which includes "the discovery and colonizing of America."[139] Also, 1 Nephi 13:30-31 records a vision of an angel to Nephi that states, "God will not suffer that the Gentiles will utterly destroy the mixture of thy seed, which are among thy brethren. Neither will he suffer that the Gentiles shall destroy the seed of thy brethren."

It appears Mormon Scripture assures the descendants of Lehi would be easily identifiable.

The LDS church itself concludes this about DNA and the Book of Mormon: "Much as critics and defenders of the Book of Mormon would like to use DNA studies to support their views, the evidence is simply inconclusive. Nothing is known about the DNA of Book of Mormon peoples." [140]

It appears the LDS leadership is concerned about the lack of a genetic link to the Lamanites as the principal ancestors of the American Indians. In 1981, the Book of Mormon had added to its introduction: "After thousands of years, all were destroyed except the Lamanites, and they are the principal ancestors of the American Indians."[141] The emergence of the negative DNA information led to a change in the 2006 edition; the introduction was reworded to a vaguer claim as the Lamanites are "among" the ancestors of the American Indians.[142]

SHOULD ONE CONSIDER LDS CHRISTIANS?

A Christian is one who has repented of his sins and trusted in the second person of the Triune Godhead as Lord and Savior. He must believe in the Trinity as

---

139   LDS.org, "The First Book of Nephi. Chapter 13," accessed July 23, 2016, https://www.lds.org/scriptures/bofm/1-ne/13.30-31?lang=eng.

140   LDS.org, "Book of Mormon and DNA Studies," accessed January 29, 2017, https://www.lds.org/topics/book-of-mormon-and-dna-studies?lang=eng&old=true.

141   Carrie Moore, Deseret News Utah, "Debate Renewed with Change in Book of Mormon Introduction," accessed February 4, 2017, http://www.deseretnews.com/article/695226008/Debate-renewed-with-change-in-Book-of-Mormon-introduction.html.

142   Ibid.

outlined in the Bible, as well as put his faith in Christ alone for his salvation and eternal life with Him.

To win converts, the LDS have attempted to masquerade as Christians. This is a deceptive approach because their theology, soteriology (how one is saved), and Christology (what they view about Christ) is completely unbiblical. As you will see, LDS, on the surface, appear Christian, but they do not believe in any core biblical tenets.

If you ever talk with Mormon missionaries, they will tell you they too are Christians who believe Jesus is the Son of God. They will even affirm the Trinity and explain how everyone needs the cross for atonement of sins. Then they will inform you that God uses modern-day prophets and apostles to speak to us because Christendom has been corrupted throughout the ages. The missionaries will also explain how their great prophet Joseph Smith received a special revelation to restore Christianity.

The unsuspecting recipient of the LDS message—true Christian or otherwise—is often surprised by how similar Mormon and biblical doctrines sound. The prophet and apostle thing may be a little bit strange, but hey, it can't be that different, right?

Wrong. Mormon theology has missed the biblical mark by a mile. The LDS "Trinity" is not one God in three persons, but three separate gods. The Father, Son, and Spirit are only one *in purpose*. When the missionaries tell you Jesus is the Son of God, they mean He is literally God's son, conceived in the celestial realm from sex between a goddess woman (one of God's "celestial wives") and *Elohim*, who is Jesus's literal father. In fact, to Mormons, He is just as much God's son as you (if you're a guy) are a son of your dad.[143]

Mormonism is not monotheistic like biblical Christianity teaches. According to the LDS, an *infinite* number of gods produce spirit children through celestial sex with their multiple wives.[144] [145] To prove polytheism is not

143   LDS.org, "Chapter 4: Jesus Christ, the Son of God," *Doctrines of the Gospel Student Manual*, accessed June 27, 2016, https://www.lds.org/manual/doctrines-of-the-gospel-student-manual/chapter-4-jesus-christ-the-son-of-god?lang=eng.

144   Rhodes, *The Challenge of the Cults*, 62.

145   LDS.org, "Journal of Discourses, Volume 2, Discourse 50," accessed October 15, 2016, https://www.journalofdiscourses.com/2/50.

condemned by the Bible, LDS will point to verses that mention many gods. This is easy to refute as these verses refer to false gods (*Isa. 45:5*).

Noted theologians in the book *To Everyone an Answer,* raise the important point that "devotion to Christ is not sufficient in itself to qualify a religious movement as authentically Christian."[146] The LDS have such a different view about the nature of God and a host of other essential doctrinal differences that one must conclude their worldview is too different to be considered "Christian."

PREEXISTENCE

Mormon doctrine teaches that we humans, including Jesus, all existed as spirit children in this heavenly realm. In the premortal state, those who are obedient to God our Father could come to earth and have a body of flesh and bones. Afterward, when humans on earth had sexual relations, the spirits in the celestial world inhabit the human bodies here. The following is a passage from the Pearl of Great Price Teacher Manual:

> The spirit children of Heavenly Father who "kept their first estate" (were obedient to God in the premortal life) have received additional opportunities by coming to earth as mortal beings, with bodies of flesh and bones. Those who were not obedient in their first estate will not receive such opportunities. Those who keep their second estate, accepting and obeying the gospel in mortality (or in the postmortal spirit world), will receive eternal glory from God.[147]

The LDS believe people existed in a "first estate" for countless years and eventually matured into "grown spirit men and women." One well-known Mormon apologist claims we dwelt in the cosmos somewhere near a planet called Kolob. We lived in the cosmos until it was time to become mortal and move onto

---

146   Francis J. Beckwith, William Lane Craig, and J.P. Moreland, *To Everyone an Answer: A Case for the Christian Worldview* (Downers Grove, IL: InterVarsity Press, 2004), 331.

147   Si.LDS.org, "Pearl of Great Price Teacher Manual," page 44, accessed February 3, 2017, https://si.lds.org/bc/seminary/content/library/manuals/institute-teacher/pearl-of-great-price-teacher-manual_eng.pdf.

the "second estate." [148] We then are sent to earth to take on flesh and bone so we can become gods one day in the afterlife. [149] [150]

DEFINING TERMS

It is important you understand LDS terms before engaging in dialogue with a Mormon. Despite the obvious differences in essential doctrine, LDS insist the Bible matches their other teachings. This point should be emphasized, as the vast differences between LDS and biblical Christianity cannot be reconciled!

WORKS-BASED GOSPEL

In your conversation with the missionaries or any LDS member, you will likely hear Jesus atoned for our sins on the cross. However, any honest Mormon will admit he believes Jesus's sacrifice was not all-sufficient, as clearly stated in LDS Scripture: "For we know that it is by grace that we are saved, after all we can do" (*2 Nephi 25:23*).

Also, the third LDS Article of Faith states, "We believe that through the Atonement of Christ, all mankind may be saved, by obedience to the laws and ordinances of the Gospel."[151] Last, the Book of Mormon states the following in Moroni 10:32:

> Yea, come unto Christ, and be perfected in him, and deny yourselves of all ungodliness; and if ye shall deny yourselves of all ungodliness, and love God with all your might, mind and strength, then is his grace sufficient for you, that by his grace ye may be perfect in Christ; and if by the grace of God ye are perfect in Christ, ye can in nowise deny the power of God.

148   Richard Abanes, *Becoming Gods* (Eugene, OR. Harvest House Publishers, 2004), 154.

149   Lds.org, "Chapter 6: Our Premortal Life," *Doctrines of the Gospel Student Manual,* accessed June 28, 2016, https://www.lds.org/manual/doctrines-of-the-gospel-student-manual/chapter-6-our-premortal-life?lang=eng.

150   LDS.org, "Becoming Like God," accessed January 29, 2017, https://www.lds.org/topics/becoming-like-god?lang=eng&old=true.

151   Lds.org, "The Articles of Faith," accessed June 27, 2016, https://www.lds.org/scriptures/pgp/a-of-f/1.3?lang=eng.

One of the important theological distinctions to understand with LDS theology is that they differentiate between salvation and eternal life. Unlike biblical Christianity, the two are not synonymous with the LDS. There is a striking pattern within the cults and the denial of the finished work of God the Son on the cross. A denial of the only true God as the only way of receiving forgiveness causes one to work for salvation.

LDS believe Jesus's death on the cross was necessary for forgiveness. However, they believe it was the down payment on salvation/eternal life. His death made it possible to be resurrected to heaven, but our place there is dependent on how righteous we were. An analogy would be one's older brother making the down payment for your car and now you need to make the rest of the payments. The down payment was necessary but was not the total payment.

When the LDS missionaries are almost done presenting their "gospel" to you, they will mention the different degrees of glory you will enter after you have been judged. The highest level, called the "celestial" kingdom, is where Heavenly Father and Jesus Christ reside. Those who live in accordance with the gospel and have been forgiven will live there in God's presence.

The second highest level is called the "terrestrial" kingdom. This kingdom is for those who refuse to accept the gospel but still live good lives. The third and lowest kingdom is called the "telestial" kingdom, where unrepentant sinners will go.[152]

In addition to three levels of heaven, two levels of hell exist. The less severe location is a temporary holding place for those who were disobedient. There, lost souls will be taught the gospel and have the opportunity to repent so they may enter one of the three celestial kingdoms. Those who are unrepentant and reject the gospel will stay in hell throughout the Millennium and be tormented but later will be resurrected to telestial glory.

The second degree of hell is a permanent location where those who have not been redeemed by Christ remain eternally. The devil, his demons, and the sons of perdition will be damned in this state forever.[153] The sons of perdition are those

---

152   The Church of Jesus Christ of Latter-Day Saints, *The Plan of Salvation* (USA: Intellectual Reserve, Inc., 2008), 14.

153   Lds.org, "Guide to the Scriptures: Hell," accessed June 27, 2016, https://www.lds.org/scriptures/gs/hell.

who followed Satan during their premortal life and those who in their mortal life served Satan instead of God.[154]

THE FALL: A BLESSING?

As stated previously, a baby's birth on earth is a result of the spirit, born in the "First Estate" to heavenly parents, being united with an earthly body due to a sexual union between mortal parents. Thus a spirit has two sets of parents: one in the pre-mortal state and one set on earth as mortals.

In Mormon theology, Adam and Eve were the first of Heavenly Father's spirit children who willingly came to earth. When they first arrived, though, they were spirit beings with bodies but were not mortal. To become flesh and blood mortals capable of reproducing, they *had* to disobey God and eat the forbidden fruit.[155] Therefore, Mormons believe The Fall was not a sin—but a blessing.[156]

IS JESUS THE BROTHER OF LUCIFER?

From a biblical perspective, one of the most dangerous Mormon doctrines is that Jesus and Satan are considered "spirit brothers." You may want to express your concerns about this topic to your Mormon friends.

Mormons believe Heavenly Father (Elohim) gathered his spirit children to discuss the plan of salvation at the Council of Heaven. Jesus and Lucifer, as the two eldest sons of God, were present. Jesus, as the firstborn son, volunteered to be the Savior of the world. Satan also volunteered, but was rejected because he planned to destroy the agency of man and dignify himself, while Jesus offered free agency and consented to Heavenly Father's plan of salvation. Consequently, Lucifer and a third of those in heaven decided to rebel. They were then cast to earth, forever denied access to mortal bodies.[157][158]

154   Lds.org, " Guide to the Scriptures: Sons of Perdition," accessed June 27,2016, https://www.lds.org/scriptures/gs/sons-of-perdition.

155   Daniel J. Kudd, BYU Religious Studies Center, "The Fortunate Fall of Adam and Eve," accessed February 3, 2017, https://rsc.byu.edu/archived/no-weapon-shall-prosper/fortunate-fall-adam-and-eve.

156   Abanes, *Becoming Gods*, 159.

157   Gayle Oblad Brown, "Premortal Life," accessed June 28, 2016, http://eom.byu.edu/index.php/Premortal_Life.

158   John Lund, "Council in Heaven," accessed March 19, 2017, http://eom.byu.edu/index.php/Council_in_Heaven.

LDS theology is just not compatible with biblical and historical Christianity. The LDS view Jesus as an evolving spirit who progressed (although He always existed as "intelligence"), which is nowhere found in the Bible. Their concept of Jesus is that He has not always been a god and is the same essence as all gods and humans but just further advanced than us. Their deficient Christology leads Mormons to think one must do works to achieve the highest level of salvation and godhood.

The Triune God of the Bible is without beginning or end, and God the Son's sacrifice is all-sufficient. For it was the Almighty on the cross, not an exalted spirit. The Bible is very clear that Jesus is the uncreated Creator—even of Satan.

LDS POLYTHEISM

What the missionaries probably won't tell you, or may not know, is that LDS theology says numerous worlds and gods exist, each with their own saviors. In fact, there has been an eternal cycle of gods sending saviors to different worlds to save humans from sin.[159] Thus, it would appear Mormonism is the most polytheistic religion in existence.

LDS teach God the Father was once a man who lived on another planet and worked His way to His Godhood (eternal life/exaltation) by obedience to the law.[160] So God has not always been God in LDS theology. Also, God the Father has a body of flesh and bones *(Doctrine and Covenants 130:22)*. This is opposite of what the Bible claims. It states very clearly that no other gods exist *(Isa. 45:5)*. As well, the Father does not have a body *(John 4:24)*, and no man can see Him *(John 1:18, John 6:46)*.

According to LDS, God lives on a planet next to a star called Kolob *(Book of Abraham 3:1-16)*.[161] Also unique to LDS doctrine is the concept of a Heavenly Mother.[162] Together with Heavenly Father, they conceive spirit children in the

---

159   Bill McKeever and Eric Johnson, *Mormonism 101* (Grand Rapids: Baker Books, 2000), 48.

160   Bruce R. McConkie, *A New Witness for the Articles of Faith* (Salt Lake City: Deseret Book, 1985), 64.

161   LDS.org, *The Book of Abraham*, accessed February 1, 2017, https://www.lds.org/bc/content/shared/content/english/pdf/language-materials/06195_eng.pdf?lang=eng https://www.lds.org/scriptures/pgp/abr/3?lang=eng.

162   LDS.org, "Mother in Heaven," accessed January March 15, 2017, https://www.lds.org/topics/mother-in-heaven?lang=eng&old=true.

pre-earth life. The 2009 LDS manual *Gospel Principles* states, "When we lived as spirit children with our heavenly parents, our Heavenly Father told us about His plan for us to become more like Him."[163]

PROGRESSION TO GODHOOD

An LDS male's goal is to progress to the status of godhood in the afterlife. So LDS start in their preexistent state as a spirit child, become a mortal man on earth, live a life of obedience and righteousness, get married in a Mormon temple, and later, in their postmortal life, they become a god. This is known as eternal progression. The official LDS website quotes from their President Gordon B. Hinckley on this issue: "Well, as God is, many may become. We believe in eternal progression. Very strongly."[164]

Mormonism expert Dr. James White emphasizes that the Mormon gospel focuses on progression to godhood. He states, "In Mormonism the idea of advancement to godhood *is the gospel of the Church*."[165] LDS manuals also quote the church's fifth president, Lorenzo Snow, who stated, "As man now is, God once was: As God now is, man may be."[166]

LDS PROOF TEXTS FOR MAN BECOMING A GOD

To justify the doctrine of deification (man can become a god), the LDS misinterpret certain verses. A common passage you may hear is John 10:34-36, where Jesus cites Psalm 82:6:

> Jesus answered them, "Is it not written in your law, 'I said, "You are gods"'? If He called them gods, to whom the word of God came (and the Scripture cannot be broken), do you say of Him whom the Father

163   LDS.org, *Gospel Principles*, page 23, accessed February 1, 2017, https://www.lds.org/bc/content/shared/content/english/pdf/language-materials/06195_eng.pdf?lang=eng.

164   LDS.org, "Becoming Like God," accessed January 29, 2017, https://www.lds.org/topics/becoming-like-god?lang=eng&old=true.

165   James R. White, *Is the Mormon My Brother?* (Birmingham: Solid Ground Christian Books, 1997), 93.

166   LDS.org, "Chapter 5: The Grand Destiny of the Faithful." Accessed March 16, 2017, https://www.lds.org/manual/teachings-of-presidents-of-the-church-lorenzo-snow/chapter-5-the-grand-destiny-of-the-faithful?lang=eng.

sanctified and sent into the world, 'You are blaspheming,' because I said, 'I am the Son of God'?"

The term "gods" in this context refers to unjust human rulers. For a discussion of this, see chapter 6 and the heading, "Because Jesus refers to certain individuals as "gods," polytheism is valid."

There's also Matthew 5:48, which states, "Therefore you shall be perfect, just as your Father in heaven is perfect." But this has been taken out of context. The previous verses *(Matt. 5:43-47)* refer to the theme of love, which makes it clear that this passage is referring to having love without limits. In fact, there is *nothing* in this verse that states one can achieve godhood. The LDS will also quote the following from 2 Peter 1:3-4:

As His divine power has given to us all things that pertain to life and godliness, through the knowledge of Him who called us by glory and virtue, by which have been given to us exceedingly great and precious promises, that through these you may be partakers of the divine nature, having escaped the corruption that is in the world through lust.

In this case, Mormons take the words "you may be partakers of the divine nature" as taking on God's nature—but again, this is out of context. The author of the book *Becoming Gods* refutes this: "By this knowledge of God we are able to partake of His nature. Partake how? By becoming gods? Hardly. We become partakers of God's nature 'having escaped the corruption that is in the world through lust.'"[167] We also note that the divine power refers to Christ who indwells the believer.

Additionally, a popular "proof-text" LDS use is Acts 17:28-29, in which Paul is talking to Athenian philosophers: "For in Him we live and move and have our being, as also some of your own poets have said, 'For we are also His offspring.' Therefore, since we are the offspring of God, we ought not to think that the Divine Nature is like gold or silver or stone, something shaped by art and man's devising."

---

167   Abanes, *Becoming Gods*, 209.

Here Paul is quoting a Greek poet to show the philosophers how even their own poets realized God could not be made of a material substance.[168] Earlier, Paul was disturbed at the idols he had seen in the city *(Acts 17:16)*. He then used Aratus's quote to show how God is also a living Being because He created living humans. The term "offspring" is not used to denote a literal birth but rather to show how God created us in His image and likeness.

Furthermore, from 1 Corinthians 15:49, the LDS will recite, "And as we have borne the image of the man of dust, we shall also bear the image of the heavenly Man." The context of this verse deals with physical resurrection, not becoming gods. This verse refers to believers who received their earthly body, like the first man Adam, and then receive their resurrected and glorified body like Jesus.

Similar to 1 Corinthians 15:49, 1 John 3:2 refers to the believers' resurrected body and nature: "Beloved, now we are children of God; and it has not yet been revealed what we shall be, but we know that when He is revealed, we shall be like Him, for we shall see Him as He is." But although a believer will be *like* Him (Jesus), the believer will not *be* Him.

In Romans 8:29, the passage "For whom He foreknew, He also predestined to be conformed to the image of His Son" refers to those who have become born again, indwelt by the Holy Spirit. They will be conformed and matured *spiritually* to be like Jesus, not to be a god.

Finally, the last passage that LDS love to quote and misrepresent is Romans 8:14-18:

> For as many as are led by the Spirit of God, these are sons of God. For you did not receive the spirit of bondage again to fear, but you received the Spirit of adoption by whom we cry out, "Abba, Father." The Spirit Himself bears witness with our spirit that we are children of God, and if children, then heirs—heirs of God and joint heirs with Christ, if indeed we suffer with *Him,* that we may also be glorified together. For I consider that the sufferings of this present time are not worthy *to be compared* with the glory which shall be revealed in us.

---

168   *MacArthur Study Bible*, annotated by John MacArthur (Dallas, TX: Word, 1997), 1666.

Verse 17 in the above passage refers to the fact that believers will be co-heirs with Christ as *children of God*. Believers will not, however, *be* God.

CHURCH FATHERS AND DEIFICATION

LDS apologists will claim the early Christian church fathers believed in deification. They believe they are justified in believing they can become gods because the early church did. However, this is a gross misinterpretation of what the early Christians taught.

The early Christian church fathers used the term "deification" in reference to the Holy Spirit dwelling in believers, which transforms them into the image of God in Christ. They did not believe that Christians became gods themselves. Author Richard Abanes describes the early church fathers' belief this way:

> Far from the LDS belief that we can be divine in nature—or become "a god" just like Heavenly Father became "a God" (which can be termed ontological deification)—the early church fathers were merely seeking to find a familiar way to express "the richness and sublime content" of salvation. They were groping for some way to describe the glory and wonder of immortality and union with God, as well as the blessedness of sanctification by (and union with) Christ.[169]

For a debate on the subject between Christian and Mormon apologists, watch the Alpha & Omega Ministries' YouTube video titled "Can Men Become Gods? James White vs. Martin Tanner."

UNIVERSALISM

LDS teach that most everyone will go to heaven. Sandra Tanner of Utah Lighthouse Ministry writes the following explanation:

> According to Mormonism, practically everyone will gain heaven. Salvation is equated with "resurrection" (immortality) and it is promised to virtually all, but the only ones who will experience "eternal life"

---

169   Abanes, *Becoming Gods*, 215.

(exaltation) are those who have been faithful LDS, married in the temple, and achieve the highest level of heaven.[170]

BAPTISM OF THE DEAD

The LDS believe the spirits of people who have died cannot attain the celestial kingdom unless a living Mormon is baptized and sealed in the temple endowment ceremony on their behalf. The official LDS website states that Joseph Smith taught this truth: "The salvation of our dead ancestors is 'essential to our salvation.' Our lives are closely tied to our ancestors' lives, for we cannot become perfect without them nor they without us."[171] This temple work is based on the LDS interpretation of 1 Corinthians 15:29: "Otherwise, what will they do who are baptized for the dead, if the dead do not rise at all? Why then are they baptized for the dead?"

While different interpretations of this verse exist, one thing is certain: it is not instructing believers that a dead person can be saved by a living person who gets baptized in their place. The Bible is very clear that we are saved by grace through faith alone *(Eph. 2:8; Rom. 3:28)*. The key to understanding this verse is to read the preceding verses, which speak of resurrection. It seems Paul is stating that those teaching baptism of the dead (likely a pagan teaching) were the same as those who denied the Resurrection of Jesus *(1 Cor. 15:20-29)*. Note he does not say "we" who baptize for the dead. Interestingly, even though it is emphasized with the LDS, the Book of Mormon never mentions the doctrine of baptism for the dead.[172] (For more information see Chapter 6, Point #23)

POLYGAMY

An important requirement for deification in the LDS church is that while on earth, LDS men must marry and become sealed in an LDS temple. A single male cannot become a god. This is described in Doctrine and Covenants

---

170 Sandra Tanner, *41 Unique Teachings of The LDS Church* (Salt Lake City: Lighthouse Ministry, 2012), 36.
171 LDS.org, "Section 128: Baptism for the Dead," accessed February 3, 2017, https://www.lds.org/manual/doctrine-and-covenants-student-manual/sections-122-131/section-128-baptism-for-the-dead?lang=eng.
172 Tanner, *Major Problems*, 230.

section 132:18-21. This puts a lot of stress on devout LDS males to marry. Men who reach the highest celestial level of heaven must practice polygamy in the heavenly kingdom:

> Brigham Young, the second president and prophet of the LDS church, explained why God introduced polygamy. All of the millions of spirit children of Heavenly Father and Heavenly Mother need to obtain physical bodies, therefore mortals need to have as many children as possible.[173]

The practice of polygamy has been heavily criticized by Christians and the secular public. But polygamy isn't just a belief. It's neither theoretical nor philosophical, but rather an action. The polygamous practices of Joseph Smith and other LDS presidents/apostles are a historical fact. The official Latter-day Saints website notes, "After receiving a revelation commanding him to practice plural marriage, Joseph Smith married multiple wives and introduced the practice to close associates."[174]

A 2014 *New York Times* article reported that LDS leaders acknowledged Joseph Smith "took as many as 40 wives, some already married and one only 14 years old."[175] Polygamy did not stop with Smith. It continued with Brigham Young, who moved the LDS community to Utah in 1847.[176] In 1862, the US government passed a series of laws to stop this practice. LDS resisted the commands for many years because the practice was supposedly commanded by God.[177]

---

173   Tanner, *41 Unique Teachings of the LDS Church*,63.

174   LDS.org, "Plural Marriage in Kirtland and Nauvoo," accessed July 26, 2016, https://www.lds.org/topics/plural-marriage-in-kirtland-and-nauvoo?lang=eng.

175   Laurie Goodstein, "It's Official: Mormon Founder Had Up to 40 Wives," accessed July 26, 2016, http://www.nytimes.com/2014/11/11/us/its-official-mormon-founder-had-up-to-40-wives.html?_r=0.

176   BYU. Harold B. Lee Library, "Plural Marriage," accessed July March 19, 2017, http://eom.byu.edu/index.php/Plural_Marriage.

177   LDS.org, "Plural Marriage in The Church of Jesus Christ of Latter-day Saints," accessed January 29, 2017, https://www.lds.org/topics/plural-marriage-in-the-church-of-jesus-christ-of-latter-day-saints?lang=eng&old=true.

Ultimately, their case was taken to the Supreme Court. In May 1887, the Court upheld the constitutionality of monogamous marriages and opened the way for church property to be confiscated. The US government gave an ultimatum to LDS to stop the practice of polygamy and enjoy the benefits of Utah statehood . . . or face closure.[178]

Under this pressure, then-LDS President Wilford Woodruff "received direction from the Lord" and in September 25, 1890, released an official statement that plural marriage would no longer be practiced.[179] LDS missionaries, however, will insist there was no connection between Woodruff's revelation and the US government's ultimatum.

LDS will also claim the Old Testament records and supports polygamy, so no one should have a problem with Smith's revelation. They will note that Abraham, David, and Solomon were polygamous. Does this prove God is okay with polygamy? No! No commandments support polygamy, and *nothing* condones polygamy in the Bible, whether it be the Old or New Testament. In fact, it's just the opposite.

Starting early on in Genesis 2:24, the Bible commands monogamous marriage of one man and one wife: "Therefore a man shall leave his father and mother and be joined to his wife, and they shall become one flesh." In Deuteronomy 17:17, God gives a command for the future kings of Israel: "Neither shall he multiply wives for himself, lest his heart turn away."

Turning away is exactly what happened in the book of Kings with Solomon, who had numerous wives and concubines and disobeyed God's command of monogamous marriage: "For it was so, when Solomon was old, that his wives turned his heart after other gods" (*1 Kings 11:4*).

Let us be very clear about this: God *tolerated* polygamy in the Old Testament, as he did many other sins, as long as people repented. Yet he let violators suffer the consequences and judgment of polygamy, spiritually and emotionally.

The New Testament is very clear on the importance of monogamous marriage as well, with several verses making this commandment unambiguous. Examples

178   Abanes, *Becoming Gods*, 227.
179   LDS.org, "The Manifesto and the End of Plural Marriage," accessed July 26, 2016, https://www.lds.org/topics/the-manifesto-and-the-end-of-plural-marriage?lang=eng.

include 1 Timothy 3:2, 12; Titus 1:6; Matthew 19:3-9; 1 Corinthians 6:15-17; and 1 Corinthians 7:2.

LDS WOMEN AND GODHOOD

LDS women can also achieve exaltation and godhood in the celestial kingdom. Remember that in LDS theology there is a Heavenly Mother and Heavenly Father. They are referred to as heavenly parents. They too had heavenly parents and the cycle regresses ad infinitum.

One of the functions of a Heavenly Mother is to bear millions of spirit children, as stated by Mormon Apostle Orson Pratt:

> In the Heaven where our spirits were born, there are many Gods, each one of whom has his own wife or wives... Each God, through his wife or wives, raises up a numerous family of sons and daughters...for each father and mother will be in a condition to multiply forever and ever. As soon as each God has begotten many millions of male and female spirits, and his Heavenly inheritance becomes too small, to comfortably accommodate his great family, he, in connection with his sons, organizes a new world, after a similar order to the one which we now inhabit, where he sends both the male and female spirits to inhabit tabernacles of flesh and bones...The inhabitants of each world are required to reverence, adore, and worship their own personal father who dwells in Heaven which they formerly inhabited.[180]

However, Heavenly Mother is not to be worshipped. Consider the words of Apostle Gordon B. Hinckley:

> Logic and reason would certainly suggest that if we have a Father in Heaven, we have a Mother in Heaven. That doctrine rests well with me. However, in light of the instruction we have received from the Lord

---

180   Orson Pratt, "The Seer. The Pre-existence of Man," accessed March 16, 2017, http://contentdm.lib.byu.edu/cdm/compoundobject/collection/NCMP1820-1846/id/18143.

Himself, I regard it as inappropriate for anyone in the Church to pray to our Mother in Heaven.[181]

MODERN-DAY PROPHETS

The LDS emphasizes prophets and apostles to speak on behalf of the Lord so they can lead the church.[182] Regarding modern-day prophets and apostles, LDS President Dieter F. Uchtdorf said, "Because Heavenly Father loves His children, He has not left them to walk through this mortal life without direction and guidance. That is why He pleads so earnestly with us through His prophets. Just as we want what is best for our loved ones, Heavenly Father wants what is best for us."

Like many other biblical doctrines, the LDS teaching on prophets and apostles has been distorted. We will correct their errors in chapter 6.

RACIAL HISTORY

Prior to 1978, Mormons of black African descent were banned from the priesthood. Furthermore, black men and women were not allowed to participate in temple endowment or sealing ordinances.[183] This racist doctrine has had different explanations by LDS theologians. An article by Brigham Young University states the following:

> According to the book of Abraham (now part of the Pearl of Great Price), the descendants of Cain were to be denied the priesthood of God (Abr. 1:23-26). Some Latter-day Saints theorized that blacks would be restricted throughout mortality. As early as 1852, however, Brigham Young said that the "time will come when they will have the privilege of all we have the privilege of and more" (Brigham Young Papers, Church Archives, Feb. 5, 1852), and increasingly in the 1960s, Presidents of the Church taught that denial of entry to the priesthood was a current

181   LDS.org, "Daughters of God," accessed March 16, 2017, https://www.lds.org/general-conference/1991/10/daughters-of-god?lang=eng.

182   LDS.org, "Prophets and Apostles: We Need Living Prophets," accessed June 28, 2016, https://www.lds.org/prophets-and-apostles/unto-all-the-world/we-need-living-prophets?lang=eng.

183   LDS.org, "Race and the Priesthood," accessed July 31, 2016, https://www.lds.org/topics/race-and-the-priesthood?lang=eng.

commandment of God, but would not prevent blacks from eventually possessing all eternal blessings.[184]

In *Mormonism 101*, the authors quote several LDS apostles and presidents who confirm this doctrine throughout history.[185] However, the LDS official website states they disagree with their past prophets, apostles, and presidents: "Today, the Church disavows the theories advanced in the past that black skin is a sign of divine disfavor or curse, or that it reflects unrighteous actions in a premortal life; that mixed-race marriages are a sin; or that blacks or people of any other race or ethnicity are inferior in any way to anyone else."[186]

NO CAFFEINE OR ALCOHOL

In 1833, Joseph Smith received a revelation from the Lord that followers should avoid alcohol, tobacco, and hot drinks (in modern times thought to mean caffeinated teas or coffee). As well, meat should be consumed "only in times of winter, or of cold, or of famine." This is found in Doctrine and Covenants section 89. This became known as the *Word of Wisdom*.

The New Testament teaches food has no legalistic restrictions *(Col. 2:16)*. And 1 Corinthians 10:31 states, "Therefore, whether you eat or drink, or whatever you do, do all to the glory of God."

ETERNALITY OF THE UNIVERSE

When speaking with Mormon missionaries, they may mention that matter is eternal because it can't be created or destroyed. However, this contradicts biblical and scientific evidence.

In the King Follett Sermon, Joseph Smith declared he knew "more than all the world put together" and that the Holy Ghost had revealed to him facts about creation other preachers did not know.[187] He stated, "Hence we infer that

184   Alan Cherry and Jessie Embry," Blacks," accessed March 16, 2017, http://eom.byu.edu/index.php/Blacks.
185   McKeever and Johnson, *Mormonism 101*, 265-272.
186   LDS.org, "Race and the Priesthood," accessed July 31, 2016, https://www.lds.org/topics/race-and-the-priesthood?lang=eng.
187   LDS.org, "The King Follett Sermon," accessed January 3, 2017, https://www.lds.org/ensign/1971/04/the-king-follett-sermon?lang=eng.

God had materials to organize the world out of chaos—chaotic matter, which is element, and in which dwells all the glory. Element had an existence from the time He had. The pure principles of element are principles which can never be destroyed; they may be organized and re-organized, but not destroyed. They had no beginning and can have no end."[188]

Smith's statement is in complete opposition to the biblical account of creation. When Genesis 1:1 states, "In the beginning God created the heavens and the earth," the Bible is affirming God created the universe out of nothing. "In the beginning" denotes time began, and "the heavens and the earth" signifies space and matter had a beginning as well. Furthermore, Hebrews 11:3 confirms *ex nihilo* creation as it states the universe was made solely by God speaking it into existence: "By faith we understand that the worlds were framed by the word of God, so that the things which are seen were not made of things which are visible."

Also, an abundance of scientific evidence shows the universe had a beginning. For example, the second law of thermodynamics tells us the universe is running down, so there must have been a time when it was wound up or created. Finally, the idea that matter is neither created nor destroyed only applies once the universe has come into being.

In summary, the LDS believe all matter is eternal including gods and humans. We have always existed as an "intelligence" who were later born to God and Heavenly Mother. We then become a spirit child of a god. This is in stark contrast to what the Bible teaches.

---

188   Ibid.

LDS vs Biblical Christianity

LDS View	Christian View
GOD THE FATHER	
Evolved spirit child of a God and Wife	Uncreated
Not eternally God, once was mortal	Eternally God
Once a man	Spirit
Had to learn as a mortal and then achieved godhood	Omniscient
God the Father Finite as God and Infinite as Intelligence	Infinite
Achieved holiness	Always been holy
One of many gods	The only true God, part of Trinity
Used pre-existent matter to make the world	Created the universe out of nothing with the other two Persons of the Trinity
Constrained to one place at a time, has a resurrected physical body.	Omnipresent
Our spirits were created by Heavenly Father and Mother God through sexual intercourse.	Created human spirits
Attained power when progressed as a mortal to godhood.	Omnipotent
JESUS	
Evolved spirit child of a God and Wife	Uncreated
One of many gods	The only true God, part of Trinity
Brother of Satan and humans	Always God
Creator of this world (not all worlds) along with other Gods, using pre-existent matter.	Created the universe out of nothing with the other two Persons of the Trinity
Achieved godhood and holiness	Always been God and holy
Constrained to one place at a time, has a resurrected physical body. Attained power when progressed as a mortal to godhood	Omnipresent
Once a man	Always God, took on humanity; so fully divine/ fully human
Our spirits were created by Heavenly Father and Mother God through sexual intercourse	Created human spirits
Son of God meaning Literally God's offspring	Son of God, meaning the second Person of the Trinity

LDS vs Biblical Christianity

LDS View	Christian View
HOLY SPIRIT	
Evolved spirit child of a God and Wife	Uncreated
Not eternally God	Eternally God
A spirit man, spirit son of God the Father; does not have a body of flesh and bones, but "is a personage of Spirit"	Person
Achieved godhood	Omniscient
Finite, although his influence can be everywhere	Infinite, Omnipresent
Can influence believers and dwell in believers hearts if one has been baptized and obedient to the laws and ordinances	Indwells all believers
Achieved holiness	Always been holy
One of many gods. A separate god of the LDS Trinity, a separate substance god than the Father and Jesus	A member of the Trinity; part of the substance of the one True God
MAN	
Pre-mortal spirit being born literally from God and his Wife, then born to earthly parents	Born to earthly parents only
Potential to achieve Godhood	Potential to spend eternity with God
Brother of Lucifer (Satan)	No relation to Satan
Sinner in need of salvation through repentance, faith, and works	Sinner in need of salvation through repentance and faith
SATAN	
Fallen spirit brother of Jesus and other mortals	Created angel who rebelled against God and cast out of heaven
Involved in the discussion of the plan of salvation at the Council of Heaven	Played no role in God's plan of salvation

SUMMARY POINTS FOR DIALOGUE WITH LDS

- Bible condemns the occult *(Deut. 18:9-12; Rev. 21:8)*; why was Joseph Smith involved in it?
- Where is the archaeological evidence for Israelites inhabiting the Americas?
- Why doesn't DNA evidence confirm the Mormon account of people groups in the Americas, especially North America?

- The Bible claims God has always existed and there were no Gods before Him *(Isa. 44:6-8, 45:5, 45:21-22)*. How do you reconcile this with LDS theology that states God the Father progressed to godhood as a human and had a Father God before Him?
- The Bible tells us Jesus is God; He is the Creator *(John 1:3; Col. 1:16)*. Why does LDS theology contradict this by stating He is the spirit brother of Satan? Why has Jesus not always been God as the Bible teaches?
- LDS doctrine promotes polytheism while Christianity is monotheistic.
- Why is Jesus's atonement satisfactory for salvation but not eternal life? Why does the Bible state works are not involved in a believer's reward of eternal life with God but LDS requires works?
- LDS theology changes throughout time. For example, polygamy is no longer commanded (by mainstream LDS but still practiced by other LDS sects), and blacks were once banned from the LDS priesthood.
- Are you aware of the thousands of changes to the Book of Mormon?

CHAPTER 4
IS JESUS REALLY GOD?

Most people would agree Jesus is the most influential person in human history. Those with a deeper understanding of history would even agree He is the most extraordinary person who ever lived. In fact, no one has made an impact on world history like Jesus had and continues to have. Tim LaHaye notes in his book *Jesus, Who Is He?* that Jesus is unparalleled in His impact in regard to moral influence, artistic influence, humanitarian influence, scholastic influence, and ability to inspire devotion.[189]

But some secular people—we'll call them "skeptics"—acknowledge the historical Jesus. The thing is, they refuse to admit He is God and dismiss anything that seems remotely "supernatural" to them.

However, it gets a little trickier when it comes to the "Christian" cults. In a typical conversation with a JW or LDS, he'll try to convince you that

---

189   Tim LaHaye. *Why Believe in Jesus?* (Eugene, OR.: Harvest House Publishers, 2004), 17-18.

Jesus is the *son* of God or *a* god, but not the *true* God. He'll even go so far as to reassure you that he believes Jesus has somewhat of a divine *aspect* to Him, but that He is not God Almighty. The Bible, however, clearly states Jesus is divine.

Even the New World Translation, which is relied upon by millions of JWs (and has taken verses out that say Jesus is God), quite clearly states Jesus is God Almighty. This will be further demonstrated in chapter 6. The Bible version used by LDS *also clearly* states Jesus is God. Yet these cults have been confused and misled by their *other* books and by the prophets who have contradicted this fundamental biblical doctrine.

Let's now look to the final court of arbitration: God's inspired and inerrant Word, the Bible. We will review clear and convincing verses that demonstrate Jesus is God. This is not an exhaustive review, as many verses that support this truth exist. As ambassadors of Jesus Christ, every Christian should know and deeply understand the following verses.

OLD TESTAMENT PREDICTED JESUS WOULD BE GOD— ISAIAH 9:6

For unto us a Child is born,
Unto us a Son is given;
And the government will be upon His shoulder.
And His name will be called
Wonderful, Counselor, Mighty God,
Everlasting Father, Prince of Peace *(Isa. 9:6)*.

In this verse, the prophet Isaiah was prophesying approximately seven hundred years before the birth of Jesus. His message was that the Messiah to come would be *the* Mighty God.

The Bible is clear throughout the Old and New Testament: There is only one, true God. Isaiah 9:6 can only mean that the Messiah would be *a Son*, *God*, and "everlasting"—or, in other words, *eternal*. Likewise, in the New Testament, we read that Jesus is *a Son (John 3:16)*, *God (John 1:1, 20:28)*, and *eternal (1 John 1:2; Rev. 1:8,17)*.

Isaiah 9:6 also proves the term "Son of God" denotes both eternality and divinity. This is because the Child born was to be a Son, God, and everlasting. Therefore, when a Jew heard Jesus declaring Himself to be the Son of God, he must have thought about this passage.

Note Isaiah 9:6 in the NWT refers to the Messiah as the "Eternal Father," making it clear in the JW Bible that Jesus is eternal.

JESUS CLAIMED TO BE GOD—JOHN 8:24, 58

Therefore I said to you that you will die in your sins; for if you do not believe that I am *He,* you will die in your sins *(John 8:24).*

Jesus said to them, "Most assuredly, I say to you, before Abraham was, I AM" *(John 8:58).*

Jesus used the term "I AM" to denote His self-existence, immutability, and eternality. This is the name of Yahweh God in the Old Testament (*Exod. 3:14; Deut. 32:39; Isa. 41:4, 43:10*).

In John 8:24, the word "He" has been added by the translators to clarify that Jesus is referring to Himself as God.

In the original Greek, the phrase "I am" is translated ego eimi,[190] which are the same words Jesus used in verses 24 and 58. After Jesus declared a second time to be the "I Am" in verse 58, His Jewish opponents picked up stones to kill Him because He claimed to be God (*Lev. 24:16*).

In the New World Translation, verse 24 reads, "I am the one," and verse 58 says, "I have been," instead of "I am." This is an obvious cover-up of the deity of Jesus by the Watch Tower. In the 1985 publication of the Kingdom Interlinear Translation of the Greek Scriptures, published by the Watch Tower, verses 24 and 58 read, "I am," in the Greek-English interlinear![191]

---

190 Kurt Aland et al., *The Greek New Testament, Fourth Revised Edition (Interlinear with Morphology)* (Deutsche Bibelgesellschaft, 1993).

191 New World Bible Translation Committee, *The Kingdom Interlinear Translation of the Greek Scriptures* (Brooklyn: Watchtower Bible and Tract Society of New York, 1985), 447, 451.

JESUS AGREES WITH THE CONCLUSION
OF THOMAS THAT HE IS GOD—JOHN 20:26-29

> And after eight days His disciples were again inside, and Thomas with them. Jesus came, the doors being shut, and stood in the midst, and said, "Peace to you!" Then He said to Thomas, "Reach your finger here, and look at My hands; and reach your hand *here,* and put *it* into My side. Do not be unbelieving, but believing." And Thomas answered and said to Him, "My Lord and my God!" Jesus said to him, "Thomas, because you have seen Me, you have believed. Blessed *are* those who have not seen and *yet* have believed."

Thomas, a disciple of Jesus, saw and touched Him after His Resurrection and concluded that Jesus was Lord and God. Who would know better than a disciple who saw the risen Lord?

Note "God" is spelled with a capital "G," as it is in the New World Translation. Also, notice how Thomas says *to* Jesus, "My Lord and my God!" This is not an exclamation, but a direct confession of faith from Thomas to Jesus.

Accepting Thomas's conclusion would've been blasphemous if, in fact, Jesus wasn't God—and because Jesus is sinless (*Heb. 4:15; 1 Pet. 2:22; 2 Cor 5:21; 1 John 3:5; 1 Pet. 1:18-19*), He would not commit the sin of blasphemy. Instead, Jesus confirms and commends the conclusion of Thomas.

JESUS IS EQUAL WITH GOD—JOHN 5:18

> Therefore the Jews sought all the more to kill Him, because He not only broke the Sabbath, but also said that God was His Father, making Himself equal with God (*John 5:18*).

Jesus made a comment to the Jews that He was working on the Sabbath and that it was okay because His Father was also working. God is always in control and sustaining the universe—and like the other members of the Trinity, Jesus, as God, is always working.

Additionally, Jesus referred to God as His Father, which enraged the Jews. They saw God as having no equal. Thus, Jesus, by claiming to be God's Son and working on the Sabbath, just as His Father, put Him on an equal level as God.[192]

JESUS IS LORD OF THE SABBATH—
MATTHEW 12:8; MARK 2:28; LUKE 6:5

> And He said to them, "The Son of Man is also Lord of the Sabbath" *(Luke 6:5).*

After the Pharisees accused Jesus's disciples of breaking the Sabbath because they gleaned grain in a field, Jesus explained to them that the Sabbath was made for man and how they had done nothing wrong biblically. Jesus correctly interpreted the Sabbath because He is Lord over it. The Bible states: "For the Son of Man is Lord even of the Sabbath" *(Matt. 12:8).*

Here's another instance where Jesus is referred to as Lord of the Sabbath, an ownership that only God has the right to. As noted in *A Commentary on the Holy Scriptures:*

> He is both the principle and the object of the sabbath; He rests in God, and God in Him: hence He is the Mediator of proper sabbath-observance, and the Interpreter of the sabbath law. Even the Jews admitted that the authority of the Messiah was greater than that of the laws of the sabbath[193]

Obviously, because God instituted the Sabbath, only He is Lord over it.

JESUS IS WORSHIPPED—MATTHEW 14:33, 28:9, 28:17; HEBREWS 1:6; REVELATION 4:11, 5:13

> Then those who were in the boat came and worshiped Him, saying, "Truly You are the Son of God" *(Matt. 14:33).*

---

192   Edwin A. Blum, "John," in *The Bible Knowledge Commentary: An Exposition of the Scriptures*, ed. J. F. Walvoord and R. B. Zuck, Vol. 2 (Wheaton, IL: Victor Books, 1985), 290.

193   John Peter Lange and Philip Schaff, *A Commentary on the Holy Scriptures: Matthew* (Bellingham, WA: Logos Bible Software, 2008), 217.

And as they went to tell His disciples, behold, Jesus met them, saying, "Rejoice!" So they came and held Him by the feet and worshiped Him *(Matt. 28:9)*.

When they saw Him, they worshiped Him; but some doubted *(Matt. 28:17)*.

Let all the angels of God worship Him *(Heb. 1:6)*.

You are worthy, O Lord, to receive glory and honor and power; For You created all things, And by Your will they exist and were created *(Rev. 4:11)*.

And every creature which is in heaven and on the earth and under the earth and such as are in the sea, and all that are in them, I heard saying:

"Blessing and honor and glory and power

Be to Him who sits on the throne,

And to the Lamb, forever and ever!" *(Rev. 5:13)*

(Note: The NWT has changed the previous verses so the word "obeisance," rather than "worship," refers to Jesus. However, they have not changed Revelation 5:13. We will explore how to use the NWT and still prove Jesus is God further in chapter 7.)

In about fourteen verses in the New Testament, Jesus is worshipped. For at least eight of these verses, the context demonstrates that the term "worship" is exactly as what it states. It's possible that the other six verses may mean to honor or to show reverence.

Nevertheless, we have provided clear verses that show Jesus was worshipped. And, of course, only God is to be worshipped (Ex. 20: 3-5, 34:14; Lk. 4:8). It would be blasphemous for Jesus to accept worship if He were not God.

Even God the Father tells us in Hebrews 1:6 that the Son is to be worshipped as God. Also, in Revelation 5:13, the Father and Son are receiving worship. Hence, the Father and Son must both be God—or part of the Triune Godhead— to receive worship.

Revelation 5:13 is an excellent verse to use with the JWs, especially when using their corrupted Bible. Isaiah 42:8 states that Yahweh will not give glory to anyone but Himself. However, Jesus receives glory in Revelation 5:13. Therefore, Jesus is Yahweh.

You can also use John 17:5 to further prove the point that Jesus must be Yahweh. Jesus states, "And now, O Father, glorify Me together with Yourself, with the glory which I had with You before the world was." Here we have Jesus asking the Father for the glory that is only for Yahweh. This further shows us that Jesus is God.

JESUS FORGAVE SINS—MARK 2:5; LUKE 7:48

When Jesus saw their faith, He said to the paralytic, "Son, your sins are forgiven you" *(Mark 2:5).*

Then He said to her, "Your sins are forgiven" *(Luke 7:48).*

Who would disagree that only God can forgive sins? Certainly, a man or spirit creature would not be able to do that. The Pharisees understood only God can forgive sins, because the Bible states in Isaiah 43:25 that Yahweh blots out sins, and in Psalm 103:3, David says Yahweh forgives sins. In Luke 5:21, we read, "And the scribes and the Pharisees began to reason, saying, 'Who is this who speaks blasphemies? Who can forgive sins but God alone?'"

The religious leaders of Jesus's day made it very clear that it would be blasphemy for anyone other than God to forgive sins. Jesus forgave sins on His own authority and would not do so if He wasn't God because He was sinless. Therefore, since Yahweh alone forgives sins, and Jesus forgave sins, what can we conclude about Jesus?

JESUS RECEIVES THE SPIRIT OF BELIEVERS—ACTS 7:59

And they stoned Stephen as he was calling on *God* and saying, "Lord Jesus, receive my spirit" *(Acts 7:59).*

The Old Testament states that a believer's spirit entered the presence of God when he died *(Ps. 23:6; Job 29:25-27).* Jesus confirmed this in the New Testament in Matthew 22:31-33: "But concerning the resurrection of the dead, have you not read what was spoken to you by God, saying, 'I am the God of Abraham, the

God of Isaac, and the God of Jacob'? God is not the God of the dead, but of the living."

If the spirit of a believer is sent to the presence of God upon death and Stephen cried out to Jesus to receive his spirit because he knew death was imminent, then Stephen must have believed Jesus was God.

NEW TESTAMENT WRITERS STATED JESUS WAS GOD

Let this mind be in you which was also in Christ Jesus, who, being in the form of God, did not consider it robbery to be equal with God, but made Himself of no reputation, taking the form of a bondservant, *and* coming in the likeness of men. And being found in appearance as a man, He humbled Himself and became obedient to *the point of* death, even the death of the cross. Therefore God also has highly exalted Him and given Him the name which is above every name, that at the name of Jesus every knee should bow, of those in heaven, and of those on earth, and of those under the earth, and *that* every tongue should confess that Jesus Christ *is* Lord, to the glory of God the Father (*Phil. 2:5-11*).

For Jesus to be in the *form* of God, it would mean He would have to be God, because there is only one God..

Paul also writes that Jesus did not consider it to be a problem (robbery) for Him to be equal with God (because He is part of the Trinity). Also, only the one, true God should be worshipped and bowed down to. Here, we read God the Father will command everyone to bow down to God the Son ("bend the knee" in the NWT). This is an allusion to Isaiah 45:23, which says every knee shall bow and take an oath to Yahweh.

Furthermore, when Jesus is referred to as Lord in a religious sense, the Greek term *Kyrios* is used, which refers to "Yahweh."[194]

Looking for the blessed hope and glorious appearing of our great God and Savior Jesus Christ *(Ti. 2:13)*. The Apostle Paul refers to Jesus as "God and Savior." (Verse has been corrupted in NWT.)

---

194   Gerhard Kittel, Gerhard Friedrich, and Geoffrey William Bromiley, *Theological Dictionary of the New Testament* (Grand Rapids, MI: W.B. Eerdmans, 1985), 488.

The prophet Isaiah affirmed in the Old Testament that Yahweh would be both God and Savior: "And *there is* no other God besides Me, a just God and a Savior; *There is* none besides Me" (*Isa. 45:21*). Consider also Romans 9:5: "According to the flesh, Christ *came,* who is over all, *the* eternally blessed God. Amen." (Verse has been corrupted in NWT.)

Similar to Philippians 2:5-11, Paul, in the following verses, tells the reader that Jesus is the eternal God who came in the flesh:

For in Him all the fullness of Deity dwells in bodily form *(Col. 2:8-9, New American Standard Bible).*

That God was in Christ reconciling the world to Himself *(2 Cor. 5:19).* (Verse has been corrupted in NWT.)

The fullness of God dwells in the person of Christ. Moreover, God dwells in Christ because Christ is God. "To those who have obtained like precious faith with us by the righteousness of our God and Savior Jesus Christ" *(2 Pet. 1:1).* (Verse has been corrupted in NWT.)

The Apostle Peter affirms in his own words that Jesus Christ is God *and* Savior. This matches Isaiah 43:11: "I, *even* I, *am* the LORD, And besides Me *there is* no savior." So even the Old Testament stated that God alone would be the savior.

JESUS RAISED HIMSELF FROM THE DEAD—JOHN 2:19-22

Jesus answered and said to them, "Destroy this temple, and in three days I will raise it up."

Then the Jews said, "It has taken forty-six years to build this temple, and will You raise it up in three days?"

But He was speaking of the temple of His body.

Therefore, when He had risen from the dead, His disciples remembered that He had said this to them; and they believed the Scripture and the word which Jesus had said *(John 2:19-22).*

The Apostle John quotes Jesus as specifically stating that He would be killed, and in three days, He would raise His body to life again by Himself. If Jesus were a mere "spirit creature," as the JWs believe, or "one god amongst many," as the LDS believe, how could He have raised Himself from the dead?

Both LDS and JWs will agree God raised Jesus from the dead *(Rom. 10:9; 1 Pet. 1:21)*. They will also concede the Father raised Jesus from the dead *(Gal. 1:1; Eph. 1:20)*. Even the Spirit raised Jesus from the dead *(Rom. 8:11)*, which shows the Triune nature of God.

However, Jesus alone raised Himself from the dead. Recall that in John 2:19, Jesus says, "Destroy this temple, and in three days I will raise it up." The Apostle John then clarifies what this temple is in verse 21: "But He was speaking of the temple of His body." Therefore, because God raised Jesus from the dead, but Jesus raised Himself from the dead, Jesus is God. But one may ask, "How can a dead person raise themselves to life?"

Recall the reply of Jesus when the thief on the cross asked Jesus to remember him when He went into His kingdom. Jesus replied in Luke 23:43, "Assuredly, I say to you, today you will be with Me in Paradise." Note that Jesus stated that "today" the thief would be with Him in paradise. As God, His spirit always existed and continued to when He was on the cross and when His human body died.

Do note that the NWT adds a comma, so Luke 23:43 reads, "And he said to him: 'Truly I tell you today, you will be with me in Paradise.'" Simply point out that Jesus's spirit was still alive since He proclaimed His victory over death to the fallen angels in hades *(1 Pet. 3:19-20)*. Furthermore, Philippians 2:5-11 tells us Jesus was God who took on a human nature, so of course He would be alive after His body died on the cross. That is why He stated the thief would be with Him immediately in the heavenly realm (paradise) instead of waiting three days when His physical body was resurrected.

When you use this verse in your witnessing encounters (and we recommend that you do), there are only two objections you will hear:

1. Jesus wasn't talking about Himself.
2. It is impossible because a dead person can't raise themselves up.

However, notice how John clarifies that Jesus is talking about the temple of His body. Additionally, Jesus's spirit would have remained because it went to Heaven just like He told the thief on the cross.

(Note: JWs might say humans don't have a spirit. Simply point out that their theology is in direct contradiction to Scripture (Rom. 8:16; Heb. 4:12). Also, when you use this verse with Mormons, emphasize how Jesus is one Person of the Godhead who played a role in His Resurrection. One God raised Jesus from the dead, not three separate gods.)

JESUS IS THE CREATOR—JOHN 1:3; COLOSSIANS 1:16; HEBREWS 1:10

All things were made through Him, and without Him nothing was made that was made *(John 1:3)*.

For by Him all things were created that are in heaven and that are on earth, visible and invisible, whether thrones or dominions or principalities or powers. All things were created through Him and for Him *(Col. 1:16)*.

And: You, LORD, in the beginning laid the foundation of the earth, And the heavens are the work of Your hands (Heb. 1:10).

The book of Genesis starts with this fact: "In the beginning God created the heavens and the earth." We also read in Isaiah 44:24 that Yahweh created the universe by Himself:

I *am* the LORD, who makes all *things,*
Who stretches out the heavens all alone,
Who spreads abroad the earth by Myself.

It only stands to reason that if God created the universe by Himself, and Jesus is given credit for creating the universe, then Jesus must be God. We see also in John 1:3, Colossians 1:16, and Hebrews 1:10 that Jesus is clearly the Creator.

(Note: As we will show later, JWs have changed Colossians 1:16. However, you can still use John 1:3 and emphasize God alone created the universe. Jesus could not just play a "part" in creation because the Bible strictly says Yahweh alone is the Creator.)

With LDS—and JWs—you should also point out that Jesus cannot be created if He created *all* things.

FIRST CENTURY CHURCH FATHERS BELIEVED AND TAUGHT JESUS WAS GOD

Several early church fathers believed Jesus was God. Next to the apostles, they would have the most credibility as to whether Jesus was believed to be God in early Christianity. We will review some of the earliest.

Ignatius (AD 35-117) was the bishop of Antioch in Syria and thought to be a disciple of John. He is best known for the seven letters he penned before his martyrdom at Rome. In a letter to Polycarp, he wrote, "Jesus Christ our God" (*Eph. 1; Rom. 1*).[195]

Polycarp (AD 69-155) lived during the time of some of the twelve apostles. Early church tradition holds he was taught by the Apostle John. He was an early church father and bishop of Smyrna.[196] In his writings, he refers to Jesus as "our Lord and God" (*Phil. 12*).[197] He too was martyred for his faith.

Polycarp passed on what he had learned from the Apostle John to Irenaeus (AD 120-202), who became an important theologian and bishop in Gaul (modern-day France). Irenaeus wrote an apologetic work called *Against Heresies* in which he referred to Jesus as, "Our Lord, and God, and Saviour, and King."[198]

---

195   Paul P. Enns, *The Moody Handbook of Theology* (Chicago: Moody Press, 1989), 410.
196   Alexander H. Pierce, ed. John D. Barry et al. "Polycarp," *The Lexham Bible Dictionary* (Bellingham, WA: Lexham Press, 2012).
197   Enns, *Moody Handbook*, 410.
198   Newadvent.org, *Against Heresies* (Book 1, Chapter 10), translated by Alexander Roberts and William Rambaut, From *Ante-Nicene Fathers*, Vol. 1, edited by Alexander Roberts, James Donaldson, and A. Cleveland Coxe, (Buffalo, NY: Christian Literature Publishing Co., 1885), accessed July 7, 2016, http://www.newadvent.org/fathers/0103110.htm.

Irenaeus went on to disciple Hippolytus (AD 170-236), who wrote a massive treatise called *Refutation of All Heresies*. He followed the orthodox teachings of the Christians before him and wrote in his apologetic work *Against Noetus*, "Christ Jesus the Son of God, who, being, God, became man." Hippolytus also advocated the Triune nature of God in this same work.[199]

Thus, we have a successive chain from the Apostle John in the first century to Hippolytus in the third that shows how Jesus was always thought of as God incarnate.[200] Therefore, any Christian who believes Jesus is God today has not been *deceived*. Rather, they've followed the biblical and *historical trail of evidence*, given to us by the earliest Christians. All in all, it's obvious Jesus is called God in the Bible and by the early church fathers. Thus, He should be worshiped and referred to as the true God.

The JWs take out most verses that refer to Jesus as God directly, but we will show you later how to use their corrupted Bible (New World Translation) to prove Jesus is God. With the LDS, you must stick to practical exegesis (interpretation of the Bible) and not allow them to insert Mormon philosophy and theology into the Bible.

---

199   Newadvent.org. *Against Noetus*, translated by J.H. MacMahon, From *Ante-Nicene Fathers*, Vol. 5, edited by Alexander Roberts, James Donaldson, and A. Cleveland Coxe. (Buffalo, NY: Christian Literature Publishing Co., 1886), revised and edited for New Advent by Kevin Knight, accessed July 7, 2016, http://www.newadvent.org/fathers/0521.htm.

200   Warner J Wallace, *Cold-Case Christianity* (Colorado Springs: David C. Cook, 2013), 216-221.

CHAPTER 5
IS THE TRINITY BIBLICAL?

One of the most common modern-day myths propagated by cults is that the Trinity is a heretical concept formulated centuries after the life of Jesus Christ. Search the Internet even just briefly, and you'll find many have been misled to believe the Trinity was invented by the Roman Emperor Constantine or that it has been adapted from pagan religions.

The JWs attack the Trinity because the word itself is not mentioned in the Bible and they believe it is not a true doctrine. The Mormons, on the other hand, believe in a completely different Trinity that contains multiple Gods—much different than Bible-believing Christians. This chapter will teach you how to defend the Trinity historically, biblically, and logically.

DEFINING THE TRINITY

To articulate the Trinitarian position correctly, first we must define what the Trinity is. The *Tyndale Bible Dictionary* provides an excellent summary:

The word 'Trinity' does not appear in the Bible; it was created by scholars to describe the three members of the Godhead. Throughout the Bible, God is presented as being Father, Son, and Spirit—not three 'gods' but three personas of the one and only God (see, e.g., Mt 28:19; 1 Cor 16:23–24; 2 Cor 13:13). The Scriptures present the Father as the source of creation, the giver of life, and God of all the universe (see Jn 5:26; 1 Cor 8:6; Eph 3:14–15). The Son is depicted as the image of the invisible God, the exact representation of his being and nature, and the Messiah-Redeemer (see Phil 2:5–6; Col 1:14–16; Heb 1:1–3). The Spirit is God in action, God reaching people—influencing them, regenerating them, infilling them, and guiding them (see Jn 14:26; 15:26; Gal 4:6; Eph 2:18). All three are a tri-unity, inhabiting one another and working together to accomplish the divine design in the universe (see Jn 16:13–15).[201]

Some would claim the Trinity is a logical contradiction. Yet when you really understand the meaning of the Trinity, you will not find any fallacious reasoning:

The doctrine of the Trinity, however, does not affirm that God is both one and three in the same sense or relationship. Rather, it affirms that God is one and only one in His essence, but He is three in His persons. Therefore, the Trinity is not contradictory. *Person* and *essence* are different. *Person* reveals who He is, and *essence* refers to what He is. So the Trinity does not refer to three whos in one *who* (which would be a contradiction), but three whos in one *what* (which is not a contradiction).[202]

Despite the JW and LDS claim that the Trinity is a pagan concept, it is, in fact, rooted in Christian history. The term "Trinity" emerged in early

201   Walter A. Elwell and Philip Wesley Comfort, *Tyndale Bible Dictionary* (Wheaton, IL: Tyndale House Publishers, 2001), 1,275.

202   Ron Rhodes, *5-Minute Apologetics for Today* (Eugene, OR: Harvest House Publishers, 2010), 139.

Christian history as the designation for the uniquely Christian monotheistic understanding of God the Father, God the Son, and God the Holy Spirit as tri-unity.

Just because the term "Trinity" is not found in the Bible does not mean it's heretical. It is simply a term to describe a truth taught in Scripture. Think about it for a minute: "Bible" is derived from *biblia* in Latin and *biblos* in Greek, which translate to mean "book." Both the JWs and LDS use it, even though it's not found in the Bible.

The Jehovah's Witnesses' claim that the term Trinity is unbiblical is self refuting since they also use terms not found in the Bible to describe or define something theological. Also, the term "Jehovah" itself is manmade and not technically found in Scripture. Therefore the JWs have an ineffective argument.

UNDERSTANDING THE TRINITY

When believers are trying to explain deep theological concepts to non-Christians, we often must use language and analogies they are familiar with. For example, a common analogy I use when explaining the Incarnation and the difference between Christianity and religion is as follows: Religion is man trying to get to God through works, prayers, and being a "good person." Christianity is God reaching down to man through Jesus Christ and doing the work for us. God became a man through Jesus and did all the work for us on the cross. All we must do is repent and receive Him as Lord and Savior.

The Bible reveals to us theological truths about the nature of God in language we can understand. So when we are explaining God, who is on the divine level, we must use language accessible on the human level. The cults will often accuse Christians of describing God in too complex of a way. They insist that a Tri-personal Being is too hard to understand. If God wants us to know Him, why can't He just explain Himself plainly?

The truth is, the God of the Bible is the most personal Being conceivable. The Father, Son, and Spirit have from all eternity been in constant communion with one another. They then extend that communion to us when one enters God's family.

Jesus is the only-begotten Son of God. Now, begotten does not mean He is "made," but rather that He has the same nature as His Father. Just as a human father begets a human son, God the Father begot God the Son. However, this analogy fails because it implies God the Father created His Son just like Him at some point. We have already established Jesus is eternal, so He is eternally-begotten of the Father.

If God were to make a "son," he could not have the same nature—just like a Father could only "beget" a son, not make one. For if He made a son, then the son would be of a different nature. He could make a statue of His son, not a person who is the same kind as Himself. (Yes, I realize this analogy is not sufficient because I am describing timeless persons in a time-bound universe. Just please realize I am not saying Jesus was created.)

Yet Christians are called the "sons of God" *(Gal 3:26)*. Since humans are made in God's image, we are like God but not of the same *nature* as His only-begotten Son. That is simply all begotten means: Jesus has the same divine nature as His Father, which human beings do not have.

I struggle to explain the Trinity in an analogous fashion because humans live on a level where one person is one being and two beings are two separate people. Yet on the divine level, God exists as one Being yet three persons.

Think of it this way: You can draw a straight line in a one-dimensional level. On a two-dimensional level, you can draw a square, which is four straight lines. On a three-dimensional level, you can draw a cube, which is made up of six squares. A world of one dimension is a straight line. In a world of two dimensions, many lines make up one figure (the square). In a world of three dimensions, you have many figures (the squares), which make up one solid body (the cube).

Because God is in the "divine" dimension, you have multiple persons who still remain the same Being. The Father, Son, and Spirit remain three distinct persons yet comprise the one Being called Yahweh God.

Just like we could not conceive a cube if we could only perceive one dimension, it is difficult for us to conceive of a Tri-personal Divine Being in our earthly dimension. However, once we realize God is not confined to the human dimension, but the heavenly, we begin to understand God exists in ways which would not be possible in our realm.

Amazingly, God desires us to take part in the fellowship He has. We see this in the everyday Christian life. When a Christian prays, he is trying to pray to his Heavenly Father. However, when he pictures God, he imagines Jesus Christ, the God-Man. Then, God the Spirit is prompting him to pray and speak his heart to God. This is how the Triune God partakes in fellowship with the Christian every day.[203]

In his book *The Faith*, Chuck Colson states an obvious differentiation of the Christian faith with that of other religions: "The Trinity also answers the deepest needs of the human heart, offering a depth of spirituality unknown in any other religion."[204] Colson also tells the story of a Muslim apologist who contended that the Trinity was idolatry. But after studying biblical support of the Trinity, as well as first century support for the death and Resurrection of Christ, the apologist converted to Christianity.[205]

In His infinite mercy and love, God wants us to partake in the relationship all three persons of the Godhead have eternally shared. Although humans cannot fully grasp the depths of God's Being, His nature is not contradictory. For this reason, "the Word became flesh and dwelt among us" *(John 1:14)*. God became a man so we could understand Him like never before and through faith in His Son share in God's communion forever.

WHAT ABOUT CONSTANTINE AND THE TRINITY?

A common accusation levied against the doctrine of the Trinity by JWs, LDS, and others is that it was forced upon Christianity by the Roman Emperor Constantine. But history tells us this was not the case.

In AD 325, one of the most important church councils in Christian history took place. It was fueled by an earlier controversy in AD 318 between two eminent church leaders in Alexandria, Egypt. This doctrinal debate was over the divinity of Christ and the relationship between the Father and Son.

---

203   C.S. Lewis, *Mere Christianity* (New York: Harper Collins, 1980), 157-158; 160-163.
204   Charles Colson and Harold Fickett, *The Faith: What Christians Believe, Why They Believe It, and Why It Matters* (Grand Rapids, MI: Zondervan, 2008), 104.
205   Ibid., 104-105.

It all started when Alexander of Alexandria declared the unity of the Trinity in one of his sermons, which prompted a priest named Arius to accuse the bishop of Sabellianism (that is, God is manifested in different roles or modes instead of persons). Arius was much like the JWs in that he did not hold the Son of God to be eternal nor fully divine. Arius believed the Son was created by the Father and not of the exact essence of God—that is, Jesus possessed some divine attributes but was not eternal. [206] In fact, Arius was known to have stated, "There was a time when the Son was not."[207]

To promote unity and stabilize his Empire, Constantine called for the Council of Nicea (in modern-day Turkey). Participants included 318 bishops (although many sources claim a number closer to three hundred) that represented Arianism (including Arius), orthodox and anti-Arianist Christians, and a third group, who believed in the deity of Jesus but wanted to make it clear that Jesus and the Father were different persons.[208] Most of the council was Eastern.[209]

Contrary to what LDS and Watch Tower leaders teach, Constantine mandated the convening of the council but then "deferred to the bishops themselves and allowed them to proceed largely without his interference."[210] Before the council convened, Emperor Constantine supported the Arians' view.[211] However, when he convened the council, he allowed the bishops to come to their own conclusion.

When no consensus between the parties occurred, the Western representatives requested a meeting with Constantine and his advisors. They met and made the case that this doctrinal matter had been resolved by the church father Tertullian generations ago. Tertullian used the Latin phrase *"una substantia, tres personae,"* which translates "one substance, three persons."[212]

Constantine's advisors agreed, and the motion went to council for a vote, which passed with an overwhelming majority. All but two bishops and

206   Wilhite, *The Gospel According to Heretics*, 108-113.
207   ChristianityToday.com, "Athanasius," accessed February 5, 2017, http://www.christianitytoday.com/history/people/theologians/athanasius.html.
208   James R. White, Christian Research Institute website, "What Really Happened at Nicea?," accessed June 15, 2016, http://www.equip.org/article/what-really-happened-at-nicea/.
209   Ibid.
210   Wilhite, *The Gospel According to Heretics*, 116.
211   Ibid.
212   Ibid.

Arius agreed to sign the resulting creed.[213] On AD June 19, 325, a formal principle called the Nicene Creed was established. The creed reaffirmed that Jesus Christ was "true God from true God . . . of one substance with the Father."[214] The creed would be updated a few centuries later at the Council of Constantinople in AD 381, where all forms of Sabellianism and Arianism were condemned as heretical.[215]

Dr. James White has summarized Constantine's actual role, based on historical writings:[216]

> There is no question that Constantine wanted a unified church after the Council of Nicea. But he was no theologian, nor did he really care to any degree what basis would be used to forge the unity he desired. Later events show that he didn't have any particular stake in the term *homoousios* and was willing to abandon it if he saw that doing so would be of benefit to him. As Schaff rightly points out with reference to the term itself, "The word . . . was not an invention of the council of Nicea, still less of Constantine, but had previously arisen in theological language, and occurs even in Origen [185-254] and among the Gnostics . . ." Constantine is not the source or origin of the term, and the council did not adopt the term at his command.

The orthodox Christians of the early centuries revolted against heresies and taught the truth of Scripture and God. We should follow the examples of the earliest Christians and defend the truth as well. With God, Scripture, and history, the truth will be revealed.

In conclusion, Jesus's divinity was not *invented* by Constantine or by certain leaders. The Council of Nicea simply was a ratification of what

213   White, "What Really Happened at Nicea?"
214   Ergun Caner and Ed Hindson, *The Popular Encyclopedia of Apologetics* (Eugene, OR: Harvest House Publishers, 2008), 150.
215   Ergun Caner and Ed Hindson, *The Popular Encyclopedia of Apologetics, 150-151* (Eugene, OR: Harvest House Publishers, 2008), 150-151.
216   James R. White, Christian Research Institute, "What Really Happened at Nicea?, " accessed June 15, 2016, http://www.equip.org/article/what-really-happened-at-nicea/.

was already taught in Scripture. Also, as mentioned earlier, Constantine originally supported the Arian view that Jesus was not divine in the way the Father was (which is what the JWs believe today). The writings of Tertullian had already solved the issue of the relationship between the three persons of the Trinity many years earlier.[217] Furthermore, history records the Bishops voted on this matter, and it was not decreed by Constantine in some totalitarian way.

WHAT THE EARLY CHURCH FATHERS THOUGHT OF THE TRINITY BEFORE THE FOURTH CENTURY

It can be easily demonstrated through *multiple* early church fathers that the doctrine of the Trinity was not a late fourth-century invention. The doctrine and term had been in use at least two centuries earlier. Make sure to emphasize these historical facts to the cult member you are witnessing to.

During his martyrdom, Polycarp (AD 70-156), a disciple of the Apostle John, prayed to God the Father using Trinitarian language:

> For this cause, yea and for all things, I praise Thee, I bless Thee, I glorify Thee, through the eternal and heavenly High-priest, Jesus Christ, Thy beloved Son, through whom with Him and the Holy Spirit be glory both now [and ever] and for the ages to come. Amen.[218]

Polycarp glorified God the Father, Jesus Christ, and the Holy Spirit. Of course, we know God does not share His glory *(Isa. 42:8)*. The fact that one of the early Christian leaders glorified three persons shows the Triune nature of the God he believed in.

Additionally, early church father and theologian Quintus Septimius Florens Tertullian used the word "Trinity" in his writings. Tertullian became a Christian in his thirties and wrote numerous works on apologetics and dogmas. He was known to have had a "superior education, including literary, rhetorical, and legal

---

217   Wilhite, 116.

218   "The Martyrdom of Polycarp," earlychristianwritings.com, accessed January 10, 2017, http://www.earlychristianwritings.com/text/martyrdompolycarp-lightfoot.html.

training, and instruction in Greek and Latin." He also served as an elder or minister at his local church. [219]

According to the book *Who's Who in Christian History*, "Tertullian's use of the Latin *trinitas* (was) the first application of the term *trinity* to Deity."[220] Thus, it would be a fallacy to say that the concept of the Trinity is pagan if one of history's most prolific Christian minds coined the term *long* before the fourth century.

Another early Christian who taught that God was a Trinity was Dionysius, the Bishop of Rome from AD 259-260. He held to a Trinitarian view of God and sought to combat Sabellianism (again, that God exists in three modes or manifestations and not three persons), Tritheism (meaning three gods make up the Trinity), and subordinationism (which means the Son is not eternal or divine and not equal to the Father) in his writings.[221]

In his work *Against the Sabellians*, Dionysius explained how God was not made up of three deities but of three persons:

> For these indeed rightly know that the Trinity is declared in the divine Scripture, but that the doctrine that there are three gods is neither taught in the Old nor in the New Testament. [222]

Additionally, he explained how three persons could comprise the Godhead:

> That admirable and divine unity, therefore, must neither be separated into three divinities, nor must the dignity and eminent greatness of the Lord be diminished by *having applied to it* the name of creation, but we must believe on God the Father Omnipotent, and on Christ Jesus His Son, and on the Holy Spirit. Moreover, that the Word is united to the

219   J.D. Douglas and Philip W. Comfort, "Tertullian," in *Who's Who in Christian History* ed. K.J. Bryer (Wheaton, IL: Tyndale House, 1992), 665-666.
220   Ibid.
221   Jackson, ed., *New Schaff-Herzog Encyclopedia*, 52.
222   Philip Schaff, "Dionysius Alexandrinus Archiepiscopus—Against the Sabellians," accessed June 12, 2016, http://www.documentacatholicaomnia.eu/03d/0190-0264,_Dionysius_Alexandrinus,_Against_the_Sabellians_[Schaff],_EN.pdf.

God of all, because He says, 'I and the Father are one;' and, "I am in the Father, and the Father is in Me." Thus doubtless will be maintained in its integrity *the doctrine of* the divine Trinity, and the sacred announcement of the monarchy.[223]

In summary, it can be easily demonstrated through multiple early church fathers that the doctrine of the Trinity was not a late fourth-century invention. The doctrine and term were in use long before the council. To declare otherwise would be a false assertion.

When the cults accuse the Trinity of being "invented" by Constantine in the fourth century, just point out that the Trinity can be proven biblically, Constantine was anti-Trinitarian before the council, and the council was a ratification of *doctrine already taught by the earliest Christians.*

JEHOVAH'S WITNESSES AND ARIANISM

The Watch Tower has ingrained in JWs' minds that the Trinity is heretical and a pagan invention. Because JWs believe in Jesus as a lesser being than the Father, they unknowingly partake in the heresy of Arianism. Additionally, JWs have been taught to believe the Holy Spirit is a personal or active force that was also created in the past.

Although they will readily agree Jehovah is the one, true God, JWs contradict their own claim to be monotheistic because they state Jesus is "a god" in John 1:1, but then call Him God with a capital "G" in John 20:26-29 and Isaiah 9:6. By referring to Jesus as "a god" in John 1:1 and then in other verses "God" with a capital "G," their New World Translation shows inconsistency and confuses the reader as to what type of God Jesus is. Furthermore, this demonstrates how they are not monotheistic because they "honor" or do "obeisance to" Jesus as a "lesser god."

In addition to the Watch Tower's blunder in calling Jesus "God" with a capital "G," they unknowingly ascribe deity to the Holy Spirit. Their New World Translation states the Holy Spirit is God in Acts 5:3:

---

223   Ibid.

But Peter said: "An·a·ni'as, why has Satan emboldened you to lie to the holy spirit and secretly hold back some of the price of the field? As long as it remained with you, did it not remain yours? And after it was sold, was it not in your control? Why have you thought up such a deed as this in your heart? You have lied, not to men, but to God."

The verse shows how it is impossible to lie to an "active force." Also, here we see Ananias lied to God, which, in the context, is the same as the Holy Spirit.

JEHOVAH'S WITNESSES, "A GOD," AND I HAVE BEEN

We will briefly examine two major translation errors in the NWT. First, their translation of John 1:1c as "the Word was a god" instead of "the Word was God." Second, their translation of John 8:58 of Jesus saying, "I have been," instead of "I AM."

All major Bible translations render John 1:1 as "God" and 8:58 as "I am." The JWs have purposefully mistranslated these verses to suite their manmade theology. Second, the majority of Bible versions translate these verses the way they do for grammatical reasons.

When translators are converting the Greek to English, they look at the context of the passage and don't just isolate one clause. John 1:1 in full in the New King James Version reads, "In the beginning was the Word, and the Word was with God, and the Word was God." John is conveying three vital truths in this one verse: the Word is eternal, the Word is personal, and the Word is deity.

The clause in question, John 1:1c, is *qualitative*, meaning it tells us about the *nature* of the Word, which is divinity. If one was to render John 1:1c any other way, he would be ignoring the monotheism in the Bible, verse three, which tells us the Word made everything that has ever been made, and other Greek translation laws, which are beyond the scope of this book.[224]

In the case of John 8:58, the present tense verb *eimi* is used (I am). However, the JWs translate it as a perfect tense verb (I have been). Dr. James White explains why the majority of Bible versions translate John 8:58 as I am:

---

224   James White, *The Forgotten Trinity* (Bloomington, MN: Bethany House, 1998), 55-57.

So why should John 8:58 not be rendered in this way? Why do so few translations follow this path? Because to so translate is to miss the entire context and content of what is being said! The vast majority of translators see, as many commentators do, that there is a clear differentiation being made here between the derivative existence of Abraham and the eternal existence of the Lord Christ. That this is understood by the translators of our modern editions can be seen from a look at the translations that render this phrase either as "I am" or "I Am" or "I AM." … This writer is not aware of a single version, produced by a team or group of scholars, that renders ego eimi at John 8:58 in a perfect tense.[225]

Hopefully this assures you it is the Watch Tower, not the Christians, who have mistranslated the Greek text. We have found it helpful to point out all other major translations (including the KJV, which JWs used before the NWT) translate John 1:1c as "God" and John 8:58 as "I am."

MORMONISM HAS A DIFFERENT TRINITY

LDS also believe in the heresy of polytheism. They have a different definition of the Trinity or Godhead. They teach that the Father, Son, and Holy Ghost are three separate gods. In other words, they are polytheistic; they believe in multiple gods instead of the one, true God in three persons as revealed in the Bible.

LDS theology teaches that Christians have been in error regarding the Trinity since its inception. The LDS website states, "Latter-day Saints reject the doctrines of the Trinity as taught by most Christian churches today."[226] Instead, they hold to a polytheistic view that, along with their other "holy books," contradicts the multitude of verses in the same version of the Old and New Testament they use—the King James Bible—which teaches monotheism (there is only one, true

---

225   Aomin.org., James White, "Purpose and Meaning of 'Ego Eimi' in the Gospel of John in Reference to the Deity of Christ," accessed on January 10, 2017, http://vintage.aomin. org/EGO.html.

226   Daniel C. Peterson and Stephen D. Ricks, "Comparing LDS Beliefs with First-Century Christianity," accessed May 15, 2016, https://www.lds.org/ensign/1988/03/comparing-lds-beliefs-with-first-century-christianity?lang=eng.

God). Additionally, they believe the Father, Son, and Holy Ghost were created. According to the Mormon faith, there is actually an infinite number of gods, an endless succession of Father Gods.

In his own words, the prophet and founder of Mormonism, Joseph Smith, taught polytheism:

> I will preach on the plurality of Gods . . . I wish to declare I have always and in all congregations when I preached on the subject of Deity, it has been the plurality of Gods. It has been preached by the Elders for fifteen years. I have always declared God to be a distinct personage, Jesus Christ a separate and distinct personage from God the Father, and that the holy Ghost was a distinct personage and a Spirit: and these three constitute three distinct personages and three Gods. If this is in accordance with the New Testament, lo and behold! We have three Gods, anyhow, and they are plural; and who can contradict it?[227]

The reality is, Joseph Smith was contradicting what the Holy Bible teaches and the consensus of the early church Fathers about the nature of God.

The current LDS church agrees with Joseph Smith's position on the Trinity (Godhead) as they state: "The true doctrine of the Godhead was lost in the apostasy that followed the Savior's mortal ministry and the deaths of His Apostles. This doctrine began to be restored when 14-year-old Joseph Smith received his First Vision."[228]

Ask LDS leaders for hard evidence that the Godhead (and the lost gospel, as they claim) was lost in apostasy, considering that the entirety of the Bible teaches there is only one, true God in three persons who are part of the same divine substance. The LDS church also defines a different God than biblical Christianity because they state He is not eternal, but finite. For instance, one of the famous Mormon apostles, Brigham Young, noted this about the Father:

---

227 Joseph Fielding Smith, ed., *Teachings of the Prophet Joseph Smith* (Salt Lake City: Deseret Book Company, 1977), location 5, 195.

228 LDS.org, "Godhead," accessed May 15, 2016, https://www.lds.org/topics/godhead?lang=eng.

And who is the Father? He is the first of the human family; and when he took a tabernacle, it was begotten by *his Father* in heaven, after the same manner as the tabernacles of Cain, Abel, and the rest of the sons and daughters of Adam and Eve; from the fruits of the earth, the first earthly tabernacles were originated by the Father, and so on in succession.[229]

Unfathomably, LDS doctrine teaches that Heavenly Fathers have physical bodies that allow them to have sexual relations with their heavenly wives. Section 130 of Doctrine and Covenants affirms this in verse 22: "The Father has a body of flesh and bones as tangible as man's."[230]

In contrast, the biblical Father is spirit and without a physical body *(John 1:18, 4:24)*. Mormon theology differs greatly than what the Bible teaches about God the Father. Why Mormon apologists claim the Bible does not contradict the Book of Mormon and their other inspired books is puzzling.

TRINITY INVOLVED IN SALVATION

The JWs and LDS will tell you they are grateful for "Jesus Christ, their Savior." But what they will *not* be quick to admit is that a "lesser god" is the one who died and rose for them. This directly contradicts the Bible, as Scripture tells us our salvation comes from Almighty God:

Truly my soul silently waits for God; From Him comes my salvation *(Ps. 62:1)*.

For the grace of God that brings salvation has appeared to all men *(Ti. 2:11)*.

For God did not send His Son into the world to condemn the world, but that the world through Him might be saved *(John 3:17)*.

---

229   Brigham Young, "*Journal of Discourses*. Self-Government—Mysteries—Recreation and Amusements, Not in Themselves Sinful—Tithing—Adam, Our Father and Our God," accessed March 7, 2017, http://jod.mrm.org/1/46.

230   LDS.org., "Doctrine and Covenants Section 130," accessed June 12, 2016, https://www.lds.org/scriptures/dc-testament/dc/130?lang=eng.

That is, that God was in Christ reconciling the world to Himself, not imputing their trespasses to them, and has committed to us the word of reconciliation (*2 Cor. 5:19*).*

(**Note: the NWT reads, "God was by means of Christ reconciling a world to himself." However, this does not match up with their 1985 Greek Interlinear, which reads, "God was in Christ,"²³¹ like other non-Watch Tower versions.)*

Other verses clearly identify God as the Savior:

To God our Savior,
Who alone is wise,
Be glory and majesty,
Dominion and power,
Both now and forever.
Amen (*Jude 1:25*).

But when the kindness and the love of God our Savior toward man appeared (*Ti. 3:4*).

I, *even* I, *am* the Lord,
    And besides Me *there is* no savior (*Isa. 43:11*).

When showing a person of a cultic faith the error of his ways, point out that if only God (or Jehovah) is the Savior, then Jesus *must* be God. Here are some verses you can compare the previous ones with:

But has now been revealed by the appearing of our Savior Jesus Christ, *who* has abolished death and brought life and immortality to light through the gospel (*2 Tim. 1:10*).

For there is born to you this day in the city of David a Savior, who is Christ the Lord (*Luke 2:11*).

---

231   *The Kingdom Interlinear Translation of the Greek Scriptures*, 800.

Looking for the blessed hope and glorious appearing of our great God and Savior Jesus Christ (*Ti. 2:13*).*

(*Note: The NWT reads, "Of the great God and of our Savior, Jesus Christ." This is an obvious cover-up, and does not match up with the Greek text.)

Here's a sample question you could ask: "because Isaiah 43:11 says Yahweh is the only Savior, and 2 Timothy 1:10 says Jesus is our Savior, would it not follow that Jesus is Yahweh?"

Furthermore, the Bible is *very clear* that *each* member of the Trinity is involved in salvation:

- The Father formulated the plan of salvation before the foundation of the world (*Eph. 1:3-4*). He also decreed and carried out the plan of salvation in His sovereignty (*Rom. 8:29-30*).
- Jesus willingly offered Himself as a sacrifice to make salvation possible. He suffered and died on the cross for the sins of mankind (*Isa. 53:1-12; John 3:16*). Also, Jesus acts as the Mediator between God and man because He is the God-Man (*1 Tim. 2:5*).
- The Holy Spirit regenerates believers to a new life (*Eph. 4:30*) and empowers believers so sin does not reign over them (*Gal. 5:22-23*).

NEW TESTAMENT AND THE TRINITY

As we stated earlier in this chapter, the cults believe there is no real scriptural basis for the doctrine of the Trinity. But the truth is, apart from any creeds or early Christian writings, if you carefully read the Bible—and, specifically, the New Testament—you will conclude that God is Triune.

In Exodus 3:14, when Moses is sent by God to go and lead the Israelites out of Egyptian captivity, he asks God what he should say when they ask who sent him. God says to tell them that, "I AM has sent me to you."[232] God also declares that He is, "I AM WHO I AM." This gives us the understanding that God is an eternal, self-existent Being. In other words, God is self-sufficient. He doesn't need anyone's help.

---

232   *The Holy Bible: New International Version* (Grand Rapids, MI: Zondervan, 1984).

At first, this may seem like a contradiction. After all, the Bible teaches that Yahweh is the one, true God (*Deut. 6:4; Isa. 45:5*); yet Jesus, the Father, and the Spirit are all God. Is that not three gods? But, like we talked about earlier, God is not confined to the human dimension of time and space, so it is not a logical contradiction for Him to be Tri-personal.

When talking to cults and anyone who denies the Trinity, emphasize the three persons in the one nature that is God. God is "One" in the sense of His essence (the essence of Yahweh) but not in the sense of His persons.

God's nature (the what) is Yahweh, the eternal, self-existent Creator. God's personhood (the who), is three persons who share that same essence and are of the same substance, yet carry out different functions.[233] For example, God the Father sent God the Son to die for the sins of the world and be resurrected from the dead to save mankind. God the Spirit then dwells in believers who put their trust in the Son and then sanctifies the believer to become more like God.

Christian apologist Nabeel Qureshi gives us vital insight into the difference between being and person:

> *Person* is not the same as *being*. Your being is the quality that makes you *what* you are, but your person is the quality that makes you *who* you are . . . Unlike a human being, which has only one person, God has three persons. He is one being, Yahweh, in three persons: Father, Son, and Spirit. He's more than able to exist like that because he is God.[234]

However, at times, different members of the Trinity all perform the same action, as they are one in their purpose of carrying out the plan of salvation. For example, all three members of the Trinity raised Jesus from the dead.

One of the easiest ways to prove the Trinity biblically to the cults is to ask cultists if they believe God raised Jesus from the dead. They will agree with you because it is a biblical truth (*Acts 2:24, 32; Rom. 10:9; 1 Pet. 1:21*). However, the Bible clearly states that each *person* of the Godhead raised Jesus from the dead.

---

233   Norman Geisler, *The Big Book of Christian Apologetics* (Grand Rapids, MI: Baker Books, 2012), 554.

234   Nabeel Qureshi, *No God but One: Allah or Jesus?* (Grand Rapids, MI: Zondervan, 2016), 56.

First, Scripture plainly states that the Father raised Jesus from the dead (*Gal. 1:1; Eph. 1:20*). The JWs or LDS have often heard God or the Father raised Jesus from the dead but not the other members of the Trinity.

But to avoid confusion, emphasize that *God* raised Jesus from the dead (*Rom. 10:9*). When the Bible says God raised Jesus from the dead, it is often referring to all three members of the Trinity. This is true throughout the Bible, unless it specifies which person. Emphasize this when talking to non-Trinitarians so they do not think you are advocating that Jesus is the Spirit or the Father.

Remember, in addition to the Father, the Son played a role in the Resurrection. Jesus declared He would raise *Himself* from the dead. After cleansing the temple in John 2, Jesus was questioned by the Jews for a sign after declaring the temple to be His Father's house and purging it of vendors:

> Jesus answered and said to them, "Destroy this temple, and in three days I will raise it up." Then the Jews said, "It has taken forty-six years to build this temple, and will You raise it up in three days?" But He was speaking of the temple of His body. Therefore, when He had risen from the dead, His disciples remembered that He had said this to them; and they believed the Scripture and the word which Jesus had said (*John 2:19-22*).

Notice that Jesus does not give glory to any other when declaring He would raise Himself from the dead.

The common objection to these powerful verses is that Jesus is using symbolic language. However, notice verse 21 of John chapter two: "He was talking about the temple of His body"—the "temple" He would raise up in three days was His body. The Apostle John specifically wrote verse 21 so the reader would understand Jesus was declaring that He would raise Himself up physically from the dead because He was God.

Last, the Spirit also raised Jesus from the dead. In Romans 8:9-11, we read the following:

But you are not in the flesh but in the Spirit, if indeed the Spirit of God dwells in you. Now if anyone does not have the Spirit of Christ, he is not His. And if Christ *is* in you, the body *is* dead because of sin, but the Spirit *is* life because of righteousness. But if the Spirit of Him who raised Jesus from the dead dwells in you, He who raised Christ from the dead will also give life to your mortal bodies through His Spirit who dwells in you.

Here we read God the Holy Spirit raised Jesus from the dead, and this same Spirit dwells in all believers.

Thus, we have strong evidence from Scripture, when describing the Resurrection, that the Triune Godhead raised Jesus from the dead. Each person of the Trinity played a part, yet collectively the same essence of God raised Jesus from the dead.

Note that JWs will often ask how Jesus could raise Himself from the dead if He died on the cross. Kindly point out to them that only his body died and His spirit was still alive. Remember how Jesus told the thief on the cross He would see him in paradise the same day they were crucified *(Luke 23:43)*?

Jesus Himself also spoke of God's Triune nature. Consider His words in the Great Commission, given in Matthew 28:18-20:

All authority has been given to Me in heaven and on earth. Go therefore and make disciples of all the nations, baptizing them in the name of the Father and of the Son and of the Holy Spirit, teaching them to observe all things that I have commanded you; and lo, I am with you always, *even* to the end of the age.

Notice that Jesus said, "In the *name* of the Father and of the Son and of the Holy Spirit." The fact Jesus commanded His disciples to baptize in the *name* of the Father, Son, and Spirit implies they make up the one, true God, who is Yahweh (the LORD). As one theologian noted, "We should notice that the word *name* is singular; Jesus does not say that his followers should baptize in the 'names' of Father, Son, and Holy Spirit, but in the 'name' of these three. It points to the fact that they are in some sense one."[235]

Also remember, when you are defending the Trinity, to remind the skeptic that the writers of the New Testament, with the exception of one, were monotheistic Jews. (Luke was probably a Gentile, but he was certainly monotheistic.) For example, in James 2:19, we read, "You believe that there is one God. You do well. Even the demons believe—and tremble!" The book itself was written by Jesus's half-brother James, a former Jew, and was aimed at early Christians who had converted from Judaism.[236]

Indeed, this is reminiscent of the Hebrew Shema prayer ("Hear, O Israel: The LORD our God, the LORD *is* one") (in essence) as well as Isaiah 42:8, which says, "I *am* the LORD, that *is* My name; And My glory I will not give to another, Nor My praise to carved images."

Considering that James was one of the first NT books written, there is no doubt the earliest Christians were monotheistic. But did they believe the Father, Jesus the Messiah, and the Holy Spirit were all God?

If we look at the writings of Paul, a former Pharisee and persecutor of Christians, he unequivocally believed God was Triune. In Titus 2:13, he refers to Jesus as "our great God and Savior." He also declares in Romans 9:5 that Christ is the eternally blessed God (corrupted in NWT). Additionally, he uses Jesus and Yahweh interchangeably. This is clear in Romans 10:9-12:

> That if you confess with your mouth the Lord Jesus and believe in your heart that God has raised Him from the dead, you will be saved. For with the heart one believes unto righteousness, and with the mouth confession is made unto salvation. For the Scripture says, "Whoever believes on Him will not be put to shame." For there is no distinction between Jew and Greek, for the same Lord over all is rich to all who call upon Him. For "whoever calls on the name of the LORD shall be saved."

235   Leon Morris, *The Gospel According to Matthew* (Grand Rapids, MI: InterVarsity Press, 1992), 748.

236   *MacArthur Study Bible*, 1924.

In verse 11 of Romans chapter 10, Paul is referring to Isaiah 28:16, 49:23, and Jeremiah 17:7, which state that those who put their trust in Yahweh will be secure. Paul then applies these verses to Jesus, who is the incarnation of Yahweh. Furthermore, Paul recites a verse in Joel that uses Yahweh's name and refers it back to Jesus. Joel 2:32 states, "And it shall come to pass that whoever calls on the name of the Lord shall be saved." Verse 13 of Romans chapter 10 is then referring to Jesus in the place of Yahweh—and the only way this could make any logical sense is if Jesus is Yahweh.

Furthermore, even God the Father refers to Jesus as God and proclaims that His reign is eternal in Hebrews 1:8: "But to the Son *He says:* 'Your throne, O God, *is* forever and ever; A scepter of righteousness *is* the scepter of Your kingdom.'" Of course, the Watch Tower has changed this verse, even though it does not correspond to the Greek.

In addition to the Son, the New Testament teaches the divinity of the Spirit of Yahweh as well, 2 Cor 3:17 states "The Lord is the Spirit", which means Yahweh is the Holy Spirit. "Yahweh of the O.T. is the same Lord who is saving people in the New Covenant through the agency of the Holy Spirit. The same God is the minister of both the Old and New Covenants.[237]

We must realize Yahweh is not just Father God, but that this is the name of the Triune God. When talking to JWs or other non-Trinitarians, we must make clear that Yahweh is the name of the one God essence that all three persons of the Trinity share equally.

Another passage which teaches the divinity of the Holy Spirit is found in the story of Ananias and Sapphira. We read in Acts 5:1-4:

> But a certain man named Ananias, with Sapphira his wife, sold a possession. And he kept back *part* of the proceeds, his wife also being aware *of it,* and brought a certain part and laid *it* at the apostles' feet. But Peter said, "Ananias, why has Satan filled your heart to lie to the Holy Spirit and keep back *part* of the price of the land for yourself? While it remained, was it not your own? And after it was sold, was it not in your

---

237   Ibid., 1,768.

own control? Why have you conceived this thing in your heart? You have not lied to men but to God."

Peter is enraged at Ananias for giving deceptively. He declares Ananias has lied to the Holy Spirit, which is the same as lying to God. Therefore, the Holy Spirit is God. (The NWT has not corrupted this verse.) Additionally, the Holy Spirit is called eternal in Hebrews 9:14: "How much more shall the blood of Christ, who through the eternal Spirit offered Himself without spot to God, cleanse your conscience from dead works to serve the living God?" (Verse corrupted in NWT.) Obviously, only God is eternal—so the Holy Spirit must be God.

There is little controversy that the Father is called God, but here are some biblical references for your review: Ephesians 4:6; Galatians 1:3; Romans 1:7; and 1 Corinthians 1:3.

On a final note, oftentimes JWs will accuse Christians of saying that Jesus is the Father—but, as we mentioned earlier, that would be the heresy known as Sabellianism. Also, always make sure to emphasize with Mormons how the Trinity must be made up of three different persons, not gods, in order to avoid the heresy of polytheism. So we must be clear in choosing and defining words.

OLD TESTAMENT AND THE TRINITY

Although the Trinity is not as clearly taught in the Old Testament as it is in the New, it is nevertheless strongly implied. As Dan Story, author of *Defending Your Faith*, has written, "Although the doctrine of the Trinity is fully revealed in the New Testament, its roots can be found in the Old Testament."[238]

Similarly, theologian Augustus Hopkins Strong, in his systematic theology book, summarizes the doctrine of the Trinity in the Old Testament as follows:

Our general conclusion with regard to the Old Testament intimations must therefore be that, while they do not by themselves furnish a sufficient basis for the doctrine of the Trinity, they contain the germ of

---

238   Dan Story, *Defending Your Faith* (Grand Rapids, MI: Kregel Publications, 1997), 101.

it, and may be used in confirmation of it when its truth is substantially proved from the New Testament.[239]

Certainly, key passages in the Old Testament, as theologian John Feinberg states, suggest "(the) plurality in the Godhead."[240]

To demonstrate how the Trinity can be inferred from the OT, we will review a few different aspects of it:

- the Old Testament title Elohim
- instances where the Son or Messiah is deemed God
- scriptural examples of the Holy Spirit-given deity

Additionally, we'll review verses that show the distinctness of each person in the Godhead. We won't, however, review passages that denote the Father as God, because this is generally accepted within theological and even cultic circles.

ELOHIM

Theologian John Feinberg finds the word Elohim a very strong indication of a plurality of persons and not just a symbol of power. While "there are . . . more substantial OT indications of plurality in the Godhead,"[241] he says, some interesting aspects about the grammatical usages of Elohim exist.

For instance, Feinberg notes that nouns and verbs usually agree in number. What is unusual is that Elohim is a plural noun:

[Elohim] is so commonly used to refer to Israel's one God, Yahweh, that it is most often used with a singular verb. . . . In fact, it is so typical to use this plural noun with a singular verb that it becomes significant when a plural verb is used with elohim to refer to Israel's God.... In Gen 20:13 elohim is used with a plural verb for "caused to wander," and in

239   Augustus Hopkins Strong, *Systematic Theology* (Philadelphia: American Baptist Publication Society, 1907), 322.

240   John Feinberg, *No One Like Him: The Doctrine of God* (Wheaton, IL: Crossway Books, 2001), 448.

241   Ibid., 449.

Gen 35:7 God is spoken of as having 'revealed' (plural in the Hebrew) himself to Jacob. In 2 Sam 7:23 we are told that Israel's God (elohim) went (halecu-third person plural) to redeem Israel.[242]

He notes passages like Genesis 1:26 and comments, "God says, 'Let us make man in our image'; the verb 'make' (naaseh) is plural, and so is 'our.'"[243] He also refutes the accusation that the "us" refers to God and His angels. Of course, this cannot be textually correct because human beings are made in the image of God, not angels.[244]

Furthermore, it should be noted that this is a figurative use of the word "image" (ṣelem). *The Bible Knowledge Commentary* states, "God does not have a human form. Being in God's image means that humans share, though imperfectly and finitely, in God's nature, that is, in His communicable attributes (life, personality, truth, wisdom, love, holiness, justice), and so have the capacity for spiritual fellowship with Him."[245]

In his book *Systematic Theology*, Professor Wayne Grudem also comments on this passage:

What do the plural verb ("let us") and the plural pronoun ("our") mean? Some have suggested they are plurals of majesty, a form of speech a king would use in saying, for example, "We are pleased to grant your request." However, in Old Testament Hebrew there are no other examples of a monarch using plural verbs or plural pronouns of himself in such a "plural of majesty," so this suggestion has no evidence to support it.[246]

Therefore, we have strong evidence that the God of the Old Testament was made up of a plurality of persons based on the language structures of the Hebrew

---

242   Ibid., 449.

243   Ibid., 450.

244   Ibid., 450.

245   Allen Ross, ed., *The Bible Knowledge Commentary: An Exposition of the Scriptures* (Wheaton, IL: Victor Books, 1985).

246   Wayne Grudem, *Systematic Theology* (Grand Rapids: MI: Zondervan Publishing, 1994), 227.

tongue. For further reference, two other similar passages where plural pronouns for God are used are Genesis 3:22 and 11:7.

THE SON IS GOD

If you exegete (that is, analyze) the OT carefully and pay close attention to key verses, it can provide profound evidence for the deity of the Messiah and Son of God. One of the clearest pieces of evidence for the deity of the Messiah is found in Psalm 45:6-7:

> Your throne, O God, is forever and ever. A scepter of righteousness is the scepter of Your kingdom. You love righteousness and hate wickedness; Therefore God, Your God, has anointed You with the oil of gladness more than Your companions.

Many detractors attempt to describe God being anointed as a type of earthly king. However, this is fallacious:

> The psalmist's intention is to address the King, whom he has already declared to be more than man (ver. 2), as "God." Is **for ever and ever**. A dominion to which there will never be any end. This is never said, and could not be truly said, of any earthly kingdom. When perpetuity is promised to the throne of David (2 Sam. 7:13–16; Ps. 89:4, 36, 37), it is to that throne as continued in the reign of David's Son, Messiah. **The sceptre of thy kingdom is a right sceptre**; literally, *a sceptre of rectitude* (comp. Ps. 67:4; 96:10).[247]

The writer of Hebrews 1:8 clarifies this as he quotes Psalm 45:6-7 and references the passage to the Son. (Psalm 45:6 is corrupted in the NWT.)

Additionally, many verses in the Old Testament ascribe deity to a person known as the Angel of the LORD, who is distinct from Yahweh but shares His essence. For example, in Genesis 16:10, the Angel of the LORD speaks

---

247   H. D. M. Spence-Jones, ed., *The Pulpit Commentary: Psalms Vol. I.* (New York: Funk & Wagnalls Company, 1909).

to Hagar and tells her, "I will multiply your descendants exceedingly." This would indicate an act of God. Then in Genesis 16:13, Scripture says, "Then she called the name of the LORD who spoke to her, You Are the God Who Sees." MacArthur notes how Hagar was interacting with God the Son:

> This special individual spoke as though He were distinct from Yahweh, yet also spoke in the first person as though He were indeed to be identified as Yahweh Himself, with Hagar recognizing that in seeing this Angel, she had seen God. Others had the same experience and came to the same conclusion. The Angel of the Lord, who does not appear after the birth of Christ, is often identified as the pre-incarnate Christ.[248]

Many other examples of the Angel of the LORD being referred to as God in the Old Testament exist. In Genesis 32, for instance, Jacob wrestles with God, who is presumably the pre-incarnate Christ because the Father does not have a body. Also, in Exodus 3:2, the Angel of the LORD appeared to Moses from the midst of a bush. But in verse 4 of this same chapter, it is God who called to Moses from the midst of the bush, signifying the Angel of the Lord and God are one and the same. Additional examples of the Angel of the LORD appearing to others include Judges 13:6, Numbers 22:22-35, Judges 6:11-23 and 13:17.

It's important to note that when the Angel of the LORD does appear to people, He is often worshiped. Theologian John Feinberg makes an insightful point about this:

> Exodus 34:14 is very clear that only God is to be worshipped, not mere humans or even angels, but in neither Exodus 3 nor Judges 13 does the angel of the Lord refuse the various acts of reverence and worship. This suggests, when joined with Exodus 34:14, his divine nature.[249]

---

248   *MacArthur Study Bible*, 37.
249   *No One Like Him: The Doctrine of God*, 452-453.

In the Old Testament, we also find references to the coming Messiah being eternal. In Isaiah 9:6, the Messiah is described as "Mighty God and Everlasting Father." Theologian R. C. Sproul comments that these and other terms in the passage "express His divine and human qualities, giving assurance that He is indeed 'Immanuel.'"[250]

In Micah 5:2, the Messiah would be born in Bethlehem and be "everlasting." Likewise, in Psalm 110:4, the Messiah is said to be "a priest forever." Obviously, because God is the only One who is eternal, the Messiah would have to be God.

One of the clearest examples of Jesus appearing in the OT is found in Isaiah 6. We've used this passage with JWs before, and it worked surprisingly well. Verses 1-5 read, as follows:

In the year that King Uzziah died, I saw the Lord sitting on a throne, high and lifted up, and the train of His *robe* filled the temple. Above it stood seraphim; each one had six wings: with two he covered his face, with two he covered his feet, and with two he flew. And one cried to another and said:

"Holy, holy, holy *is* the LORD of hosts;
The whole earth *is* full of His glory!"
And the posts of the door were shaken by the voice of him who cried out, and the house was filled with smoke.
So I said:
"Woe *is* me, for I am undone!
Because I *am* a man of unclean lips,
And I dwell in the midst of a people of unclean lips;
For my eyes have seen the King,
The LORD of hosts."

Recall that no man may see God and live *(Exodus 33:20)*, which is why Isaiah cried out in distress. Yet Isaiah said he saw God, for this was not just a vision or hallucination. Considering this, who did Isaiah see, and how did he not

---

250   R.C. Sproul, *The Reformation Study Bible* (Phillipsburg, NJ: Presbyterian and Reformed Publishing Company, 2005), 963.

die? John 12:41 tells us Isaiah saw Jesus because He has declared or made known the Father (*John 1:18*).

The JWs were quite surprised when we showed them how Isaiah would have died if he had seen Father Jehovah. If you use this passage with the Mormons, explain to them how no one can see God except through Jesus. Therefore, Joseph Smith could have never seen God the Father. We don't recommend using this as the first verse to prove Jesus is God, but it can be extremely useful if you ever have an in-depth discussion with a non-Trinitarian.

THE HOLY SPIRIT IS GOD

Although the Old Testament verses that show the deity of the Holy Spirit are not as obvious compared to that of the Messiah, verses in the Old Testament exist that suggest the Holy Spirit is God.

In his book *The Holy Spirit*, John Walvoord makes a profound statement regarding the deity of the Holy Spirit: "The Holy Spirit is presented in Scripture as having the same essential deity as the Father and the Son and is to be worshipped and adored, loved and obeyed in the same way as God. To regard the Holy Spirit in any other way is to make one guilty of blasphemy and unbelief."[251]

Because the Holy Spirit is given the attributes of a person, He is not just a mere force. Walvoord comments on this by saying, "The most tangible and conclusive evidence for the personality of the Holy Spirit is found in His works."[252] We read about His work in creation (*Gen. 1:2*), empowering (*Zech. 4:6*), teaching (*John 16:13*), guidance (*Isa. 48:16; Rom. 8:14*), comforting (*John 14:26*), prayer (*Rom. 8:26*), convincing the world of sin, righteousness, and judgment (*John 16:8*), His commands (*Acts 8:29, 13:2, 16:7*), and restraint of sin (*Gen. 6:3; Isa. 59:19, 2 Thess.2:7*).[253]

To further explore the idea that the Holy Spirit is one of three Trinitarian persons, we must examine the creation of the universe. Remember Yahweh alone made the universe (*Isa. 44:24*), so anyone else who created the universe must be God. As we have already mentioned, Genesis 1:2 indicates the Holy

251   John F. Walvoord, *The Holy Spirit. A Comprehensive Study of the Person and Work of the Holy Spirit* (Grand Rapids, MI: Zondervan, 1991), 5.
252   Ibid., 6.
253   Ibid.

Spirit was involved in creation; and in Job 33:4, Elihu (Job's friend) states, "The Spirit of God has made me." It would be blasphemous to state someone other than God created a person. Yet inspired Scripture tells us in Job that the Holy Spirit was involved in creation. Therefore, the Spirit must be Yahweh if He created the world.

The Holy Spirit is also given the divine attribute of omnipresence. In Psalm 139:7, we read, "Where can I go from Your Spirit? Or where can I flee from Your presence?" Of course, the only omnipresent Being is God.

God the Spirit is also distinguished as a different person than the Father and Messiah. For example, Isaiah 48:16 reads, "Come near to Me, hear this: I have not spoken in secret from the beginning; From the time that it was, I was there. And now the Lord God and His Spirit Have sent Me." All three persons are separate and distinct. Another great verse demonstrating the distinctness of the persons is Isaiah 63:7-14.

The bottom line is that the Old Testament not only *suggests* the Trinity, but it also connects the bridge to the New Testament in proving the Triune nature of God. With progressive revelation, the New Testament more clearly ascribes deity to the Father, Son, and Holy Spirit. Therefore, one can harmonize the doctrine of the Trinity through the whole of Scripture. This would be expected because Old and New Testament Scriptures are inspired by God *(2 Tim. 3:16; 2 Pet. 1:21)*.

CONCLUSION

In summary, the "Trinity" is a term developed by the earliest Christians to describe what the Bible declares about the nature of God: there is one God who exists in three persons. All three persons are co-eternal, co-distinct, co-equal, and all fully God. To deny this clear teaching of Scripture would be to deny the true God and, therefore, fall into heresy. Furthermore, the Trinity is the only doctrine that maintains monotheism while ascribing personhood to each member of the Godhead.

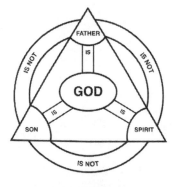

Support for the concept of the Trinity is so clearly seen throughout Scripture that it can even serve as a springboard for evangelism to those skeptical of the Bible's doctrinal integrity. Make sure you understand it well enough to explain it. Here's a simple definition you can use: God the Creator is made up of three co-distinct, co-eternal, and co-equal persons. To easily prove the Trinity, show how each member of the Trinity raised Jesus from the dead.

CHAPTER 6
APOLOGETICS FOR
COMMON CULTIC ATTACKS

Jehovah's Witnesses and Latter-day Saints bring up common ideas to prove not only their doctrinal stance that Jesus is not Almighty God but also several *other* nonbiblical theological beliefs they have. In this chapter, we will review the main ideas they use and provide the proper apologetic (defense) of these attacks to prepare you for your future encounters. We pray this will help you demonstrate the truth with confidence and clarity. Here are a few key points JWs and LDS will make:

1. It is important we know "Jehovah" is God's name.
2. Christians are supposed to be witnesses of Jehovah.
3. We had a preexistent state.
4. "Firstborn" means Jesus was created.

5. "Begotten" means "created."

6. "Beginning of the Creation" means Jesus was created.

7. Proverbs 8 teaches Jesus was created.

8. The fact that God is the head of Christ means Jesus isn't God.

9. "Son of God" means Jesus is not equal with Father God.

10. Jesus is a "Mighty God" but not "Almighty God."

11. "My Father is greater than I" means Jesus is not God.

12. Jesus praying means He is not God.

13. Jesus not knowing the day or hour means Jesus is not God.

14. Jesus's question, "Why do you call Me good?" means Jesus is not good— or God.

15. Because Jesus refers to certain individuals as "gods," polytheism is valid.

16. The NT supports the notion that prophets are necessary.

17. God does nothing apart from His prophets.

18. The Bible prophesies an apostasy of the early church.

19. The Apostle Paul predicted all of Christendom would need to be restored.

20. The Bible prophesies of a "restored church."

21. Having a certain knowledge of God is a requirement for salvation.

22. Baptism is necessary to be saved.

23. Baptism on behalf of the dead is biblical.

24. The Mormon Church has the priesthood.

25. The Bible and Christianity have been changed throughout the ages.

26. Jesus can't be God because He said, "My God, My God, why have You forsaken Me?"

27. 1 Thessalonians 4:16 teaches Jesus is Michael the Archangel.

28. God is only one in purpose, not essence.

29. Because Jesus is called a Man in 1 Timothy 2:5, He's not God.

30. The Book of Mormon is true and Joseph Smith is a prophet because I feel this is so, and I have seen a change in my life.

31. Jesus can't be God because He is subject to the Father.

32. Joseph Smith saw God the Father.

33. Jesus is Michael the Archangel.

POINT #1: IT IS IMPORTANT WE KNOW "JEHOVAH" IS GOD'S NAME

Know that Jehovah is God. He is the one who made us, and we belong to him. We are his people and the sheep of his pasture *(Ps. 100:3, NWT).*

When you first engage with the JWs, they will most likely tell you how important it is to use the correct name for God. They will use Psalm 100:3 or 83:18 to demonstrate this.

COUNTERPOINT #1:

You can respond to this in two ways. First, you can point out how "Jehovah" is a manmade term (see chapter 2). Second, you can explain how the most personal name for God is Jesus Christ.

Use John 20:28, Isaiah 9:6, or Philippians 2:5-11 to demonstrate how God condescended to the form of a man to save us.

POINT #2: CHRISTIANS ARE SUPPOSED TO BE WITNESSES OF JEHOVAH

"You are my witnesses," declares Jehovah *(Isa. 43:10).*

When you converse with the JWs, they will emphasize how their organization is being obedient to God because of their focus on the name Jehovah.

COUNTERPOINT #2:

Again, let's consider the context of this chapter. Verse 1 of Isaiah 43 tells us Jehovah is talking to Israel. Ask the JWs if they are Jewish Israelites in the time of Isaiah. They will say no. So let them know this verse does not apply to them.

Then, go to Acts 1:8, which says, "But you will receive power when the holy spirit comes upon you, and you will be witnesses of me in Jerusalem, in all Judea and Samaria, and to the most distant part of the earth" (NWT). Here, Jesus is commanding the earliest Christians to be witnesses of Him. Ask the JWs why they are not being obedient to God and calling themselves witnesses of Jesus Christ.

Point out that nowhere in the New Testament does it say Christians are to be witnesses of Jehovah. Christians are to be witnesses of Jesus Christ because He is God (Jehovah), as fully revealed in the New Testament.

POINT #3: WE HAD A PREEXISTENT STATE

Before I formed you in the womb I knew you; Before you were born I sanctified you; I ordained you a prophet to the nations *(Jer. 1:5)*.

The LDS are convinced the Bible supports their manmade doctrines, so they will often take texts that do not support their teachings and misinterpret them. Missionaries will use the above verse as a "proof" text that we all had a preexistent state in the heavenly realms—meaning humans existed in a spirit world before being born on the earth.

COUNTERPOINT #3:

The reality is, the passage says nothing about a spiritual preexistence, a premortal realm, or spirit children. Rather, the verse is referring to God's omniscience and His plan for Jeremiah to be a prophet. God sovereignly chose Jeremiah for ministry before he was born.

Notice how Jeremiah did not know God, but God knew Jeremiah, thus refuting the notion that Jeremiah was with God prior to his birth on earth.[254] LDS are reading something into the verse that is just not there.

The Bible *actually* says God formed the physical component of man and his spiritual component instantaneously: "And the LORD God formed man *of* the dust of the ground, and breathed into his nostrils the breath of life; and man became a living being" *(Gen. 2:7)*. There was no preexistent spiritual existence.

POINT #4: "FIRSTBORN" MEANS JESUS WAS CREATED

He is the image of the invisible God, the firstborn over all creation *(Col. 1:15)*.

---

254   Bill McKeever and Eric Johnson, mrm.org, "Jeremiah 1:5," accessed August 16, 2016, http://www.mrm.org/jeremiah-1-5.

It is very common for a JW or LDS to point out that Colossians 1:15 shows Jesus was created. After all, "firstborn" implies something was created, doesn't it?

COUNTERPOINT #4:

Actually, it doesn't, particularly in the context of this verse. Let's address the definition of "firstborn." The term in the original biblical Greek translation is *prototokos*, which means "preeminent one" or "sovereign." If the verse had intended to convey Jesus was the "first created," it would have used the Greek term *protoktisis*—but, in fact, that word is never used to describe Jesus in the New Testament.

Wuest's Word Studies in the Greek New Testament says it is impossible the term "firstborn" refers to a literal beginning:

The word "firstborn" is *prōtotokos* (πρωτοτοκος). The Greek word implied two things, *priority* to all creation and *sovereignty* over all creation. In the first meaning we see the absolute pre-existence of the Logos. Since our Lord existed before all created things, He must be uncreated. Since He is uncreated, He is eternal. Since He is eternal, He is God. Since He is God, He cannot be one of the emanations from deity of which the Gnostic speaks, even though He proceeds from God the Father as the Son. In the second meaning we see that He is the natural ruler, the acknowledged head of God's household. Thus again, He cannot be one of the emanations from deity in whom the divine essence is present but diffused. *He is Lord of creation.*[255]

Now look at how "firstborn" is used in the Bible. It can mean the first one born in the family, particularly the eldest son. In ancient times, the firstborn was given a double inheritance to protect the son when there was a polygamous marriage.[256]

---

255   Kenneth S. Wuest, *Wuest's Word Studies from the Greek New Testament: For the English Reader* (Grand Rapids, MI: Eerdmans, 1997).

256   Elwell and Beitzel, *Baker Encyclopedia,* 791.

But "firstborn" also often referred to preeminence or superiority. For example, Psalm 89:27 tells us David was firstborn, yet he was the youngest in his family. In Jeremiah 31:9, Ephraim is called the firstborn, even though He was Joseph's second son. Manasseh was actually the eldest son, according to Genesis 41:51-52.[257] In Exodus 4:22, Israel is called God's firstborn son. Of course, Israel was *not* the first nation on earth.

Whenever Jesus is referred to as the firstborn, it is in regard to his sovereignty and supreme authority. Hebrews 1:6 confirms this: "But when He again brings the firstborn into the world, He says: 'Let all the angels of God worship Him.'"

Only God is to be worshipped; thus, the Bible wouldn't ever command a created being or lesser god to be worshipped. Furthermore, when Jesus is called "the firstborn from the dead" in Colossians 1:18, it refers to His Resurrection. Jesus was obviously not the first person to die—rather, He was the first to be resurrected from the dead and never die again. Revelation 1:5 also calls Jesus the firstborn from the dead but is obviously referring to the same concept as in Colossians 1:18.

Because the cultist has already brought you to Colossians, we have found it useful to ask the unbeliever about Colossians 1:15, which tells us Jesus is the image of the invisible God. The word "image" in the Greek is *eikōn*. According to most commentaries, including *The New American Commentary*, the context in which the word is being used means "manifestation." Thus J. B. Phillips translated it as "visible expression," and by it, Paul meant Jesus brought God into the human sphere of understanding. He manifested God. The terminology is similar to Hebrews 1:3, in which Jesus is called the "exact representation" of God, and John 1:18, which states Jesus "has made him known." The point is, in Christ, the invisible God became visible. He shared the same substance as God and made God's character known in this earthly sphere of existence. The revelation of God in Christ is such that we can see Him, even with all of our limitations.[258]

---

257 Ron Rhodes, *Reasoning from the Scriptures with the Jehovah's Witnesses* (Eugene, OR: Harvest House Publishers. 2009), 131.

258 Richard R. Melick, *Philippians, Colossians, Philemon, vol. 32, The New American Commentary* (Nashville: Broadman & Holman Publishers, 1991), 215.

We often ask the unbeliever how Jesus could be the image of God if He is not God Himself. Then we lead into John 1:18 and demonstrate how we can only see God through Jesus. This is especially powerful because no man may see God and live *(Exod. 33:20)*.

Additionally, as Jesus stated in John 14:9, "He who has seen Me has seen the Father." This shows how He is the expression of the Father; they share the same divine substance. They are different Persons, but of the same divine essence or nature in the Trinity.

Then we explain how the true God is reaching down to the JW or LDS through Jesus Christ, who is Himself Almighty God. Even though the passage is supposed to be a problem for Christians, you can turn it around and make it into an effective evangelistic tool.

(Note: The cultists may say Jesus is the image of God just like humans are made in the image of God. However, humans are made in the image of God, while Jesus is the uncreated image of God.)

In addition to showing how Jesus is the only way we may see God, it is helpful to continue with Colossians 1:16 to further demonstrate Christ's preeminence: "For by Him all things were created that are in heaven and that are on earth, visible and invisible, whether thrones or dominions or principalities or powers. All things were created through Him and for Him" *(Col. 1:16)*. In this verse, Paul is telling us that Jesus is the Creator. He created everything in the universe. If He was the Creator, then how could he be created?

A common objection is that Jesus helped in the creation of the universe. But keep in mind that Yahweh alone created the universe *(Isa. 44:24, 45:12,18-19)*. So the obvious conclusion is that Jesus is Yahweh or Jehovah—and thus has never been created but created all things.

The New World Translation used by JWs tries to get around the obvious implication that Jesus is Yahweh by changing Colossians 1:16 to say that "by means of him all other things were created." The word "other" is not in *any* Greek manuscript.

In fact, the translators of the New World Translation took the liberty of inserting the word "other" *twice* in verse 16 and *twice* in verse 17 where it speaks of Jesus being the Creator:

Because by means of him all *other* things were created in the heavens and on the earth, the things visible and the things invisible, whether they are thrones or lordships or governments or authorities. All *other* things have been created through him and for him. Also, he is before all other things, and by means of him all other things were made to exist (emphasis ours).

This is a blatant cover-up of Jesus's deity! The 1985 Greek Interlinear of the New World Translation, in fact, has the word "other" in brackets—and the editors of this translation admit that brackets mean the words were inserted by the translators.[259] Also, the 1985 Watch Tower Bible—as well as the JW Tract Society's Greek text, called the Kingdom Interlinear Translation of the Greek Scriptures—affirms the addition of the words.

However, when the 2013 "improved" version came out, the word "other" had no brackets around it all. At least the 1985 version was honest about the insertion. Point this out in your conversation with the JWs, and ask them why the Watch Tower would lie to others by inserting the words without brackets.

Colossians 1:16 ends by telling the reader this: "All things were created through Him and for Him." Again, we see Jesus is the Creator, and we know creation was made for the glory of God. Yet, as we mentioned earlier, the New World Translation editors once again inserted the word "other," stating that "All *other* things have been created through him and for him."

And you may have guessed, the New World Translation editors made two more unwarranted insertions with the word "other": "Also, he is before all *other* things, and by means of him all *other* things were made to exist" (emphasis ours).

Ask your JW visitor why the editors of the New World Translation would dishonestly insert the word "other" in Colossians 1:16 to 1:17 *four* times. Point out how it is not in the original Greek or any other prominent Bible version. The real answer is obvious. Without inserting the word "other," the reader would clearly understand Jesus is the Creator Jehovah.

---

259   *The Kingdom Interlinear Translation of the Greek Scriptures*, 6.

Inevitably, the JWs will bring this up in the discussion of Jesus. Here is a powerful question to ask them after you have explained what firstborn means: "Where does it clearly state in Scripture that Jehovah created Jesus?" They will only try to show you Colossians 1:15 or a few other passages we'll refute later. When they do use Colossians, ask them if creation created Jesus, since it states in their version He is the firstborn of all creation. Using *their* logic, it was creation that must have given "birth" to Jesus!

Then politely explain what the verse means. Once again, ask if there is a verse that explicitly states Jehovah created Jesus. They will not be able to show you one. Ask them why Jesus is referred to as the Creator in John 1:2. In reply, they will tell you He was Jehovah's agent in creation. Next, show them how their doctrine contradicts Isaiah 44:24, 45:12, and 45:18-9, which state Jehovah alone was the Creator. The only logical conclusion is that Jesus is Jehovah (Yahweh).

Furthermore, go to the next sentence following verse 16 (Colossians 1:16) for further support that Jesus is the Creator. Remember in Colossians 1, Paul has the preeminence of Jesus in mind, "And He is before all things, and in Him all things consist." Again, only God is before all things—not some lesser deity, like LDS claim, or a created spirit creature, as the JWs say. This verse explicitly states Christ sustains the universe because in Him all things consist.

In his commentary on Colossians, Dr. Richard Melick has an excellent insight on Colossians Chapter 1, verse 17:

The summary includes two statements of significance to the readers. The first is, "He is before all things." Clearly this comment has a time orientation, and it teaches that before creation Jesus existed. Since for the ancients priority in time often meant priority of person, this argument not only stresses Jesus' role in creating but also gives him a prominent position with respect to creation. The second statement is, "In him all things hold together." The work of creation included the continual sustaining of what was created. Looking to the present, ongoing routine of creation, therefore, Paul stated that Jesus keeps things in order. The

Creator has not forgotten the creation. He daily maintains a balance in the universe.[260]

Colossians chapter 1, verses 16-17 refute the LDS position that Jesus was an evolved spirit. Jesus could not have been created if He is the Creator; and if He sustains *all things*, there could not have been a time when He did not exist.

POINT #5: "BEGOTTEN" MEANS "CREATED"

For God so loved the world that He gave His only begotten Son that whoever believes in Him should not perish but have everlasting life *(John 3:16, NKJV).*

LDS and JWs have been wrongly taught that the word "begotten" denotes procreation or creation.

COUNTERPOINT #5:

Does the term "begotten" show Jesus was created /procreated and not God? Definitely not! You can point to several references to explain why. The *Tyndale Bible Dictionary* states, "The word traditionally translated 'only begotten' does not carry the idea of birth at all. Literally, it means 'only one of its kind,' 'unique.' This can be readily seen in the way it is used in the NT and in the Septuagint (the Greek translation of the OT)."[261] Also, the *Holman Treasury of Key Bible Words* explains, "People have a mistaken idea about the term 'only-begotten' because the English term 'begotten' connotes a birth. By contrast, the Greek word *monogenēs* denotes a 'one and only son'; it does not convey the idea of a birth."[262]

We can get more insight from John 1:18 where some versions also use the term "begotten Son" in terms of denoting His uniqueness as God the Son. Several modern literal translations, such as the New American Standard Bible (NASB), print the verse as, "No one has seen God at any time; the only

---

260   Melick, *Philippians, Colossians, Philemon,* 220.

261   Walter A. Elwell and Philip Wesley Comfort, *Tyndale Bible Dictionary* (Wheaton, IL: Tyndale House Publishers, 2001), 978.

262   Eugene E. Carpenter and Philip W. Comfort, *Holman Treasury of Key Bible Words: 200 Greek and 200 Hebrew Words Defined and Explained* (Nashville: Broadman & Holman Publishers, 2000), 349.

begotten God who is in the bosom of the Father, He has explained *Him*." The English Standard Version (ESV), on the other hand, translates the verse to say, "No one has ever seen God; the only God, who is at the Father's side, he has made him known."

Furthermore, the reading in all the earliest manuscripts indicates that Jesus in this verse is called "God," as well as "the one and only." This perfectly corresponds to the first verse of John's prologue, where the Word is called "God" and is described as the Son living in intimate fellowship with the Father.[263]

The discovery of two ancient manuscripts, Papyrus 66 and Papyrus 75, in the middle part of the last century, are dated A.D. 150-225. Both have the reading *monogenēs theos*, which convinced modern translators to go with "one and only God" over and against "only begotten Son. Their decision is also helped by the fact that other early manuscripts (Codices Vaticanus, Sinaiticus, Ephraemi Rescriptus) and some early versions (Coptic and Syriac) support the text, as do many church fathers (including Irenaeus, Clement, Origen, Eusebius, and Didymus).[264]

Last, you can also point out that in Hebrews 11:17, Isaac is called "the only begotten" of Abraham—yet Abraham had several sons. Isaac wasn't even the first one born, but he *was* a unique son. So the context here also tells us that *begotten* means "unique one" and not "created."

POINT #6: "BEGINNING OF THE CREATION" MEANS JESUS WAS CREATED

> And to the angel of the church of the Laodiceans write, "These things says the Amen, the Faithful and True Witness, the Beginning of the creation of God" *(Rev. 3:14).*

Some misinterpret the end of this verse, "the Beginning of the creation of God," to mean Jesus was the first of God's creations, but a simple analysis of the Greek can solve this misunderstanding.

---

263   Carpenter and Comfort, *Holman Treasury*, 350.
264   Ibid.

COUNTERPOINT #6:

Whenever this point has come up, we explain how, in context, the Greek word for beginning, *arche*, means "originator" (or, alternately, "first cause"). And, of course, we always invite the unbeliever to check the Greek for himself.

The Complete Word Study Dictionary: New Testament states, "Christ is called 'the beginning' because He is the efficient cause of the creation; 'the head' because He is before all things, and all things were created by Him and for Him (*John 1:1–3; Col. 1:16–17; Heb. 1:10*)."[265] Thus, Jesus is not the first creation of God, but the cause of creation.

POINT #7: PROVERBS 8 TEACHES JESUS WAS CREATED

The LORD possessed me at the beginning of His way,

Before His works of old. I have been established from everlasting,

From the beginning, before there was ever an earth. When there were no depths I was brought forth, When there were no fountains abounding with water *(Prov. 8:22-24).*

COUNTERPOINT #7:

That Proverbs 8 teaches Jesus was created is an argument quite easy to refute. The first nine chapters of Proverbs deal with the personification (giving human characteristics to something nonhuman) of wisdom *(Prov. 1:2-3).* In addition, we read in Proverbs that wisdom is called a "sister" in 7:4, "her" in 8:1, and "she" in 8:2, 3, as well as a "woman who cries out in the streets" *(Prov. 1:20-21).* (Note: Use KJV with 8:1-3 or NWT with 7:4).

We obviously know Jesus is not a woman, so this is a failed attempt to prove Jesus was created. In fact, there is not a verse in the Bible that states Jesus was created. Just the opposite is true. We read that Jesus is eternal (*Mic. 5:2; 1 John 1:2; Rev. 22:13*). Jesus is also the Creator who created everything, including all the spirits. Therefore, he could not have been created (*John 1:1–3; Col. 1:16–17; Heb. 1:10*).

---

265   Spiros Zodhiates, *The Complete Word Study Dictionary: New Testament* (Chattanooga, TN: AMG Publishers, 2000).

When the JWs bring this point up, show them how the first nine chapters of Proverbs are about the personification of wisdom. If they persist, ask them how Jesus could be a "she" if He was a man.

POINT #8: THE FACT THAT GOD IS THE HEAD OF CHRIST MEANS JESUS ISN'T GOD

> But I want you to know that the head of every man is Christ, the head of woman is man, and the head of Christ is God *(1 Cor. 11:3)*.

When engaging with the Jehovah's Witnesses, you may find them confused when Jesus and God the Father are referred to as separate persons. Because God and Christ are seen as separate, and God is the head of Christ, JWs think this means Jesus is *not* God and, therefore, an inferior being.

COUNTERPOINT #8:

First, when Jesus and God are separated, the term "God" can refer to God the Father or the rest of the Godhead. Second, context is everything. Notice how Paul is making a comparison in authority, not equality.

Men are under the authority of Christ; women are to follow men in terms of roles (especially spiritual leadership); and Christ is under the authority of the Father. If the JW is to make the case that Christ is unequal to the Father, then that must mean women are unequal to men. Of course, men and women are created in the image of God *(Gen. 1:27)* and, therefore, are equal beings.

Similarly, Christ is subject to the Father in terms of authority *(1 Cor. 15:28)* but is not inferior in nature. Consider the words of Jesus Himself:

> My sheep hear My voice, and I know them, and they follow Me. And I give them eternal life, and they shall never perish; neither shall anyone snatch them out of My hand. My Father, who has given *them* to Me, is greater than all; and no one is able to snatch *them* out of My Father's hand. I and *My* Father are one *(John 10:27-30)*.

The context makes it clear that the Father and Son keep the believer secure and are involved in his salvation. Thus, since they are united in will and power, they must also be one in nature or essence.[266] Additionally, Jesus referred to God as His own Father, which presupposes them both possessing a divine nature *(John 5:18)*.

When talking to JWs, simply point out their reasoning would make women of lesser value. Tell them the Watch Tower has taught them to think Jesus is a lesser god, when the Bible clearly states He is the true God but plays a different role than His Father.

POINT #9: "SON OF GOD" MEANS JESUS IS NOT EQUAL WITH FATHER GOD

> Among the spirit children of Elohim, the first-born was and is Jehovah, or Jesus Christ, to whom all others are juniors (Joseph F. Smith, Gospel Doctrine, 70).

Today, official Mormon doctrine teaches Jesus Christ is literally the son of God the Eternal Father. Recall that the Mormon Father God has flesh and bones and is not Spirit as the Bible teaches *(John 4:24)*.

Although it has changed over time, the 1992 publication of *Gospel Principles* from the Church of Jesus Christ of Latter-day Saints states, "Thus, God the Father became the literal father of Jesus Christ. Jesus is the only person on earth to be born of a mortal mother and immortal father."[267]

In his "Analysis of the Articles of Faith" published in a 1922 issue of *Millennial Star*, the seventh president of the LDS church, Heber J. Grant, wrote, "We believe absolutely that Jesus Christ is the Son of God, begotten of God, the first-born in the spirit and the only begotten in the flesh; that He is the Son of God just as much as you and I are the sons of our fathers."[268]

---

266   John Peter Lange and Philip Schaff, *A Commentary on the Holy Scriptures: John* (Bellingham, WA: 2008), 332.

267   The Church of Jesus Christ of Latter-day Saints, *Gospel Principles* (Salt Lake City: The Church of Jesus Christ of Latter-day Saints, 1992), 64.

268   The Church of Jesus Christ of Latter-Day Saints website, "Chapter 4: Jesus Christ, the Son of God," *Doctrines of the Gospel Student Manual*, accessed May 1, 2016, https://www.

Unfathomably, Apostle James Talmage taught that God the Father had sex with the Virgin Mary to produce Jesus: "That Child to be born of Mary was begotten of Elohim, the Eternal Father, not in violation of natural law but in accordance with a higher manifestation thereof; and, the offspring from that association of supreme sanctity, celestial Sireship, and pure though mortal maternity, was of right to be called the 'Son of the Highest.'"[269]

Mormonism states that Jesus was an evolved spirit in the heavenly realm but that he acquired a human body after Heavenly Father had sexual relations with Mary! But the bigger issue here is that JWs and LDS, as well as other non-Trinitarians, feel the term "Son of God" must mean Jesus is a lesser being than God the Father.

COUNTERPOINT #9:

In the Old Testament, the term "Son of God" is used in different ways. For example, it describes the nation of Israel through the Exodus (*Hosea 11:1*). Also, it is a title given to the monarch at the time of enthronement (*Ps. 2:7*). Additionally, angels are called "sons of God" (*Job 38:7*). In all these examples, the term does not designate a physical relationship, but rather a divine call to obedience in the role of salvation.[270]

Also, Isaiah 9:6 gives us valuable insight into what the term "Son of God" means:

For unto us a Child is born,

Unto us a Son is given;

    And the government will be upon His shoulder.

    And His name will be called

    Wonderful, Counselor, Mighty God,

    Everlasting Father, Prince of Peace.

---

    lds.org/manual/doctrines-of-the-gospel-student-manual/chapter-4-jesus-christ-the-son-of-god?lang=eng.

269   LDS.org, "Chapter 4:Jesus Christ, the Son of God," accessed March 7, 2016, https://www.lds.org/manual/doctrines-of-the-gospel-student-manual/chapter-4-jesus-christ-the-son-of-god?lang=eng.

270   Paul J. Achtemeier, *Harper's Bible Dictionary* (San Francisco: Harper & Row, 1985), 979.

The Child will be a Son, God, and Everlasting. No wonder the Jews accused Jesus of blasphemy for calling Himself the Son of God *(John. 10:33)*. This verse tells us the Messiah would be a Son but also divine in His nature.

In the New Testament, when Jesus is called the "Son of God," it does not mean God had a son through sexual union. Rather, it references Christ's divine nature and relationship with the Father. The term occurs thirty-seven times in the New Testament. *Easton's Bible Dictionary* emphasizes that the term Son of God refers to Jesus's nature:

> The sonship of Christ denotes his equality with the Father. To call Christ the Son of God is to assert his true and proper divinity. The second Person of the Trinity, because of his eternal relation to the first Person, is the Son of God. He is the Son of God as to his divine nature, while as to his human nature he is the Son of David (Rom. 1:3, 4. Comp. Gal. 4:4; John 1:1–14; 5:18–25; 10:30–38, which prove that Christ was the Son of God before his incarnation, and that his claim to this title is a claim of equality with God).[271]

Jesus is the Son of God also in the sense of His virgin birth. The power of the Most High through the Holy Spirit *(Luke 1:35)* caused the Virgin Mary to give birth to a Son. Because the Son was not conceived through sexual relations but through the power of God, Jesus is God's Son in the human sense as well.

To say the term "Son of God" refers to a created—and therefore lesser—being would mean Jesus Christ had a beginning. But the Bible states in numerous passages (e.g. *Rev. 22:13; 1 John 1:2*) that Jesus is *eternal*, without a beginning or end. We've already quoted a few of these in detail earlier in this book.

As previously shown, Jesus is the eternal Creator and shares *the same*—that is, *equal*—divine essence as His Father *(John 10:30)*. And, of course, because Jesus is the Creator *(John 1:1–3; Col. 1:16–17; Heb. 1:10)*, He could not have been created.

---

271   M. G. Easton, *Easton's Bible Dictionary* (New York: Harper & Brothers, 1893).

Furthermore, because God is love (*1 John 4:8*) there must be a plurality of persons unto whom God can love. God *creating* a being to love would violate His nature, because God is eternally loving. Therefore, the person who God loves must be internal to Himself.

God's love is extended throughout the Triad of persons who have eternally loved. Love requires a relationship, which is only possible with the Triune God and is on full display in the intimate relationship between the Father and Son.[272]

Another way to look at the term "Son of God" would be to call Jesus "God the Son." Because Jesus is called "God"—and there is only one, true God, and He is also called "Son," referring to His relationship within the Triune Godhead—the use of "God the Son" is perfectly legitimate. As Jesus stated in John 14:9, "He who has seen Me has seen the Father." Jesus is the expression of the Father because they are of the same substance—although not the same person.

Now here's where your conversation with LDS gets complicated. Today, some LDS apologists will state God did not have a sexual relationship with Mary, thereby contradicting what past LDS apostles have stated.[273] It is found clearly in the writings of LDS leaders and apologists *throughout history* that they believe this sexual union *did* occur and that the Holy Spirit was *not* involved. LDS Apostle Brigham Young himself, while speaking on behalf of the LDS church, made this statement:

> When the Virgin Mary conceived the child Jesus, the Father had begotten him in his own likeness. He was *not* [emphasis added] begotten by the Holy Ghost . . . Jesus, our elder brother, was begotten in the flesh by the same character that was in the garden of Eden, and who is our Father in

272   William Lane Craig and Shabir Ally, "The Concept of God in Islam and Christianity," Campus Crusade for Christ and the Islamic Information Center & Dawah Center International, McMaster University, Hamilton, ON, Canada, March 2002, Debate accessed October 16, 2016, YouTube on reasonablefaith.org channel.

273   Fairmormon.org website, *Does the Church of Jesus Christ of Latter-day Saints Teach that God Had SEX with Mary?* accessed May 1, 2016, http://www.fairmormon.org/wp content/uploads/2012/02/Did_God_have_Sex_with_Mary.pdf.

Heaven . . . Now, remember from this time forth, and forever, that Jesus Christ was not begotten by the Holy Ghost.[274]

Joseph Fielding Smith (1876-1972) was a president of the LDS church and an apostle. He too believed in the sexual union between Heavenly Father and Mary, as he stated in *Religious Truths Defined*:

The birth of the Savior was a natural occurrence unattended with any degree of mysticism, and the Father god was the literal parent of Jesus in the flesh as well as in the spirit. He is the only person ever born on this earth in the flesh with an immortal Father.[275]

If an LDS makes a similar argument, you can respond by pointing to Scripture. The Bible teaches clearly that Jesus was conceived by the power of the Holy Spirit (*Matt. 1:18-20*), not by the Virgin Mary having relations with Heavenly Father. After all, that would contradict what it means to be a virgin (*Isa. 7:14; Matt. 1:23; Luke 1:34*).

A note on your interaction with the LDS missionaries: Do not allow those you meet with to tell you their organization teaches Jesus was conceived by the Holy Spirit. Sometimes, the missionaries preach fallacious doctrine out of ignorance; yet other times, they do not want to admit they believe a bizarre doctrine that contradicts the Bible. Politely show them what their leaders have taught in the past regarding Jesus being created through sexual union.

In actuality, LDS believe Jesus was birthed twice—once in the celestial realm, and once on earth—just as *every* person has two births. In the case of Christ, He was "the first and foremost of subsequent billions of spirit children created through sexual intercourse between the male earth god and his celestial wife. Later, to produce the body for this special spirit child, the earth god again

---

274 *Journal of Discourses,* "Self-Government—Mysteries—Recreation and Amusements, Not in Themselves Sinful Tithing—Adam, Our Father and Our God," pages 50-51, accessed May 1, 2016, http://jod.mrm.org/1/46.

275 Joseph Fielding Smith Jr., *Religious Truths Defined* (Salt Lake City: Bookcraft Inc., 1959), 44.

had sexual intercourse, this time with the 'virgin' Mary, who then became Jesus' earthly mother."[276] Watch Tower theology states, "As God's firstborn Son, Jesus was a spirit creature in heaven before he was born as a human on earth."[277]

Jehovah's Witness theology understands Jesus as being God's Son because He was created just like Adam, who is referred to also as "son of God" in the genealogy of Luke 3:38.[278] Of course, we have already gone over why Jesus is eternal. Obviously the Watch Tower has drawn their conclusions based on their opinions rather than Scripture.

Furthermore, this view does not match up with two thousand years of biblical, orthodox Christian doctrine. JWs do not understand that Jesus was eternally the Son of God and is a separate person of the Trinity, not a created being.

POINT #10: JESUS IS A "MIGHTY GOD" BUT NOT "ALMIGHTY GOD"

For unto us a Child is born, Unto us a Son is given;
And the government will be upon His shoulder. And His name will be calledWonderful, Counselor, Mighty God, Everlasting Father, Prince of Peace *(Isa. 9:6).*

JWs often claim Jesus is a "Mighty God," but He is not Almighty God. The Watch Tower has deceived them into thinking this is a good argument.

COUNTERPOINT #10:

There is only one, true God, as we read in Isaiah 44:6-8:

Thus says the LORD, the King of Israel,
And his Redeemer, the LORD of hosts:
"I am the First and I am the Last;
Besides Me there is no God."

---

276   John Ankerberg and John Weldon, *Encyclopedia of Cults and New Religions* (Eugene, OR: Harvest House Publishers, 1999), 298.

277   JW.org, *Why Is Jesus Called God's Son?*, accessed May 1, 2016, https://www.jw.org/en/bible-teachings/questions/jesus-gods-son/.

278   Ibid.

Also, in James 2:19, we read, "You believe that there is one God. You do well. Even the demons believe—and tremble!"

Point out to the JW that Jehovah is called "Mighty God" in Isaiah 10:21. Using Watch Tower logic, Jehovah should *also* be an inferior god. In addition to being called "Mighty God," Jesus, on the other hand, is *also* called "the Almighty" in the book of Revelation. Revelation 1:8 refers to Jesus as "the Lord Almighty," indicating He is God Almighty.

Of course, the Watch Tower changed Revelation 1:8 in the New World Translation to hide this fact by inserting the word Jehovah instead of Lord: "'I am the Alpha and the Omega,' says Jehovah God, 'the One who is and who was and who is coming, the Almighty.'"

Ask the JWs whose Revelation they are reading. If they do not say, "Jesus," ask if they agree that Revelation 1:7 ("every eye will see Him, even those who pierced Him") is referring to Jesus.

Next, ask why the New World Translation editors switched the word "Lord" to "Jehovah" when *their own Greek Interlinear* uses the term "Lord."[279] Point out there is no other verse where Jehovah is speaking in Revelation *except in this insertion* by the Watch Tower. You can also use the KJV to point out the blatant cover-up of Jesus's deity.

POINT #11: "MY FATHER IS GREATER THAN I" MEANS JESUS IS NOT GOD

You heard me say to you, "I am going away, and I will come to you." If you loved me, you would have rejoiced, because I am going to the Father, for the Father is greater than I *(John 14:28)*.

JWs often cite this verse to show Jesus Christ is not Almighty God and is a lesser god than Jehovah. Interestingly, through taking this position, they make themselves polytheists (which they deny) by believing in more than one god. More on that in a moment.

---

279   *The Kingdom Interlinear Translation,* 1,059.

COUNTERPOINT #11:

The context of this verse is that Jesus is referring to the Father being greater than Himself because He had not yet returned to His glory in heaven. Philippians 2:5-11 tells us exactly how to view John 14:28. We read how, being God, Jesus humbled Himself and took on human form:

> Have this mind among yourselves, which is yours in Christ Jesus, who, though he was in the form of God, did not count equality with God a thing to be grasped, but emptied himself, by taking the form of a servant, being born in the likeness of men. And being found in human form, he humbled himself by becoming obedient to the point of death, even death on a cross. Therefore God has highly exalted him and bestowed on him the name that is above every name, that at the name of Jesus every knee should bow, in heaven and on earth and under the earth, and every tongue confess that Jesus Christ is Lord, to the glory of God the Father.

These passages demonstrate how Jesus, at times, set aside some of His divine prerogatives (taking the form of a servant). John 14:28 is not talking about the nature of Christ, but rather the position of Christ in His humbled incarnation state.

As scholar Ron Rhodes notes, Jesus did not say the Father is "better" but used the term "greater." "Greater" refers to the position of Jesus. If He used the term "better," then it would have meant the Father had a better nature.[280] Because Jesus was God and man, He could not be in a "greater" position in His earthly state.

Greek and New Testament Scholar Dr. James White makes an insightful commentary in regard to John 14:28: "So we can see that rather than denying the deity of Christ, John 14:28 implies it, for the position into which the Son was returning is a position fit only for deity, not for mere creatures."[281] Because Jesus was both God and man, He could not be in a "greater" position in His earthly state.

---

280 Ron Rhodes, *Reasoning from the Scriptures with the Jehovah's Witnesses*, 147.
281 James White, *The Forgotten Trinity*, 90-91.

A simple way to respond to the JWs is to say, "In this verse, Jesus is speaking from His humanity. Philippians 2 tells us Jesus is God but took on human form to be obedient to God the Father. Plus, the verse says 'greater,' not 'better.' Also, are you saying you believe in multiple gods—even though there is only one, true God? If so, is Jesus a true God or false god?"

POINT #12: JESUS PRAYING MEANS HE IS NOT GOD

When Jesus had spoken these words, he lifted up his eyes to heaven, and said, "Father, the hour has come; glorify your Son that the Son may glorify you, since you have given him authority over all flesh, to give eternal life to all whom you have given him" *(John 17:1-2)*.

COUNTERPOINT #12:

The question of Jesus praying almost always comes up when talking to unbelievers. However, the refutation is quite simple: Jesus prayed simply because He took on humanity. We have found it helpful to use Philippians 2:5-11 to explain how Jesus took on the form of a man while remaining God to save us.

His prayers are an example of the relationship the Father had with the Son—that is, the relationship between the Persons of the Trinity. Note Jesus is not praying to Jehovah but to the "Father." This denotes the intimacy between God the Son and God the Father.

We read in John 17:5 that Jesus prays to the Father to "glorify Me together with Yourself, with the glory which I had with You before the world was." Jesus is asking the Father to glorify Him with the same glory He has always possessed. This shows how Jesus was awaiting to return to the glory He once had in the heavens. The Father will glorify the Son, and the Son will glorify the Father.

Isaiah 48:11 shows Yahweh will give glory to no one but Himself. So if Jesus is glorified with Yahweh (Jehovah) and receives glory from Him, then He must be equal to God and thus *be* God. And, of course, we are told multiple times in the book of John that Jesus is God *(John 1:1, 8:58, 10:30, 20:28)*.

In conclusion, because Jesus was a monotheistic Jew, He of course prayed to God.

POINT #13: JESUS NOT KNOWING THE DAY OR HOUR MEANS JESUS IS NOT GOD

But concerning that day or that hour, no one knows, not even the angels in heaven, nor the Son, but only the Father *(Mark 13:31-32)*.

COUNTERPOINT #13:

Jesus had two natures on earth: a divine nature as God (*John 1:1, 8:58, 20:28; Heb. 1:8, 1;10; Col 2:9*) and a human nature (*John 1:14; 1 Tim. 3:16*). As God, Jesus took on human flesh.

Philippians 2:5-11 tells us that, being God, Jesus humbled Himself and took on human form. We read: "Have this mind among yourselves, which is yours in Christ Jesus, who, though he was in the form of God, did not count equality with God a thing to be grasped, but emptied himself, by taking the form of a servant, being born in the likeness of men."

In reference to Jesus's humanity, He never knew the time of His second coming. Yet in regard to His divinity, several examples in the New Testament show Jesus's omniscience—an attribute only God would have. Examples include Luke 5:4-6; John 2:24, 16:30, 21:17, 11:11, and 18:4; Acts 1:24; Mark 2:8; and Matthew 21:2.

So Jesus *could* have veiled His knowledge in light of His hour of return, and the Holy Spirit *may* have known the hour. However, if we look at the cultural context, we can get a much better understanding of what Jesus may have been alluding to when He said only the Father knows.

This insightful information comes from Matt Slick, president and founder of the Christian Apologetics and Research Ministry. As he explains, when a man was going to marry a woman in the time of Jesus, it was usually prearranged. The bridegroom would be living with his family, and he would begin to build an addition onto his father's house where he and his future wife would live. It was the custom for the father of the home to be the one who designated *when* the addition was finished. This meant that only the father knew when the son would be told to go get the bride. But does this mean that the son would *not* know when he had to go to get the bride? Not necessarily.

You see, a wedding was a community affair, to which many people would be invited. In a culture where there is no Internet, phone, or radio, things were done well in advance so people could plan ahead. They needed advance notice so people could allot the necessary time to put their animals away for the day and plan not to work in the field that day or have business dealings that day.

Furthermore, a wedding feast also meant large amounts of food would have to be prepared for all the guests to have something to eat. These kinds of arrangements were not done on the spur of the moment. The arrangements were done weeks, sometimes months, in advance to make sure no one would miss the wedding feast due to a spontaneous invitation.

But to maintain the respect and dignity of the father's place in the home, it would naturally be said "only the father knows" when it would be time for the son to go get the bride. This did not necessarily mean the son *didn't know*—because the community would *have* to know within a reasonable degree of accuracy when the wedding would occur. Therefore, Jesus may have been alluding to the phraseology of the wedding and wedding feast culture— wording that did not necessarily mean He didn't know or the Holy Spirit didn't know the time of His return. [282]

When this accusation is raised, inform the cultist how Jesus was alluding to a Jewish custom. The father of the bridegroom would announce when the time was for the marriage. Out of respect, it was said only the father knew when his son should get his bride. Similarly, God the Father would summon His Son, the Bridegroom, to meet His bride *(Rev. 19:7)*.

POINT #14: JESUS'S QUESTION, "WHY DO YOU CALL ME GOOD?," MEANS JESUS IS NOT GOOD—OR GOD

Now as He was going out on the road, one came running, knelt before Him, and asked Him, "Good Teacher, what shall I do that I may inherit eternal life?" So Jesus said to him, "Why do you call Me good? No one

---

282   Matt Slick, Christian Apologetics & Research Ministry, Carm.org., "If the Holy Spirit Is God, Why Didn't He Know the Time of Christ's Return?," accessed June 15, 2016, https://carm.org/bible-difficulties/matthew-mark/if-holy-spirit-god-why-didnt-he-know-time-christs-return.

is good but One, that is, God. You know the commandments: 'Do not commit adultery,' 'Do not murder,' 'Do not steal,' 'Do not bear false witness,' 'Do not defraud,' 'Honor your father and your mother.'" And he answered and said to Him, "Teacher, all these things I have kept from my youth." Then Jesus, looking at him, loved him, and said to him, "One thing you lack: Go your way, sell whatever you have and give to the poor, and you will have treasure in heaven; and come, take up the cross, and follow Me." But he was sad at this word, and went away sorrowful, for he had great possessions *(Mark 10:17-22)*.

Many claim this verse proves Jesus was not good and thus purely a man, devoid of all divinity.

COUNTERPOINT #14:

When examined properly, this passage in Mark *proves* Jesus is God. Jesus basically answered the young man in a rhetorical fashion to prove a point. In other words, He said, "Do not refer to me as a good teacher, since only God is good. Refer to me as God, or do not call me good." Jesus then went on to show the rich young ruler how *he* is not good because of his inability to follow the law.

Also, Jesus commands the young man to leave everything and follow Him instead of his possessions. This is similar to the greatest commandment in Deuteronomy 6:5: "You shall love the LORD your God with all your heart, with all your soul, and with all your strength." Jesus, as God, commanded the rich ruler to leave all and follow Him, because He, as God, is worthy of full commitment.

The only question that needs to be asked is, "Does the Bible teach that Jesus was good?" If so, there is no reason to think that Jesus was not good. If He is good, then He is God. Fortunately, the Bible is very clear on this issue in several books and verses:

For our sake he made him to be sin who knew no sin, so that in him we might become the righteousness of God *(2 Cor. 5:21)*.

He committed no sin, neither was deceit found in his mouth (*1 Pet. 2:22*).

For we do not have a high priest who is unable to sympathize with our weaknesses, but one who in every respect has been tempted as we are, yet without sin (*Heb. 4:15*).

You know that he appeared in order to take away sins, and in him there is no sin (*1 John 3:5*).

Knowing that you were ransomed from the futile ways inherited from your forefathers, not with perishable things such as silver or gold, but with the precious blood of Christ, like that of a lamb without blemish or spot (*1 Pet. 1:18-19*).

So we can see clearly that Jesus is sinless, good, and, therefore, God. He is asking a rhetorical question to prove His divinity.

POINT #15: BECAUSE JESUS REFERS TO CERTAIN INDIVIDUALS AS "gods," POLYTHEISM IS VALID

The Jews picked up stones again to stone Him. Jesus answered them, "I showed you many good works from the Father; for which of them are you stoning Me?" The Jews answered Him, "For a good work we do not stone You, but for blasphemy; and because You, being a man, make Yourself out to be God." Jesus answered them, "Has it not been written in your Law, 'I said, you are gods'? If he called them gods, to whom the word of God came (and the Scripture cannot be broken), do you say of Him, whom the Father sanctified and sent into the world, 'You are blaspheming,' because I said, 'I am the Son of God'?" (*John 10:34-36*)

The above passage comes up often when talking with the LDS and JWs. Because both religious groups are polytheistic, they attempt to prove Jesus was fine with polytheism and numerous gods exist.

COUNTERPOINT #15:

Like the verses in Colossians, you can make these supposed refutations of Jesus's divinity work toward your advantage in proving the deity of Jesus.

In the quoted verse, Jesus was telling the Jews their anger was irrational by pointing out that in Psalm 82, sinful human rulers were called "gods"— which the Jews had no problem with. These rulers would "die like men" (*Ps. 82:7*) because they were unjust (*Ps. 82:2*). Jesus, on the other hand, had proven His divinity through His miracles. Therefore, Jesus was perfectly legitimate in referring to Himself as the divine Son of God.

When the LDS or JWs bring this or any other verse up that refers to someone else as God rather than Yahweh (the Triune God), we tell them they are false gods. *Any* god, other than the Triune Yahweh, is a false god. And remember, lower case "gods" always bow down to capitalized "G" God.

Once you have refuted the allegation that polytheism is valid, point out how the Jews wanted to kill Jesus because He claimed to be God (*John 10:33*). Show the unbeliever the Jews' reaction when He claimed to be the divine Son of God. In their eyes, to be God's Son would mean you were on the same footing as God Almighty. This passage is often quoted, so make sure to emphasize that any other god than Yahweh is false and the Jews wanted to kill Jesus because He claimed to be God.

POINT #16: THE NT SUPPORTS THE NOTION THAT PROPHETS ARE NECESSARY

> And He Himself gave some to be apostles, some prophets, some evangelists, and some pastors and teachers *(Eph. 4:11)*.

LDS try to use this and other verses that appeal to apostles and prophets in support of their doctrines.

COUNTERPOINT #16:

The New Testament provides several examples of the Apostle Paul mentioning prophets and prophecy in regard to spiritual gifts. However, it does not support the Mormon definitions of these offices.

An apostle of Jesus Christ was one who had been with Jesus from His baptism to ascension (*Acts 1:21-22*). He must have been an eyewitness to the Resurrection too. Apostles of the church, such as Barnabas, Silas, and Timothy, were also sent and taught by the apostles of Jesus Christ *(2 Cor. 8:23).*[283] However, the LDS definition of an apostle stands in stark contrast:

> An "apostle" is an ordained leader in the Melchizedek Priesthood in The Church of Jesus Christ of Latter-day Saints. Apostles are chosen through inspiration by the President of the Church, sustained by the general membership of the Church, and ordained by the First Presidency and Quorum of the Twelve Apostles by the laying on of hands.[284]

LDS have obviously made up their own definition of an apostle. *None* of them have been eyewitnesses to the Resurrection or taught by the original followers of Jesus.

LDS also quote Ephesians 4:11 to support their claim that prophets and new revelations are necessary. According to them, "Like the prophets of old, prophets today testify of Jesus Christ and teach His gospel. They make known God's will and true character. They speak boldly and clearly, denouncing sin and warning of its consequences. At times, they may be inspired to prophesy of future events for our benefit."[285]

Once again, however, the LDS definition of a prophet is not biblical. As we will explain further in chapter 8, there has been no need for prophets and doctrinal revelations since the completion of Scripture.

When Paul refers to prophecy and prophets in his epistles (*1 Cor. 14; Eph. 2,4*), he is talking about those who have been chosen by God to proclaim the gospel for the building up and benefit of others (*1 Cor. 14:3-4*) *not* individuals selected by the church. [286]

---

283   *MacArthur Study Bible*, 1809.

284   The Church of Jesus Christ of Latter-Day Saints, "Apostle," accessed August 15, 2016, https://www.lds.org/topics/apostle?lang=eng.

285   The Church of Jesus Christ of Latter-Day Saints, "Prophets," accessed August 15, 2016, https://www.lds.org/topics/prophets?lang=en.

286   Don Stewart, Blue Letter Bible, Blueletterbible.org, "Who Were the New Testament Prophets?" accessed August 15, 2016, https://www.blueletterbible.org/faq/don_stewart/don_stewart_389.cfm.

It is also important to note the Greek word for prophet (*prophétes*) doesn't always refer to someone who predicts the future. Often, it refers to someone speaking forth God's message or the Word of God.[287] Occasionally, prophets in the NT prophesied about future events (*Acts 11:27, 21:11*) that always came to pass. It appears, however, that predictive prophecy ceased after the time of the apostles, as some of the earliest Christians were given by the Holy Spirit to authenticate who they were in a time of paganism.

Today, a Christian may have the gift of prophecy, which simply means he proclaims God's Word. It does not mean he receives new doctrine not taught in Scripture. In conclusion, when the LDS church has predicted the future, its "prophets" have not done so accurately—and thus have not been under the inspiration of the Holy Spirit (see chapter 9).

POINT #17: GOD DOES NOTHING APART FROM HIS PROPHETS

Surely the Lord GOD does nothing, unless He reveals His secret to His servants the prophets *(Amos 3:7)*.

Mormon missionaries may bring up this verse from Amos up to show the necessity of prophets.

COUNTERPOINT #17:

Like many of these verses that supposedly support LDS doctrine, the missionaries have taken Amos 3:7 out of context. To begin with, the first two chapters of Amos describe the judgment to come upon Israel, Judah, and other nations. Second, God posed a series of questions in the beginning of chapter 3 of Amos to show how certain actions produce certain results. However, God is merciful and decided to warn His creation through prophets instead of keeping silent. He wanted to give them the chance to repent before the judgment.[288]

You can also simply point out that, in the OT, God *did* use prophets, but they are no longer necessary because Jesus fulfilled that role. Ask the

---

287 Biblehub.com 4396, "Prophétes," accessed August 15, 2016, http://biblehub.com/str/greek/4396.htm.

288 *MacArthur Study Bible*, 1,279.

cultist to look at Hebrews 1:1-2, which states Jesus fulfilled the role of prophet.

In summary, explain to the Mormon missionaries how this verse does not apply to them. Then explain how we need no new revelation since Jesus came.

POINT #18: THE BIBLE PROPHESIES AN APOSTASY OF THE EARLY CHURCH

Both LDS and JWs will claim the Bible prophesies a total apostasy of the early church took place and God has chosen their respective group to restore it. For the JWs, it is the Watch Tower that will lead the restoration. For the LDS, it is their prophets.

COUNTERPOINT #18:

Galatians 1:6-8 is a verse commonly misused by the cults in an attempt to prove all of Christendom is apostate. However, this verse does not talk about a total apostasy.

> I marvel that you are turning away so soon from Him who called you in the grace of Christ, to a different gospel, which is not another; but there are some who trouble you and want to pervert the gospel of Christ. But even if we, or an angel from heaven, preach any other gospel to you than what we have preached to you, let him be accursed (*Gal. 1:6-8*).

Rather, it talks about a "different gospel." And interestingly, the JW and LDS have a different gospel than historic and biblical Christianity.

There's another verse that they will likely quote, yet it likewise states nothing about a total apostasy of the early Church:

> Let no one deceive you by any means; for that Day will not come unless the falling away comes first, and the man of sin is revealed, the son of perdition (*2 Thess. 2:3:*).

The *actual* context of this verse is about a future person near the end times before the return of Christ who will deceive others.

One more common verse used is Acts 20:30-31:

Also from among yourselves men will rise up, speaking perverse things, to draw away the disciples after themselves. Therefore watch, and remember that for three years I did not cease to warn everyone night and day with tears.

Ask the person who is claiming this verse refers to an apostasy of the early church how he arrived at such an interpretation. There is no language being used of a total apostasy.

JWs and LDS could bring up other verses, but the point would be the same: there is no language stating a total apostasy would occur in the early church or at any point in the church's history. The LDS need to realize there is no such thing as a "Restoration of the Gospel of Jesus Christ." The JWs, too, must come to grips with the fact that the gospel has been preserved. Jesus said, "Heaven and earth will pass away, but My words will by no means pass away" *(Matt. 24:35).* Also, Isaiah 40:8 states, "The grass withers, the flower fades, but the word of our God stands forever."

These groups are calling Jesus and God's Word false if they say the Bible's message has been lost. Christians must reform their doctrine so it follows Scripture, not restore it through human philosophy.

POINT #19: THE APOSTLE PAUL PREDICTED ALL OF CHRISTENDOM WOULD HAVE TO BE RESTORED

During your conversation with the LDS missionaries, they will undoubtedly bring up how Joseph Smith revealed the truth because all of Christendom had apostatized. They will use verses such as 1 Timothy 4:1 to support their view that a "restoration" of the gospel was necessary: "Now the Spirit expressly says that in latter times some will depart from the faith."

COUNTERPOINT #19:

Neither this passage nor the other numerous passages that warn of false teachings support the LDS claim. Why? Because there have been apostates and false teachings since the beginning. Just one example would be Judas Iscariot. He was a follower of Christ, yet apostatized.

You must ask the missionaries to point out how Bible-based Christianity has been corrupted and at what exact period of history did Christendom fall away to false teachings. They will surely not be able to do so.

Point out to them that you believe the same doctrine as the original apostles believed. *They* are the ones adding new doctrine, which is unnecessary and forbidden (*Jude 3; Rev. 22:8*).

You can also use the same argument with the JWs, as they claim Bible-believing Christians have been deceived since Christendom has fallen away. Also, as previously stated, they make out Jesus to be a liar if they say the Bible has been changed (*Matt. 24:35*).

POINT #20: THE BIBLE PROPHESIES OF A "RESTORED CHURCH"

And that He may send Jesus Christ, who was preached to you before, whom heaven must receive until the times of restoration of all things, which God has spoken by the mouth of all His holy prophets since the world began (*Acts 3:20-21*).

The LDS believe they are the restored church and prophets since the time of Joseph Smith, so they misinterpret this passage.

COUNTERPOINT #20:

This talks about a future event when Jesus returns before the Millennial Kingdom. It could also be referring to the restoration of Israel. However, no matter the interpretation, it would be farfetched to consider it a reference to the Latter-day Saints.

To claim the church would need to be restored is a contradiction of what Jesus Christ proclaimed during His earthly ministry in Matthew 16:18: "And I also say to you that you are Peter, and on this rock I will build My church, and the gates of Hades shall not prevail against it." Once again, LDS make out Jesus to be a liar if they say all of Christendom has fallen away.

POINT #21: HAVING A CERTAIN KNOWLEDGE
OF GOD IS A REQUIREMENT FOR SALVATION

This means everlasting life, their coming to know you, the only true God, and the one whom you sent, Jesus Christ *(John 17:3, NWT)*.

According to JW theology, one must have a specific knowledge of God to be saved.

COUNTERPOINT #21:

First off, this does not contradict the fact that salvation is attained by repentance and faith. In John 17:3, Jesus is alluding to OT passages, such as Jeremiah 31:34, which state man will know God personally. We can only know the Father through the Son. This is why Jesus includes *Himself* when He mentions knowing the true God, as the only way to see God is through the Son *(John 1:18, 14:7; Matthew 11:27)*.[289]

In his first epistle, the Apostle John further mentions knowledge of God when he says, "I write to you, little children, because you have known the Father" *(1 John 2:13)*. And how may we know the Father to receive eternal life? John tells us, "These things I have written to you who believe in the name of the Son of God, that you may know that you have eternal life, and that you may *continue to* believe in the name of the Son of God" *(1 John 5:13)*.

Just as John 3:16 and many other verses state, belief in the Son of God—not special knowledge—is necessary for eternal life. We may know the Father through belief in Jesus Christ, as He is the Mediator between God and Man *(John 14:6; 1 Tim. 2:5)*.

We've found it helpful to show JWs the following verse regarding John 17 (using the New World Translation) that shows Jesus is not a spirit creature. The first verse of the chapter reads: "Jesus spoke of these things, and raising his eyes to heaven, he said: 'Father, the hour has come. Glorify your son so that your son may glorify you.'" And verse 5 states, "So now, Father, glorify me at your side with the glory that I had alongside you before the world was."

---

289   D. A. Carson, *The Gospel According to John, The Pillar New Testament Commentary* (Grand Rapids, MI: InterVarsity Press, 1991), 555–556.

Hold on a second, why is a spirit creature asking to be glorified? The Bible says God gives His glory to no one else. For example, look at Isaiah 42:8 in the New World Translation: "I am Jehovah. That is my name; I give my glory to no one else, Nor my praise to graven images."

If Jesus is asking to be glorified by Jehovah, but Jehovah does not give glory to any other, then either Jesus is Jehovah or He is blaspheming. Make sure to bring this up when the JW has you read from John 17, as it is irrefutable.

To sum this up, ask the JW why Jesus includes Himself when speaking of the true God. Remember, if He is not the true God, then He is a false god. Also, from a human standpoint, Jesus would, of course, refer to Yahweh as the true God because He was Jewish.

POINT #22: BAPTISM IS NECESSARY TO BE SAVED

The LDS and JWs believe baptism is necessary to receive salvation.

COUNTERPOINT #22:

Cultists may use three main verses to support this position. First, consider John 3:5: "Jesus answered, 'Most assuredly, I say to you, unless one is born of water and the Spirit, he cannot enter the kingdom of God.'" Here, the cultist has misconstrued what being born of "water" means. Jesus is not saying, "Unless you are baptized, you cannot enter into the kingdom." He is using the word in a figurative sense.

When the term "water" is used figuratively in the Old Testament, it habitually refers to renewal or cleansing, especially when it is found in conjunction with "spirit." This is explicitly taught in OT passages such as Ezekiel 36:25-27:

> Then I will sprinkle clean water on you, and you shall be clean; I will cleanse you from all your filthiness and from all your idols. I will give you a new heart and put a new spirit within you; I will take the heart of stone out of your flesh and give you a heart of flesh.

This passage shows how water and spirit come together to cleanse from sin and transform the heart.[290] Jesus is referring to the spiritual washing that takes place and is accomplished by the Holy Spirit once one believes in the Lord Jesus Christ *(John 3:16,36)*.

Here's the next verse cultists may try to use: "He who believes and is baptized will be saved; but he who does not believe will be condemned" *(Mark 16:16)*.

First, it is virtually certain that 16:9–20 is a later addition and not in the original ending of the Gospel of Mark because the manuscript evidence for the longer ending is spurious.[291] However, let's look at the verse anyway. It states that those who *do not believe* are condemned, not those who *are not baptized*. It follows logically, then, if someone were baptized but did not believe, then he would be condemned. We see this in the story of the thief on the cross *(Luke 23:32-43)*. Baptism was viewed as a response to belief as many early Christians were baptized immediately after they had believed *(Acts 2:41, 10:44-48)*.

Finally, the most difficult verse to interpret is Acts 2:38: "Then Peter said to them, 'Repent, and let every one of you be baptized in the name of Jesus Christ for the remission of sins; and you shall receive the gift of the Holy Spirit.'"

At first glance, it seems Peter is saying one must be baptized to be forgiven. However, we must look at the context and the Greek to see if that is what he is advocating. The Greek word translated into "for" is *eis*. Just like our English word "for," eis can have several meanings depending on the context. For example, if you saw a poster that read, "Jesse James wanted for robbery," "for" could mean Jesse is wanted so he can commit a robbery, or he is wanted because he has committed a robbery. Of course, the latter sense is the correct one.

So too in this passage, the word "for" signifies an action in the past. Otherwise, it would violate the entire tenor of the NT teaching on salvation by grace and not by works.[292] It was because of their repentance and faith that they were to be baptized.

---

290   D. A. Carson, *The Gospel According to John*, 195.

291   James R. Edwards, *The Gospel According to Mark, The Pillar New Testament Commentary* (Grand Rapids, MI: Eerdmans; Apollos, 2002), 497.

292   James Strong, *Enhanced Strong's Lexicon* (Woodside Bible Fellowship, 1995).

POINT #23: BAPTISM ON BEHALF OF THE DEAD IS BIBLICAL

Otherwise, what will they do who are baptized for the dead, if the dead do not rise at all? Why then are they baptized for the dead? *(1 Cor. 15:29)*

Because LDS members believe baptism is necessary for salvation, they baptize living members of their church for relatives who died and never became LDS or for those who were baptized without proper authority.[293]

They believe non-LDS spirits go to a spirit prison where they can still be evangelized and taught by spirits from paradise. If the spirit then believes, it is eligible to go to paradise only if a relative of theirs on earth is baptized by the LDS church on their behalf.[294]

COUNTERPOINT #23:

Let's point out what 1 Corinthians 15:29 does *not* state. Nowhere does it say, "Baptize living believers so the deceased can have a second chance to be born again."

The context of 1 Corinthians 15 is the Resurrection of Christ and believers. Two possibilities exist. One is Paul trying to explain how living believers are being baptized because of the faithfulness of believers who had influenced them but have since died. He is essentially asking, "If there is no resurrection, then why are people coming to Christ and being baptized?"[295]

The other possibility is Paul is stating that those teaching baptism of the dead (likely a pagan teaching) were the same as those who denied the Resurrection of Jesus *(1 Cor. 15:20-29)*. Note that he does not say "we" baptize for the dead.

Furthermore, the Bible makes it crystal clear there are no second chances. Take, for example, the story of the rich man and Lazarus in Luke 16:19-31. Upon dying, the rich man was immediately taken to Hades, while Lazarus was

---

293   The Church of Jesus Christ of Latter-Day Saints, "Baptisms for the Dead," accessed August 19, 2016, https://www.lds.org/topics/baptisms-for-the-dead?lang=eng.

294   The Church of Jesus Christ of Latter-Day Saints, "Chapter 41: The Postmortal Spirit World," accessed August 19, 2016, https://www.lds.org/manual/gospel-principles/chapter-41-the-postmortal-spirit-world?lang=eng.

295   *MacArthur Study Bible*, 1,756.

taken to Abraham's bosom, aka heaven. Although the rich man asked for help, Abraham told him of the great gulf that cannot be bridged:

> Son, remember that in your lifetime you received your good things, and likewise Lazarus evil things; but now he is comforted and you are tormented. And besides all this, between us and you there is a great gulf fixed, so that those who want to pass from here to you cannot, nor can those from there pass to us.

There are no second chances; only if you are in Christ during this life will you be saved. Hebrews 9:27 also supports this notion: "And as it is appointed for men to die once, but after this the judgment."

POINT #24: THE MORMON CHURCH HAS THE PRIESTHOOD

The LDS declare they divinely represent the New Testament priesthood, which gives *only them* the power to baptize, lay on hands for receiving the Holy Ghost, preach the gospel, and administer the ordinances.

They have two classes of priesthood: Aaronic and Melchizedek. The Aaronic is for those conferred at twelve years old and is the higher priesthood. The Melchizedek priesthood is for those conferred at age eighteen. Both priestly concepts have their origins in the Old Testament.

COUNTERPOINT #24:

The Aaronic priesthood applied only to Jewish males from the tribe of Levi who were descendants of Aaron (*Exod. 28:1; Num. 3:5-13*). This disqualifies the clear majority of Mormons. The Melchizedek priesthood refers to one individual named Melchizedek who was a king and priest in the Old Testament (*Gen. 14:18-20; Ps. 110:1*). The priesthood of Melchizedek then applied to Jesus Christ in the New Testament (*Heb. 5:5-6*).

Nowhere in the Old or New Testament is a priestly ordination given to a line of people. The New Testament teaches all Christian believers have priesthood authority (*1 Pet. 2:5,9; Rev 1:6;5:10;20:6*). Therefore, all believers have the right to baptize and interpret/preach God's Word.

Interestingly, the writer of Hebrews tells us in chapter 7 that Jesus was the High Priest who was sacrificed. Also, Jesus *alone* intercedes to God for the believer. We are told in 7:24 that the priesthood of Jesus is unchangeable and permanent and, therefore, cannot be transferred to others. Hebrews 8:13 then caps it all off by telling us the priesthood, as exemplified in the Old Testament, is "obsolete."

POINT #25: THE BIBLE AND CHRISTIANITY
HAVE BEEN CHANGED THROUGHOUT THE AGES

Almost every time we talk to LDS missionaries, they will end their message by talking about the corruption in the Bible or how Christianity has been apostate for centuries. It seems these young missionaries have been told this fallacy by their leaders and have not researched it for themselves.

COUNTERPOINT #25:

The truth is, the Bible we have today is almost identical to what was originally written. A common misconception about the Bible is how it is translated. Translators do not take the Wycliffe Bible from the Middle Ages and then translate it into modern English. Nor do they take a Spanish version of the Bible, translate it into French, then Chinese, and then English. Instead, they take the Hebrew or Greek manuscripts and translate them directly into whatever language is needed. We have had to explain this to JWs and LDS.

Although the New Testament contains hundreds of thousands of variants (places where the texts are not all the same), the majority are insignificant spelling or copyist errors. Very few are of any importance and *none* affect doctrine. In fact, the New Testament we have today is 99.5 percent the same as the original.[296]

Also, as stated previously, the earliest Christians believed Jesus was God, salvation is a gift, and there is only one, true God. Politely share this important information with the cult members you engage with. Unfortunately, their

---

296   Gregory Kokul. Equip.org., *Facts for Skeptics of the New Testament*, accessed July 26, 2016, http://www.equip.org/article/facts-for-skeptics-of-the-new-testament/.

organizations have misled them into thinking Bible-believing Christians are the heretics, when just the opposite is true.

You can also use the verses we have already talked about to prove the Bible, gospel, and the church would never fall away *(Isa. 40:8; Matt. 24:35; Matt. 16:18).*

POINT #26: JESUS CAN'T BE GOD BECAUSE HE SAID, "MY GOD, MY GOD, WHY HAVE YOU FORSAKEN ME?"

Cultists may point to Matthew 27:46 as a refutation of Jesus's divinity.

COUNTERPOINT #26:

The verse in question states, "And about the ninth hour Jesus cried out with a loud voice, saying, 'Eli, Eli, lama sabachthani?' that is, 'My God, My God, why have You forsaken Me?'"

On the cross, Jesus is quoting Psalm 22, which is a Messianic prophecy. Psalm 22 describes the crucifixion and vindication of the Messiah. The verse He cried out was Psalm 22:1a, a famous hymn of the Jewish people. Jesus was trying to show everyone how the Psalm was being fulfilled before their very eyes. Jesus was being crucified as the Psalm prophesied (verse 16) and would also be vindicated as the Psalm prophesied (verse 21).[297]

Also, keep in mind, Jesus is talking to another person of the Trinity, not Himself. It was perfectly legitimate for Him to refer to God as "My God" since He was a monotheistic Jew.

POINT #27: 1 THESSALONIANS 4:16 TEACHES JESUS IS MICHAEL THE ARCHANGEL

In their desperate attempt to prove Jesus is an angel, the JWs quote 1 Thessalonians 4:16, which states, "For the Lord Himself will descend from heaven with a shout, with the voice of an archangel, and with the trumpet of God. And the dead in Christ will rise first."

---

297   DrOakley1689, "Why Did Jesus Say 'My God, My God, Why Have You Forsaken Me' from the Cross?" online video clip, YouTube, January 16, 2016, 2017.

COUNTERPOINT #27

Hopefully you have noticed a common theme with these cultist "proof texts." You can make a verse say anything you want if you simply add doctrine to it. This verse tells us Jesus will return from heaven and be accompanied by a shout, which is the voice of an archangel. This verse does not say Jesus is the archangel or even that the shout or voice is His.

POINT #28: GOD IS ONLY ONE IN PURPOSE, NOT ESSENCE

LDS will state they believe God is one only in the sense of His purpose, not His essence. Also, JWs believe Jesus and His Father are only one in purpose and not Being as well.

COUNTERPOINT #28

First, explain to Mormons how the different persons of the Trinity perform different roles. Also, ask them if they can show you a verse that states the Godhead is only one in purpose.

Next, use John 10:30-33 to show how Jesus's declaration of being one with His Father meant He was divine.

> "I and *My* Father are one." Then the Jews took up stones again to stone Him. Jesus answered them, "Many good works I have shown you from My Father. For which of those works do you stone Me?" The Jews answered Him, saying, "For a good work we do not stone You, but for blasphemy, and because You, being a Man, make Yourself God."

Obviously, this was no shallow statement of being united with His Father in purpose. Rather, Jesus was claiming to be God. The violent reaction of the Jews shows us how we are to understand this passage.

POINT #29: BECAUSE JESUS IS CALLED A MAN IN 1 TIMOTHY 2:5, HE'S NOT GOD

> For there is one God and one Mediator between God and men, the Man Christ Jesus *(1 Tim. 2:5)*.

COUNTERPOINT #29

Jesus is referred to as the Mediator between God and men because of His human and divine nature. One commentator has explained why Jesus is called a man quite nicely: "The human nature of our Lord is here insisted upon, to show how fit he is to mediate for man, as his Godhead fits him to mediate with God."[298]

Jesus, being the eternal, sinless Son of God, is the only one who can mediate between humankind and God the Father *(John. 14:6)*. Furthermore, Jesus is the God-Man, as He was God in human flesh *(John. 1:1,14)*. Therefore, there is no contradiction because He mediates to God the Father on behalf of mankind.

POINT #30: THE BOOK OF MORMON IS TRUE AND JOSEPH SMITH IS A PROPHET BECAUSE I FEEL THIS IS SO, AND I HAVE SEEN A CHANGE IN MY LIFE

Very commonly, Mormons will lean on their emotions and experiences to convince you to join the LDS church.

COUNTERPOINT #30

We must always speak the truth in love. Some cult members are very passionate about what they believe, so we must be careful not to attack them personally, but instead address their teachings and doctrines.

That said, we cannot allow them to believe the lie that Joseph Smith is a prophet or that Mormonism is true because they feel it is. Point out how millions of people believe in their religion because of a supposed change that occurred once they joined it. Tell them a Muslim or Buddhist could say the same thing about their religion.

The question is, "What is the truth, and where do the facts point?" Explain how the predictive prophecy, eyewitness accounts, and promises by God Himself that His word will not change demonstrate how the Bible is true. Tell them a man receiving a private revelation that contradicts the teaching of Jesus, the apostles, and the earliest testimony of the church is not to be trusted.

---

298   H. D. M. Spence-Jones, ed., *1 Timothy, The Pulpit Commentary* (New York: Funk & Wagnalls Company, 1909), 34.

POINT #31: JESUS CAN'T BE GOD
BECAUSE HE IS SUBJECT TO THE FATHER

Now when all things are made subject to Him, then the Son Himself will also be subject to Him who put all things under Him, that God may be all in all *(1 Cor. 15:28).*

COUNTERPOINT #31

There is no problem with the Son being subject to the Father. Jesus was given all the authority on heaven and earth by the Father *(Matt. 28:18)* and will give it back to His Father once there is a new heaven and new earth.

Furthermore, Jesus will still be King because His reign is eternal. Revelation 11:15 clearly teaches this: "Then the seventh angel sounded: And there were loud voices in heaven, saying, 'The kingdoms of this world have become *the kingdoms* of our Lord and of His Christ, and He shall reign forever and ever!'" We see here that God and Jesus will reign forever, thus denoting He is equal to God as King of all.

POINT #32 JOSEPH SMITH SAW GOD THE FATHER

Mormon missionaries will tell you Jesus Christ and God the Father appeared to Joseph Smith in the forest.

COUNTERPOINT #32

No one can see God the Father. John 1:18 in the New American Standard Bible makes this quite clear: "No one has seen God at any time; the only begotten God who is in the bosom of the Father, He has explained *Him*." Furthermore, John 4:24 says, "God *is* Spirit, and those who worship Him must worship in spirit and truth."

Obviously, because God is Spirit and not made of physical parts, He cannot be seen. Only through the Incarnation of Jesus Christ can we see God *(John 1:18).* Also, Jesus said in John 6:46 that only He has seen the Father. Point out to the LDS missionaries how the Bible clearly states no one can see God because He is immaterial. If they ask how people saw God in the OT *(Gen. 18; Judg. 13; Isa. 6)*, explain it was God the Son, because He is God in the flesh.

In conclusion, Joseph Smith's supposed First Vision is a fraud because he claimed to see God the Father, which is impossible according to the Bible (Exodus 33:20).

POINT #33 DANIEL10:13 TEACHES JESUS IS MICHAEL THE ARCHANGEL

But the prince of the kingdom of Persia withstood me twenty-one days; and behold, Michael, one of the chief princes, came to help me, for I had been left alone there with the kings of Persia *(Dan.10:13)*.

COUNTERPOINT #33

Notice how the name of Jesus is nowhere mentioned in Daniel 10:13. The JWs have literally read words into the verse that don't exist. The JW argument would go something like this: Michael is one of the chief princes, and Jesus is called the Prince of Peace. Therefore, Jesus is Michael the Archangel. This is called a non-sequitur, as the conclusion does not follow from the first two premises.

Jesus is called Prince of Peace because of His role as the Messiah, and the name has nothing to do with being a chief angel. Furthermore, Jesus is called the "King of Kings and Lord of Lords" in Revelation 19:16. Therefore, Jesus is not just a Prince, but King.

CHAPTER 7
WITNESSING TECHNIQUES FOR JEHOVAH'S WITNESSES AND MORMONS

Most Christians can be turned into a doctrinal pretzel within a few minutes by a Jehovah's Witness and have trouble refuting twisted Mormon theology. This is because the average Christian has only a superficial understanding of the Scriptures and theology. Sadly, most Christians do not make it a priority to study God's Word or other religions' beliefs.

In Timothy 2:15, we are instructed to "Be diligent to present yourself approved to God, a worker who does not need to be ashamed, rightly dividing the word of truth." If you have a solid foundation in God's Word, we encourage you to continue studying it, and we hope this section will assist you in refuting accusations against Christian doctrine. If you do not have a solid foundation, we invite you to start reading it more often, and we hope this section will give you a better understanding of how to engage with the cults.

This chapter deals with polemics and the ability to argue against the truth claims of JW and LDS theology. The goal is to turn their attention to whether their belief is true. After exposing their false teaching, we then transition to truth claims of Christianity to show why they have been misled in their beliefs. This then sets the stage for them to receive the real Jesus and biblical salvation.

If you understand the fundamentals of biblical theology, you will have no problem refuting any false doctrines and will be able to show cultists the truth. The cultist, then, can become a doctrinal pretzel within seconds if you have sound theology and apologetics. Of course, the goal is not to win a theological debate but to lead him to the real Jesus so he may be born again through the power of the Holy Spirit. If you care enough about people, you will study God's Word and use the different witnessing approaches provided in this chapter.

Here are some important recommendations for any Christian witnessing to cultists: First, remember you are questioning the validity of their religious organization and doctrine; you are not attacking them personally. After all, you are an ambassador of Jesus Christ, and everyone is valuable in God's view.

That said, we adhere to the biblical principle of "grace to the humble and law to the proud" (*James 4:6*). At times, you may use shocking comments to get a cultist's attention. This does not mean you can use coarse language. Rather, it would be something that grabs his attention, like, "Your organization has misled you," or "Your organization has been proven to give false prophecies throughout history, so why would you trust them?"

Jesus used theological truths to shock the cultists of his day, the Pharisees and Sadducees. For example, we read the following in Matthew 22:41-46:

While the Pharisees were gathered together, Jesus asked them, saying, "What do you think about the Christ? Whose Son is He?" They said to Him, "*The Son* of David." He said to them, "How then does David in the Spirit call Him 'Lord,' saying: The LORD said to my Lord, 'Sit at My right hand, Till I make Your enemies Your footstool'? If David then calls Him 'Lord,' how is He his Son?" And no one was able to answer Him a word, nor from that day on did anyone dare question Him anymore.

Here, we see Jesus shocking the Pharisees, the presumed theologians of His time. Jesus quotes from Psalm 110:1 and points out that their own Scripture shows that King David had another "Lord" other than the LORD.

This Lord is the Messiah. The implication is that this other Lord is Yahweh because David only worshipped Yahweh. Thus, Jesus, being the Messiah, is also Yahweh. It is no wonder the Pharisees dared not question Jesus anymore. Obviously, He had a much deeper theological understanding of who the Messiah was. In a matter of seconds, Jesus used the Scriptures to prove the Messiah was Yahweh. This certainly made the Pharisees question their theology of the Messiah's identity.

Finally, if you are meeting with a cultist at a set place and time, ask him if he will answer your questions before you start. If you don't ensure you can ask questions, you'll end up listening to a thirty-minute lecture, with only five minutes to talk until he must leave. If you find a JW at a booth or catch a Mormon on his/her bicycle, just be polite, and, without revealing too much information about your beliefs, ask him questions.

Also, most importantly, pray to God and ask Him to speak through you and protect you. Pray for clarity of thought and self-control as well. Remember, we are not trying to crush a cultist in a debate, but rather control the conversation in such a way he can know the truth.

You have read over a lot of background information in this book, including the history and beliefs of JWs and LDS. As well, you have seen the strong evidence for the Trinity and deity of Jesus Christ. Now it is time to see how it works in real life.

The following are questions you should consider asking a JW or LDS. These questions will help you demonstrate who Jesus is, the nature of God, what is involved in salvation, and the problems with their respective organization's teachings.

WHO RAISED JESUS FROM THE DEAD?

This is the go-to question when witnessing to those who deny the divinity of Jesus. It is completely immune to cultic attack. We recommend you frame the question as follows: Do you believe God raised Jesus from the dead? They will say yes. Then read John 2:19-22: "Jesus answered and said to them, 'Destroy this temple, and in three days I will raise it up.' Then the Jews said, 'It has taken forty-six years to build this temple, and will You raise it up in three days?' But He was speaking of the temple of His body. After he was raised from the dead, his disciples recalled what he had said. Then they believed the Scripture and the words that Jesus had spoken."

Point out to them that Jesus must be God because He raised Himself from the dead. When they disagree, explain that because God, or Jehovah, raised Jesus from the dead and Jesus raised Himself from the dead, Jesus must be God or Jehovah. Make sure the unbeliever you are engaging with understands you are not saying Jesus is the Father.

Also, as stated previously, the cultist almost always believes Jesus is talking about the actual temple. However, the Apostle John inserted the sentence, "But He was talking about the temple of His body," to make sure the reader understood Jesus raised Himself from the dead.

Another answer you may hear is that God gave Jesus power. However, the verses say nothing about Jesus being given power, and notice how Jesus does not give glory to any other but Himself. He said "I will raise it up," not "God gave me power." It would be blasphemous for Jesus not to give credit to Almighty God if He wasn't the Almighty Himself.

The cultist may also say this is impossible because a dead person cannot raise themselves from the dead. However, point out that Jesus's spirit was still alive because it went to Heaven upon His death *(Luke 23:39-43)*. Thus, there is no problem with Jesus raising Himself if His spirit was still alive.

This question is also an excellent way to introduce the Trinity. Show the cultist where it states in Scripture that God raised Jesus from the dead *(Rom. 10:9; 1 Pet. 1:21)*, where the Father raised Jesus from the dead *(Gal. 1:1; Eph. 1:17-20)*, and where the Holy Spirit raised Jesus from the dead *(Rom. 8:11)*. Then ask, "Considering that God raised Jesus from the dead, would it not make sense to say God is Triune because three persons raised Him from the dead?"

Also, in John 10:18, Jesus proclaimed He had the power to lay his life down and raise it up again. This matches precisely to Jesus' claim in John 2:19-22.

You will find the cultist will not be able to give a reasonable answer to the question of who raised Jesus from the dead. Proceed to tell him it is important for him to know the real God of the Bible so he can receive a true salvation.

The question of who raised Jesus is a great question to ask a JW to prove Jesus is God. When you use it with the LDS, make sure you emphasize one God raised Jesus from the dead because they believe the Trinity is three gods.

WHAT CAN WE LEARN FROM DOUBTING THOMAS?

Who better to learn from about the nature of Jesus than from a skeptical eyewitness? Ask the cultist if they are familiar with the story of doubting Thomas. They will say yes. Then, ask them to read with you about it:

> And after eight days His disciples were again inside, and Thomas with them. Jesus came, the doors being shut, and stood in the midst, and said, "Peace to you!" Then He said to Thomas, "Reach your finger here, and look at My hands; and reach your hand here, and put it into My side. Do not be unbelieving, but believing." And Thomas answered and said to Him, "My Lord and my God!" Jesus said to him, "Thomas, because you have seen Me, you have believed. Blessed are those who have not seen and yet have believed" (*John 20:26-29*).

This argument too is invulnerable to cultic attack. Always ask what conclusion Thomas came to when he encountered the (physically) resurrected Christ. If he does not respond, read, "And Thomas answered and said to Him, 'My Lord and my God!'"

Then ask if Jesus commended Thomas for calling Him God with a capital "G" or rebuked him. If Jesus wasn't God, He would have sharply rebuked Thomas for blasphemy. However, he commended Thomas for his conclusion.

Cultists often respond to this by saying Thomas was excited or said it out of surprise. But if so, Thomas would be blaspheming, and Jesus surely would have rebuked him.

For the JWs, this is extremely powerful. Thomas, a monotheistic Jew who only believed in Almighty Jehovah God, calls Jesus "God." For the LDS, point out how the Jews believed in only one God, so Jesus must be one person of the Triune Godhead, not one god out of many. Ask the cultists who would know better if Jesus were the true God—the Watch Tower or the LDS organization, or Thomas, a disciple and eyewitness of Jesus. Tell them organizations formed one thousand eight hundred years after the time of Christ should not override what the original apostles said.

In summary, emphasize that Thomas said to Jesus, "My Lord and my God." This was not a mere exclamation or praise to the Father. If Jesus wasn't God, He would have rebuked Thomas because it is a sin to receive this type of worship. However, Jesus commended Thomas.

WHY IS THE MESSIAH GOD AND ETERNAL?

Start a conversation with cult members by asking them if they believe Jesus is the Messiah. Undoubtedly, they will say yes. Then ask them to read Isaiah 9:6:

> For unto us a Child is born,
>
> Unto us a Son is given; and the government will be upon His shoulder. And His name will be called Wonderful, Counselor, Mighty God, Everlasting Father, Prince of Peace.

Explain how it was prophesied seven hundred years before the birth of Jesus that the Messiah would be God and eternal. The Mormons will probably agree with you because they define "God" and "eternal" to suit their theology. However, point out that eternal means without beginning or end. So the Messiah they believe in is not biblical since Jesus has always been God.

The JWs, on the other hand, will immediately respond that the Messiah is only a "Mighty God," not "Almighty God." They reason Jesus must not be Jehovah God because He is only the "Mighty God." At this point, tell them they have committed to polytheism. Also, ask them to read Isaiah 10:20-21 in their New World Translation:

> In that day those remaining of Israel
>
> And the survivors of the house of Jacob

Will no longer support themselves on the one who struck them; But they will support themselves on Jehovah, The Holy One of Israel, with faithfulness. Only a remnant will return, The remnant of Jacob, to the Mighty God.

Then ask, "Because Jehovah is called Mighty God in Isaiah 10:21, does that mean He cannot be Almighty God?" Per JW reasoning, anyone called "Mighty God" cannot be the true Almighty God. So Jehovah cannot be Almighty God.

After you point out their flawed reasoning, show the cultists Isaiah 44:6, which states, "Is there a God besides Me? Indeed *there is* no other Rock; I know not *one*." If Jesus is only a Mighty God, then He is a false God. Ask them why they would revere a false god as their Savior. For the LDS, explain how the notion that Yahweh knows no other God would mean their polytheistic theology is unbiblical.

After you have explained the polytheistic dilemma to the cultists, share with them how Jesus is a different *person* of the Godhead, not a different God. Show them how the Bible is contradictory if you do not accept the fact God is one nature in three persons. Otherwise, you are a polytheist, which the Bible strictly condemns (*Deut. 4:35; Isa. 46:9*).

Here's another common response: eternal means lasting forever once you are born. Simply point out that the dictionary definition of eternal is "having no beginning and no end in time: lasting forever."[299]

This is highly problematic for both groups. For LDS, it means Jesus could never have been exalted to godhood since He has always been the eternal God. For the JWs, it destroys the notion that Jesus was created as Michael the Archangel because He has always existed. Sometimes, JWs may state that Jesus was eternal from the time He came to earth. Again, simply review the definition of eternal.

To further make the case Jesus is eternal, have the JW (or LDS) read verses in the New World Translation (or KJV) that also tell us Jesus is eternal. He is

---

299 *Merriam-Webster* online, accessed May 7, 2016, http://www.merriam-webster.com/dictionary/eternal.

called the First and the Last and the Alpha and Omega, all of which are terms for eternality (*Rev. 2:8, 22:13*).

Then show the JW the parallel between Jesus and Jehovah in Isaiah 44:6. The New World Translation states, "This is what Jehovah has said, the King of Israel and the Repurchaser of him, Jehovah of armies, 'I am the first and I am the last, and besides me there is no God.'"

Then ask them to read Isaiah 48:12: "Listen to me, O Jacob, and Israel, whom I have called. I am the same One. I am the first; I am also the last." For the JW, ask how Jehovah and Jesus can both be the First and the Last. The answer is simple: Jehovah and Jesus are the same Being. For the LDS, explain how Jesus is not an evolved spirit but the eternal God without beginning because the titles "First and Last" and "Alpha and Omega" denote eternality.

For the JW and LDS, you can also use Revelation 1:8 to prove Jesus is the Almighty. "I am Alpha and Omega, the beginning and the ending, saith the Lord, which is, and which was, and which is to come, the Almighty" (KJV). Of course, the NWT has changed this to say, "'I am the Alpha and the Omega,' says Jehovah God, 'the One who is and who was and who is coming, the Almighty.'"

However, using the KJV (which the JWs have on their official website), it is easy to demonstrate the bias of the NWT translation. Verse one of the chapter tells us we are reading the revelation of Jesus Christ. Furthermore, Revelation 1:7 in the NWT says, "Look! He is coming with the clouds, and every eye will see him, and those who pierced him; and all the tribes of the earth will beat themselves in grief because of him."

Obviously, verse eight is then talking about Jesus, because He is the one who was pierced and will return on clouds (*John 19:37; Matt. 24:30*). In fact, the Father never speaks in the book of Revelation, so it is obvious Jesus is speaking in verse 8 and is, therefore, the Almighty God.

IS JESUS A TRUE GOD OR FALSE GOD?

When it comes to discussing the real Jesus with the LDS and JWs, much of the discussion comes down to simple logic. When you talk to the LDS, they will stress emotion and the "spiritual" side of their religion. The JWs, on the other hand, act as if they have evidence but are often deficient in backing the case for their theological assertions. What both groups have in common, however, is that they violate elementary rules of logic.

Ask the person you are speaking with if he believes in truth and logic. He will typically respond yes. Then ask if he agrees with the statement, "Whatever is not true is false." Assuming he agrees, ask what the Bible states in terms of how many true Gods exist. The answer should be one. If he does not answer "one," let him know at least twenty-eight verses in the Old and New Testament attest to this fact. A few you can cite to demonstrate this include the following:

Hear, O Israel: The LORD our God, the LORD is one (*Deut. 6:4*)!

For You are great, and do wondrous things; You alone are God (*Ps. 86:10*).

"You are My witnesses," says the LORD,
"And My servant whom I have chosen,
That you may know and believe Me,
And understand that I am He.
Before Me there was no God formed,
Nor shall there be after Me" (*Isa. 43:10*).

Thus says the LORD, the King of Israel,
And his Redeemer, the LORD of hosts:
"I am the First and I am the Last;
Besides Me there is no God" (*Isa. 44:6*).

And this is eternal life, that they may know You, the only true God, and Jesus Christ whom You have sent (*John 17:3*).*

Since there is one God who will justify the circumcised by faith and the uncircumcised through faith (*Rom. 3:30*).

Now a mediator does not mediate for one only, but God is one (*Gal. 3:20*).

You believe that there is one God. You do well. Even the demons believe—and tremble (*James 2:19*).

(*Note Jesus Christ is linked in this verse with the only true God, and it is required to know Him for eternal life because He is God.*)

It's easiest to cite Isaiah 43:10 and James 2:19 as a concise way to summarize what has been taught throughout the Old and New Testament.

Next, ask, "Because Jesus is clearly called God in the Scriptures, then is Jesus a true God or a false God?" If necessary, refer to John 20:26-29 or Isaiah 9:6. If the cultist answers "a false God," then ask why he would honor a being who is false. Also, ask why Jesus is worshipped throughout the New Testament. If a JW states He was not worshipped but only given obeisance (honor), then ask him to read Revelation 5:13 in the New World Translation:

And I heard every creature in heaven and on earth and underneath the earth and on the sea, and all the things in them, saying: "To the One sitting on the throne and to the Lamb be the blessing and the honor and the glory and the might forever and ever."

Then, ask this: "Do you agree that we read in Revelation 5:13 that Jesus is being worshipped by all of creation and given glory in this verse?" Remember, the Lamb is referring to Jesus. Should he answer Jesus is a true God, then ask why he doesn't worship Jesus since He is the true God.

The LDS might answer He is a true God. If he does, press him to clarify by asking, "So are the Heavenly Father, the Holy Ghost, and all the other Father gods in the heavenly realm frauds?" If he says Jesus is the only true God who came to this earth, remind him Isaiah 44:8 says besides Yahweh, there is no God.

The LDS may say this verse, or others like it, are only talking about this world. However, this would be adding extra words and interpreting the text to suit Mormon doctrine. On the other hand, the JWs most likely will not answer your question because they are trapped no matter how they answer it. They will probably say He is the Son of God repeatedly because they don't know what to say.

But tell them you are asking if He is the true God worthy of our worship, not the Son of God. Ask them to think about this dilemma and remind them that if they do not understand who the real Jesus is, they cannot receive salvation (*John 8:24*). If the JWs do say Jesus is a true God, tell them Jehovah must be a false God—unless Jesus is Jehovah and He and His Father are separate persons.

It is also helpful to show the cultists verses where Jesus is worshipped, such as Matthew 2:11, 14:33, and 28:9. Obviously, the Watch Tower has changed these verses and uses the word "obeisance" instead of "worship." So you can either use Revelation 5:13 or show them the verses in the KJV Bible. With the LDS, there is no problem because they use the KJV Bible and may be fine with whichever version you have.

After going over these verses, proceed to explain how we should not worship Jesus if He was only a sinless man or angel. We have examples in the Bible of men and angels being worshipped (*Acts 10:25-26; Rev. 19:9-10*), but the worshippers were rebuked sternly. Only the eternal God deserves to be worshipped (*Deut. 6:13; Matt. 4:10*).

DOES SALVATION DEPEND ON WORKS IN ADDITION TO FAITH?

Interestingly, you'll get different answers from different people. The truth is, the leadership of both groups has taught that faith plus works is required for salvation. If the cultist answers that both are required, directing you to James 2:17, then have him read the following verses with you:

> For by grace you have been saved through faith, and that not of yourselves; it is the gift of God, not of works, lest anyone should boast (*Eph. 2:8*).

> Knowing that a man is not justified by the works of the law but by faith in Jesus Christ, even we have believed in Christ Jesus, that we might be justified by faith in Christ and not by the works of the law; for by the works of the law no flesh shall be justified (*Gal. 2:16*).

I do not set aside the grace of God; for if righteousness comes through the law, then Christ died in vain (*Gal. 2:21*).

Therefore the law was our tutor to bring us to Christ, that we might be justified by faith (*Gal. 3:24*).

You have become estranged from Christ, you who attempt to be justified by law; you have fallen from grace (*Gal. 5:4*).

Even the righteousness of God, through faith in Jesus Christ, to all and on all who believe (*Rom. 3:22*).

Not by works of righteousness which we have done, but according to His mercy He saved us, through the washing of regeneration and renewing of the Holy Spirit (*Ti. 3:5*).

Also ask, "Is it not crystal clear that salvation is dependent on faith alone?" If he brings up James 2:17 ("Thus also faith by itself, if it does not have works, is dead"), then ask if Scripture contradicts itself. He will likely say no. Explain that James 2:17-26 is talking about a Christian who claims to have faith but does not reflect Christ. The passage starts by stating, "What *does it* profit, my brethren, if someone says he has faith but does not have works? Can faith save him?" James then explains how a Christian knows he has true saving faith if he obeys God and follows His commands.

James is not talking about how to receive salvation, but rather how a Christian should act if he has been saved. This is why faith without works is dead.[300] If cultists are still insistent works are involved in salvation, then ask them what work they could possibly do that would have any impact on atoning or eradicating their sin. Let them know they have been misled by their organization regarding the role of works in salvation;

---

300   Mark Stengler Jr., Pleasetellmethetruth.org, "Does James Teach Salvation by Works?," accessed January 14, 2017, http://pleasetellmethetruth.org/2016/08/13/does-james-teach-salvation-by-works/.

they need to repent and put their faith solely in the real Jesus, not in any human work.

One way to prove beyond a doubt that works and baptism are not necessary to be saved is to show the cultists Luke 23:39-43:

> Then one of the criminals who were hanged blasphemed Him, saying, "If You are the Christ, save Yourself and us." But the other, answering, rebuked him, saying, "Do you not even fear God, seeing you are under the same condemnation? And we indeed justly, for we receive the due reward of our deeds; but this Man has done nothing wrong." Then he said to Jesus, "Lord, remember me when You come into Your kingdom." And Jesus said to him, "Assuredly, I say to you, today you will be with Me in Paradise."

Was the thief baptized before Jesus confirmed his salvation? Did the criminal perform any special work? Did he receive a certain knowledge of God? No! The criminal: (a) recognized his sinful state and displayed godly sorrow (repentance), and (b) believed in Jesus as the Messiah.

Ask the cultist why Jesus affirmed the criminal would be in paradise with Him if baptism and works were necessary for salvation. This is a powerful question to ask, as it exposes how these cults are manmade religions and provide no real relationship with God like biblical Christianity does.

WHO CREATED THE SABBATH AND IS RULER OVER THE SABBATH?

The JW will state Jehovah created and rules over the Sabbath, while the LDS will say God. Ask them to read Matthew 12:8: "For the Son of Man is Lord even of the Sabbath." Then ask, "If Jesus is Lord of the Sabbath, must not He be the one, true God?" Then ask them to read John 5:17-18:

> But Jesus answered them, "My Father has been working until now, and I have been working." Therefore the Jews sought all the more to kill Him, because He not only broke the Sabbath, but also said that God was His Father, making Himself equal with God.

Ask them, "Why did the Jews want to kill Jesus?" In response, point out the Jews understood His claim to be God, as the verse states, "making Himself equal with God." Tell them you can only be equal with God if you *are* God.

Last, emphasize this is even more clear in John 10:30-33: "The Jews answered Him, saying, 'For a good work we do not stone You, but for blasphemy, and because You, being a Man, make Yourself God.'" Then ask, "In light of the fact that God has no equals *(Isa. 46:9)*, why did Jesus not reject the accusation the Jews made if He wasn't God?"

IS JESUS YAHWEH (JEHOVAH)?

Jesus very clearly made the claim that He is Yahweh (Jehovah). We read this in John 8:24 and 56-58:

> Therefore I said to you that you will die in your sins; for if you do not believe that I am *He,* you will die in your sins.
>
> "Your father Abraham rejoiced to see My day, and he saw *it* and was glad." Then the Jews said to Him, "You are not yet fifty years old, and have You seen Abraham?" Jesus said to them, "Most assuredly, I say to you, before Abraham was, I AM."

Note that the JWs' New World Translation has mistranslated verses 24 and 58:

> That is why I said to you: You will die in your sins. For if you do not believe that I am the one, you will die in your sins.
>
> Jesus said to them: "Most truly I say to you, before Abraham came into existence, I have been."

This is another blatant mistranslation to avoid an obvious claim by Jesus to be Yahweh (Jehovah). We know this because the phrase "I Am" was also used by Yahweh in the OT. The *Holman Treasury of Key Bible Words* provides excellent insight:

> When Jesus declared, "Before Abraham was born, I am," He asserted His eternal preexistence and His absolute deity *(John 8:58)*. Abraham,

as with all mortals, came into existence at one point in time. The Son of God, unlike all mortals, does not have a beginning. He is eternal; and He is God.

This is evident in Jesus's use of the words "I AM" for Himself. This statement recalls the Septuagint (the Greek Old Testament) translation of Exodus 3:6, 14, in which God unveiled His identity to Moses as the "I AM." Thus, Jesus was claiming to be the ever-existing, self-existent God.[301] The Greek expression for I AM is ego eimi. There is no reason to translate the Greek phrase "I have been" like the New World Translation states. Interestingly, the Watch Tower publication known as the Kingdom Interlinear Translation of the Greek Scriptures quotes the word-for-word Greek as "Before Abraham to become I am."[302] Yet when they wrote the full English translation of the New World Translation, they completely changed what their Greek Interlinear states to a totally different meaning. This is ridiculous as their own Greek Scriptures translates egō eimi as "I am."

The Watch Tower's deception is also displayed in the nine "I am statements of Jesus" (John 6:35,8:12,8:24,8:58,10:9,11,11:25,14:6,15:1). Throughout the Gospel of John, Jesus uses nine powerful statements that begin with the phrase "I am." For example, in John 6:35, Jesus says "I am the Bread of Life." The Greek words for "I am" in the verse are ego eimi, just like in John 8:24, 58. However, the Watch Tower has published every occurrence of the words egō eimi as "I Am" *except* for John 8:24 and 8:58. This is not only horrendous scholarship but blasphemous dishonesty.

Furthermore, the very next verse in John 8:59 confirms that Jesus was claiming to be Yahweh (Jehovah). The Jews were outraged by what they considered blasphemy. Verse 59 states, "Then they took up stones to throw at Him; but Jesus hid Himself and went out of the temple, going through the midst of them, and so passed by." Their actions showed the significance of Jesus's words. They thought He was blaspheming God's name by claiming to be Yahweh and tried to stone Him, in accordance with Leviticus 24:16.

301   Carpenter and Comfort, *Holman Treasury,* 306.
302   *The Kingdom Interlinear Translation,* 451.

Although it is not as clear, the original Greek in verse 24 does not contain the word "He." One modern translation, the English Standard Version, states, "I told you that you would die in your sins, for unless you believe that I am he you will die in your sins." Just like verse 58, it contains the words ego eimi. Some Bible versions add in the word "He" to make it clear that Jesus is referring to Himself as Yahweh.

Of course, the Watch Tower changed the verse to suit its theology. However, it is worth nothing that their own Greek reads, "If ever for not you should believe that I am, you will die in the sins of you."[303] Ask the JWs why the New World Translation so obviously mistranslates John 8:24, 58. Why does their own Interlinear Translation state the Greek term ego eimi means "I am," yet it is not translated this way in the New World Translation? Ask what it would mean if Jesus is claiming to be the I Am. Why would the Jews want to stone Jesus if He had only claimed to exist before Abraham? Also ask, "Can you have any confidence in the New World Translation with such blatant, biased changes to the text?"

(Note: It is difficult to parallel John 8:24, 58 to Exodus 3:14 in the NWT because the corrupt Watch Tower took out the phrase "I Am" and replaced it with "I Will Become." Therefore, we recommend you have JWs use the KJV Bible, which they have on their website as an optional Bible, or simply point out that Jesus referring to Himself as I Am means He is self-existent and eternal.)

Also, ask the LDS what it means if Jesus is claiming to be the one, true God, Yahweh. Additionally, Jesus could not have been created through a sexual union if He already existed. Jesus's I AM declaration means He is self-existent and without beginning or end.

WHAT KIND OF GOD WOULD DECEIVE HIS CREATION?

The following is an extremely powerful question to ask JWs and LDS: "If God is truly loving like you claim, why would He not reveal the truth to His creation for one thousand eight hundred years until Charles Russell/Joseph Smith showed up?" We have never heard a good answer for this.

---

303   *The Kingdom Interlinear Translation of the Greek Scriptures*, 447.

If you are polite and sincere, the question can open the door for an excellent witnessing encounter to share the truth. During one of my (Mark Jr.) many witnessing encounters, I spoke with a young LDS male. I asked him why God would deceive people for one thousand eight hundred years and only recently reveal the truth through Joseph Smith. To my surprise, the young man said, "Yeah, I've actually been thinking about that." We chatted about the gospel for a while, and I encouraged him to read the book of Hebrews. When he left, he had tears in his eyes.

CHAPTER 8

CONVERSATIONS WITH JEHOVAH'S WITNESSES AND MORMONS

So far in this book, you have read about important topics such as the beliefs of JWs and LDS, biblical theology, apologetics, and polemics. Now we will take you through typical real-life conversations with a JW or LDS member. The strategies used in these conversations are aimed at getting to the heart of one's misunderstanding about the nature of God or the means of salvation.

These conversations are strongly polemic in that they are designed to expose cultists' false beliefs. Of course, the goal is to get them to think about what they believe and why they believe it and let the Holy Spirit convict them of the truth. These are just examples you can use as a guideline. Use your own personality and style when evangelizing.

Conversations #1 through #6 are specific to Jehovah's Witnesses. This is followed by #7 through #10, which are specific to LDS. Last, #11 and #12 apply to both groups.

#1 JW CONVERSATION

Strategy: Demonstrate the Messiah is Almighty God and expose their misinterpretation of Colossians 1:15, which they so often refer to.

Mark: Hello, are you guys a Christian organization?

JW: Yes, we are, absolutely.

Mark: So what do you guys believe in?

JW: Well, we believe there is one God named Jehovah who sent His Son, Jesus Christ, to be a ransom sacrifice for sinners.

Mark: Okay, so you believe Jesus is the Messiah?

JW: Yes!

Mark: That's cool. Do you enjoy studying the prophecies about the Messiah?

JW: Um, sure, they are neat.

Mark: Yeah, I was reading one in Isaiah the other day. Do you have a Bible with you? I'd like to ask you a question about it. You are a Bible teacher, right?

JW: Yes, I have a Bible right here, and all JWs are trained in the Bible. Which chapter and verse?

Mark: Would you read Isaiah chapter 9, verse 6?

JW: [*Reading out of his NWT Bible*] "His name will be called Wonderful Counselor, Mighty God, Eternal Father, Prince of Peace."

Mark: Yeah, so when I was reading that, I thought, *Wow! What an amazing prophecy that the Messiah would be both God and Eternal, which the rest of the Bible says too.*

JW: Yeah, but notice how it says "Mighty" God, not Almighty. Only Jehovah is Almighty God.

Mark: Hmm. So let me get this straight. There is only one, true Almighty God whose name is Jehovah, right?

JW: Yes.

Mark: All right, well, if there is only one, true God, then Jesus must be a false god.

JW: No, no, no, He is the Son of God. I mean, why did He pray to the Father?

Mark: Because Jesus had two natures, a human and divine nature. He was praying from His humanity.

JW: Well, He is still the Son of God. In Colossians, He is called the firstborn, so He was created.

Mark: Would you mind reading that passage, starting from verse 15?

JW: "He is the image of the invisible God, the firstborn of all creation, because by means of him all other things were created."

Mark: So you believe that "firstborn" means Jesus is created?

JW: Absolutely, He is God's firstborn.

Mark: Okay, so before that, He is called the image of the invisible God. How can you be the image of God if you are not God?

JW: Well, we are all made in the image of God.

Mark: The verse says He is the image of the invisible God, not made like Him. Also, are you saying Jesus was birthed by some kind of sexual union between a woman and Jehovah?

JW: Of course not!

Mark: "Firstborn" actually means preeminent one, like the heir or owner of creation. For example, David was called the firstborn in Psalm 89:27, but we know David was the youngest in his family. Also, the word "other" was inserted by the Watch Tower and used to be in brackets in previous New World Translation versions because it's not in the original Greek manuscripts.

JW: Well, I am not here to debate.

Mark: Me either. I just wanted to ask questions. It seems to me the Watch Tower has misled you. I'd invite you to pray to God to reveal to you the truth and read Bible versions that have not been tampered with.

#2 JW CONVERSATION

Strategy: Demonstrate the clear teaching that Jesus is God, which would mean the Watch Tower's teaching of Jesus being a spirit creature and lesser god is false.

Mark: So do you guys believe in the Resurrection?

JW: Yes, we do.

Mark: And would you agree Almighty God raised Jesus from the dead?

JW: Well, yes.

Mark: I was reading an interesting passage about the Resurrection in John 2:18-22. Would you mind reading it? I would like to get your thoughts on it.

[JW Reads passage where Jesus says He would raise Himself from the dead.]

Mark: Thanks. So since Jesus said He would raise Himself from the dead, you would agree Jesus is God then, right?

JW: Well, it says that He would raise the temple, not His body.

Mark: But verse 21 clarifies what Jesus was referring to: "But He was speaking of the temple of His body." Furthermore, verse 22 says, "After he was raised from the dead, his disciples recalled what he had said. Then they believed the Scripture and the words that Jesus had spoken."

JW: I'd have to check on that later.

Mark: No problem. Now another cool Resurrection story is found in John 20:27-29. Would you mind turning there? It's the story about doubting Thomas.

JW: This isn't a debate, right?

Mark: Nope, just a question.

[JW reads verse where it says Jesus is Lord and God.]

Mark: See, this is why I believe Jesus is God. Thomas, a disciple of Jesus for three years, called the physically resurrected Christ "God" with a capital "G."

JW: Well, this was just an exclamation. Emotions were obviously high, and he was excited. Or he was praising Jehovah.

Mark: But notice how it says, "Thomas said to Him, 'My Lord and my God.'" He was speaking directly to Jesus. Besides, it would be blasphemy to use God's name out of surprise. And if Jesus weren't God and sinless, why didn't He rebuke Thomas for his conclusion but rather commend him?

JW: I think we're done here. You just want to debate.

Mark: No, I'm just concerned the Watch Tower has misled you. Please know you are only saved through faith in Jesus Christ because He is God, just like the Scriptures say.

#3 JW CONVERSATION

Strategy: Refute the Watch Tower teaching that Jesus was created and prove He is eternal. If Jesus is eternal, then this demonstrates He is God.

Mark: Do you believe Jesus is God?

JW: No, He is the Son of God.

Mark: What does the term "Son of God" mean to you?

JW: It means Jehovah created Jesus and sent him as a ransom to die on a torture stake.

Mark: That's interesting. I have never seen any verses in the Bible that state Jesus was created. Would you show me some?

JW: Sure, go to Proverbs 8:22-24 in the New World Translation, where it states, "Jehovah produced me as the beginning of his way."

Mark: Have you studied the book of Proverbs?

JW: Absolutely. We study all the books of the Bible.

Mark: I only ask because the first nine chapters of Proverbs all deal with the personification of wisdom. Did the Watch Tower explain what personification is?

JW: No.

Mark: Well, it means giving human qualities to something nonhuman. If you look at the first nine chapters of Proverbs, it is clear that it is talking about wisdom. It tells us right at the beginning in Proverbs 1:2, "To know wisdom." Of course, Proverbs was mainly written by Solomon, who, as you know, was the wisest man to ever live in Old Testament times. You will see the word "wisdom" used throughout the first nine chapters. Even in chapter 8, it is used several times to let us know this is what the chapter is about. See Proverbs 8:1 and 8:12, which specifically use the term wisdom. Also, look at the beginning of chapter nine—the first verse uses the word "wisdom."

JW: I still believe Proverbs 8:22-24 is referring to the creation of Jesus.

Mark: Well, then do you also believe Jesus is a "sister" as described in Proverbs 7:4?

JW: Okay, I see your point. Then read Colossians 1:15, where we see Jesus is the firstborn or the created one.

Mark: Why would you think "firstborn" here refers to Jesus being created? It doesn't say He was the firstborn of Jehovah. Do you think Jehovah had other children?

JW: No, I don't.

Mark: Look at Colossians 1:18 in your version. It states Jesus is "the firstborn from the dead." Do you think here it means anything about Jesus being created?

JW: No, here it means He was raised from the dead.

Mark: Exactly, as you know, we always need to read Scripture in context. The whole first chapter of Colossians is talking about the superiority and preeminence of Jesus Christ. For example, look at verses 16 and 17 as they talk about how Jesus created everything, even all the angels in the heavenly realm.

JW: You are saying Jesus is Jehovah?

Mark: Right, God was in Jesus Christ. Jesus was God, who took on human form, as we read in Philippians 2:5-11. My friend, I recommend you reconsider who Jesus Christ is. He is not a spirit creature as your organization has taught you.

JW: I still don't believe Jesus is God Almighty. He is just a god amongst many.

Mark: It seems the Scriptures we just reviewed demonstrate quite clearly that Jesus is God. Let me ask you this: would you agree God Almighty would have to be eternal?

JW: Yes.

Mark: Okay, let's look at a few verses that show the eternality of Jesus, and remember, for something to be eternal, it means it has "no beginning and no end." Please read Isaiah 9:6. This verses tell us the Messiah would be eternal. Now, go to Isaiah 44:6 in the New World Translation. What does it say?

JW: "This is what Jehovah has said, the King of Israel and the Repurchaser of him, Jehovah of armies, 'I am the first and I am the last, and besides me there is no God.'"

Mark: Okay, now read Revelation 1:17 and 22:13. Who does it say is the first and the last?

JW: Jesus.

Mark: That's right. You see your own Scripture tells you Jesus is eternal, just like Jehovah, because Jesus is Jehovah—He is God Almighty. You see, no spirit creature or created being could save you from your sins. As you read Isaiah 43:11, you can see that only Jehovah can be the Savior of men, and we both know the New Testament refers to Jesus as the Savior. Put your faith in the real Jesus, as there is no other who can save you. Please give this some thought.

#4 JW CONVERSATION

Strategy: To Demonstrate Jesus Is the Creator and Is Jehovah God

Mark: Understanding the nature of God, or who He is exactly, is very important, don't you think?

JW: Yes.

Mark: And the same with Jesus Christ?

JW: Of course.

Mark: If I am understanding correctly, your organization teaches Jesus was a mighty God but not Almighty God.

JW: That's right. We believe Jehovah is the one, true God, the Almighty.

Mark: Where does it say in the Bible Jesus is a mighty God?

JW: Isaiah 9:6.

Mark: Right. It is a prophecy the Messiah to come would be God.

JW: The Messiah would be a mighty God but not God Almighty. There are many gods, the Bible states. For example, Satan is called the god of this world (*2 Cor. 4:4*).

Mark: Let's look at that verse in your Bible. Do you notice how the "g" is not a capitalized "G"? If it's not capitalized, it means it is not referring to the true God. In the verse you showed me in Isaiah 9:6, the word "God" uses a capital "G," referring to the true God.

JW: Jehovah is the Almighty God; Jesus is a Mighty God.

Mark: So, if I understand you correctly, if the term "mighty God" is used, it must refer to a lesser god, not God Almighty?

JW: Correct.

Mark: Would you go to Isaiah 10:21 in your New World Translation Bible and read what it says?

JW: "Only a remnant will return, The remnant of Jacob, to the Mighty God."

Mark: Please read the verses before and after and tell me whom this is referring to.

JW: It is referring to Jehovah.

Mark: Okay, then according to what you told me earlier in regard to a being given the term "mighty God," Jehovah cannot be the Almighty God.

JW: *[Silence]*

Mark: Please realize term "Jehovah" or "Yahweh" does not refer to the Father. It refers to the nature or essence of God. Jesus is Jehovah.

JW: I don't believe that.

Mark: Let me show you something I think you will find interesting. Go to Hebrews 1:10 and read what it says in your New World Translation Bible: "At the beginning, O Lord, you laid the foundations of the earth, and the heavens are the works of your hands." Who is this referring to?

JW: Jesus.

Mark: Okay. Now read Psalms 102:25 in the New World Translation: "Long ago you laid the foundations of the earth, And the heavens are the work of your hands." Who is this referring to?

JW: Jehovah.

Mark: Right, can you see how the writer of Hebrews is quoting from Psalms to show Jesus is Jehovah?

JW: I don't know about that; I think Jehovah used Jesus in the work of creation.

Mark: Well, let's see what God's Word says. Please read to me what Jehovah claims in Isaiah 44:24 in the New World Translation.

JW: "This is what Jehovah says, your Repurchaser, Who formed you since you were in the womb: 'I am Jehovah, who made everything. I stretched out the heavens by myself, And I spread out the earth. Who was with me?'"

Mark: Do you see Jehovah alone was involved in creation? Therefore, either He was lying, or it means Jesus is Jehovah.

JW: *[Silence]*

Mark: I know it's concerning for you to see these things. I just want you to know the real Jesus so you can be saved. The Jesus you have been taught does not exist. He is an invention of the Watch Tower, so He cannot save you from your sins. Would you like to meet with me for Bible studies so we can reason through these things together?

#5 JW CONVERSATION

Strategy: Demonstrate the Watch Tower and Jehovah's Witnesses cannot be God's prophets and representatives because they have a history of false prophecies.

Mark: The JW organization, called the Watch Tower, started in the 1800s, correct?

JW: Yes.

Mark: Could you please give me some insight on the prophecies made by your organization? I would like to hear the view from someone in the organization.

JW: Okay, what are you referring to?

Mark: In the years 1922, 1923, and 1924, it was prophesied Jesus would return in 1925. Of course, this did not happen.

JW: That was a long time ago. Things have changed since then.

Mark: Okay. But 1975 wasn't that long ago, and the Watch Tower prophesied in 1968 and 1974, in writing, that 1975 would be the end of human history and Christ would set up his Millennial Kingdom on earth. Many Jehovah's Witnesses even sold their homes and property in anticipation of this event.

JW: What is your goal in bringing this up?

Mark: Well, the Bible teaches God's prophets always foretell the future correctly 100 percent of the time *(Deut. 18:20-22; Jer. 28:9)*. Can you show me anywhere in the Bible where one of God's true prophets incorrectly predicted the future?

JW: Everyone makes mistakes. The book of Proverbs tell us this about Jehovah's Kingdom. Proverbs 4:18 in the New World Translation reads, "But the path of the righteous is like the bright morning light That grows brighter and brighter until full daylight." So things are becoming clearer for Jehovah's Witnesses.

Mark: Well, the first nine chapters of Proverbs are about the topic of wisdom. As you read in 4:7 in the NWT, it says, "Wisdom is the most important thing, so acquire wisdom." It appears the Watch Tower has a problem with acquiring wisdom as they have declared false prophecies. Therefore, they have disqualified themselves from being God's organization and spokespersons. As we read in your Scripture, God's true prophets cannot make false predictions. Does it concern you that the Watch Tower, which supplies the information you study about the Bible, is a false prophet? Also, the Watch Tower is not on the path of the righteous because they have deceived millions of people with their lies.

JW: *[Silence]*

Mark: God cares about you and wants you to know you have been misled by a false prophet. Please consider these things and leave that organization. Trust in God's Word, not manmade doctrines, and join a church that will come alongside you and teach the truth. Your eternal salvation is at stake.

#6 JW CONVERSATION

Strategy: Demonstrate to JWs that their New World Translation is corrupt and intentionally changes verses that clearly demonstrate the deity of Jesus. Do this using their own Greek translation, which is published by the Watch Tower.

Mark: The Jehovah's Witnesses website has a lot of Bible information on it.

JW: Oh, yes. We have the most modern Bible version and a lot of scholarly work to help one understand the Bible.

Mark: I've found the Kingdom Interlinear Translation of the Greek Scriptures interesting. I assume it's supposed to help people understand what words mean in the original Greek.

JW: Oh, yes. It's very important to know what words meant in the original Greek so that the New Testament is translated properly. There are so many Bible versions out there, and you want to make sure you have a good, literal one, like the New World Translation, which we use.

Mark: Right, well let's take a look at your Greek Interlinear.

JW: Okay.

Mark: I was looking at John 1:1. Here in your Greek Interlinear, it translates the Greek as "In beginning was the Word, and the Word was toward the God, and god was the Word." I was wondering why your corresponding English translation translates it as, "and the Word was a god?"

JW: It has to do with definite articles and things like that. Many Greek translators feel it should be "and the Word was a god."

Mark: Oh, what other versions—other than the New World Translation—have it as "a god"?

JW: I am not sure, but there are some.

Mark: Here on your website, you have other versions, including The Bible in Living English, King James, and the American Standard Version. They all translate John 1:1 as "the Word was God" and the word "God" has a capital "G," referring to the one, true God. Also, all the most commonly used versions, such as the New King James, New American Standard, and English Standard Version—you know, the ones used by seminaries and scholars—do not translate it like the Watch Tower does.

JW: That's because they are all Trinitarians. They have a bias.

Mark: Are you saying all the Greek scholars around the world are intentionally mistranslating this verse to say Jesus is God?

JW: Well, not on purpose. It's because of their theology.

Mark: Let's look in your Greek Interlinear at 2 Corinthians 5:19. Here the Greek translation states, "As that God was in Christ world reconciling to himself." Now, your New World Translation translates it as, "Namely, that God was by means of Christ reconciling a world to himself." It seems the NWT changes the whole meaning of the sentence. Your Greek, as well as the KJV, tells us God was in Christ, which would mean Christ was God.

JW: I will have to take a closer look at it.

Mark: Okay, let's also look at Colossians 2:8. Here in your Interlinear, it translates the Greek as, "Be You looking at not someone You will be the (one) leading as booty through the philosophy and empty seduction according to the tradition of the men, according to the elementary things of the world and not according to Christ; because in him is dwelling down all the fullness of the *divinity bodily*" (emphasis ours). Then in the New World Translation, it has it differently and does not say Jesus was "divinity bodily," which refers to God (divine) being in a body. Instead, it reads like this:

> Look out that no one takes you captive by means of the philosophy and empty deception according to human tradition, according to the elementary things of the world and not according to Christ; because it is in him that all the fullness of the divine quality dwells bodily.

Why would they translate it that way, contradicting the Greek as well as other versions?

JW: I will review it closer at another time.

Mark: Okay, let's take a look at John 8:58. Your Greek Interlinear translates the Greek as, "Said to them Jesus Amen amen I am saying to You Before Abraham to become I am."

Notice how in the next verse, the Jews wanted to kill Jesus for claiming to be the "I am," a term used for Jehovah to describe his eternality in Exodus 3:14 (in non-Watch Tower versions). Now, your New World Translation has something different than your Greek. It states, "Jesus said to them: 'Most truly I say to you, before Abraham came into existence, I have been.'"

Notice how the words " have been" were inserted. It is not in the Greek manuscript, as your Greek Interlinear correctly shows. Why would the New World Translation editors add the words "have been"?

JW: John 8:58 is referring to Jesus's age. He had been around a long time before. He was not claiming to be Jehovah.

Mark: Well, then why did the Jews understand Jesus to be claiming to be Jehovah since they wanted to stone him to death after He used this phrase? They would not be so angry as to stone Him if He was claiming to be ancient yet not Jehovah. Remember, the penalty for blasphemy in the Old Testament was death (*Lev. 24:16*). The Jews obviously understood this as a claim to deity.

JW: I think we have gone through enough verses for now. What's your point about all this?

Mark: There are more verses I could show you, but the point is that it is obvious there has been a deliberate changing of the text by the editors of the New World Translation where Jesus is directly referred to as Jehovah (Yahweh), the Almighty God. I am demonstrating this to you by using your own organization's Greek Interlinear to clearly show Jesus is Jehovah (Yahweh). Doesn't it concern you that your organization intentionally mistranslates verses that show the deity of Jesus and misleads people about who Jesus really is? Are you open to the truth? After all, your eternal salvation is at stake!

#7 LDS CONVERSATION

Strategy: Demonstrate the Mormon Trinity is different than the biblical Trinity and the Bible teaches there would be no new revelation.

Mark: Before we start this meeting, I just want to make sure I can ask questions. Will that be all right?

LDS: Absolutely! We love questions.

Mark: Awesome. Well, why don't you tell me who Jesus is?

LDS: Great question. Jesus is our Savior and the Son of God. We cannot be forgiven of our sins without Him.

Mark: Okay. When you say Son of God, do you mean He is God?

LDS: Yes, we believe Jesus is God. We believe in the Trinity.

Mark: Okay, but Mormons believe the Trinity is three separate gods, correct?

LDS: Yes. LDS doctrine says the Trinity is three gods: Heavenly Father, Jesus, and the Holy Ghost. But they are one in purpose.

Mark: Okay, so that would be a difference from biblical Christianity. The Bible says there is one, true God, like in Isaiah 45:5. But three persons make up this one God: the Father, Son, and Spirit. Also, I'm not sure what you mean when you say they are one in purpose since each member of the Trinity performs different tasks. For example, the Father sent the Son, not the Holy Spirit, to die on the cross.

LDS: Well, if there is only one God, then when Jesus prayed, was He praying to Himself?

Mark: Good question. Actually, Jesus was praying (communicating) to a different person of the Trinity, not a different god. In biblical Christianity, there is one God in three persons.

LDS: What do you mean by "one God in three persons"?

Mark: Let's use this illustration: The Bible clearly states God raised Jesus from the dead *(Acts 2:24; Rom. 10:9)*. However, the Bible also states three separate persons raised Jesus from the dead: God the Father in Galatians 1:1, Jesus Himself in John 2:19-22, and the Holy Spirit in Romans 8:11. Here we have a biblical example of God raising Jesus from the dead, yet each person of the Trinity raising Him.

LDS: Okay. I see where you're coming from. We just have a different take on it.

Mark: Has Joseph Smith had an influence on your viewpoint?

LDS: Yes, he was an important prophet who guided us into truth.

Mark: Could you give me a summary of who he is?

LDS: Well, Joseph Smith is probably the greatest man who ever lived. He helped restore the gospel when he received a revelation from God.

Mark: Okay. Now, this was a new revelation, correct?

LDS: Yes, a new revelation from God so the church could be restored. There has been a lot of corruption since Jesus's time, and our church has been the restored version of Christendom.

Mark: All right, so how do you reconcile Joseph's new revelation with the fact that the Bible says there is no new revelation other than what Jesus revealed. For example, Hebrews 1 says God has spoken to us through His Son and prophets no longer reveal new doctrine or teachings. Similarly, Jude 3 says the faith has been delivered once and for all at the time of Christ. And after all, the Bible is one of the Holy books you use, so I would hope you respect what it says.

LDS: Well, that would be a difference, as we do believe in modern-day prophets.

Mark: And that concerns me because it seems to me Mormon doctrine doesn't match up with what Jesus and His original disciples taught. Think about it this way: would God really allow His creation to be deceived for one thousand eight hundred years until recently when Joseph Smith received a private vision?

LDS: I think we should get going.

Mark: All right. Well, thanks for talking. Maybe give Hebrews 1 and Jude 3 a read later and think about these things.

LDS: Will do.

#8 LDS CONVERSATION

Strategy: Demonstrate we are saved by repentance and faith. As well, show how the LDS doctrine of salvation is different than the Bible, which is infallible.

Mark: So tell me, are we saved solely through repentance and faith? Moroni 10:32 teaches we must deny ourselves of all ungodliness and love God with all of our might; then we receive God's grace.

LDS: We are familiar with that verse.

Mark: So have you denied yourself of ALL ungodliness as commanded in Moroni 10:32?

LDS: That same verse says by His grace we become perfect in Christ.

Mark: Let's look at it. It states, "And if ye shall deny yourselves of all ungodliness, and love God with all your might, mind and strength, *then* is his grace sufficient for you" (emphasis ours). So it seems clear that only after you deny yourself of all ungodliness and love God with all your might, mind, and strength, is God's grace available. Do you disagree with what this verse clearly states?

LDS: No, but we also know we must do some works. Even James said faith without works is dead.

Mark: Okay, in Ephesians 2:8, it says we are saved by grace through faith and not of works. And I can show you many more verses, like in Galatians 2:16 and 21, that say the same thing. Also, in context, James is talking about professing Christians whose lives do not reflect Christ. Once you become born again, you will naturally do good works.

LDS: Well, as you know, the Bible has been changed many times. It has been translated from Greek to hundreds of other languages until it finally was translated into English.

Mark: Actually, that's not how translations work. Translators take the Greek manuscripts and translate them directly into English or Spanish or whichever language is the focus. Also, there are over fifty-five hundred Greek NT manuscripts, which all match up to each other in regard to doctrine. The New Testament we have today is 99 percent accurate compared with the original, with no major doctrinal changes. In addition, the prophet Isaiah said God's Word would endure forever *(Isa. 40:8)*, and Jesus said His words would never pass away *(Matt. 24:35)*.

LDS: I think we should be going to our next appointment.

Mark: Just think about this: You think you must work for salvation because Joseph Smith gave another gospel, a false gospel that contradicts God's Word, the Bible. My friend, it is time to know the God of the Bible.

#9 LDS CONVERSATION

Strategy: Demonstrate Joseph Smith was a sexual deviant and polygamy is contrary to the Word of God.

Mark: Hi, mind if I ask you some questions?

LDS: Sure, go ahead.

Mark: Thanks. I was trying to better understand your founding prophet, Joseph Smith. I am sure you get a lot of questions on the topic of polygamy.

LDS: Yes, we do.

Mark: Okay, I read in a 2014 *New York Times* article that the leadership of the Latter-day Saints came out and admitted Joseph Smith "took as many as 40 wives, some already married and one only 14 years old." Is that true?

LDS: I don't know the exact number, but yes, Joseph Smith did have several wives in accordance with God's command.

Mark: The Bible is one of the four Holy books the LDS use, correct?

LDS: Yes.

Mark: Can you show me any verses in the Old or New Testament where it states men should have multiple wives?

LDS: Sure. Wouldn't you agree that Abraham, David, and Solomon had several wives and were blessed by God?

Mark: It is true they had multiple wives, but this was done in defiance of God's law. For example, starting right in Genesis 2:24, it tells us marriage should be monogamous. As well, in Deuteronomy 17:17, God gives instruction about monogamy for future kings of Israel. He states, "Neither shall he multiply wives for himself, lest his heart turn away." And this is exactly what happened with Solomon, who had numerous wives and concubines. 1 Kings 11:4 tells us what happened to Solomon for his disobedience. The verse states, "For it was so, when Solomon was old, that his wives turned his heart after other gods." You see, God tolerated polygamy in the Old Testament and gave the sinners opportunities to repent. Yet polygamists like Abraham, Solomon, and David eventually suffered the consequences and judgments, both spiritually and emotionally. The New Testament is also very clear on the importance of monogamous marriage. Several verses make this commandment unambiguous: 1 Timothy 3:2, 12; Titus 1:6; Matthew 19:3-9; 1 Corinthians 6:15-17; and 1 Corinthians 7:2.

LDS: Okay, I see your point. But Joseph Smith was commanded to have multiple wives as he started God's restored church.

Mark: Did God tell the LDS women they could have multiple husbands?

LDS: No.

Mark: Why not?

LDS: I don't know. You would have to ask God.

Mark: Hmm . . . don't feel like I am attacking you personally, but is it possible Joseph Smith was a sexual deviant, coming up with this command to satisfy his own sexual desires?

LDS: I don't think so.

Mark: What about the fact he married women who were already married as well as a fourteen-year-old girl?

LDS: I haven't thought much about it; I'm not sure.

Mark: Okay, well put some thought into it. Do you really believe God would have His leading prophet marry women who were already married or a fourteen-year-old girl?

LDS: We don't practice polygamy anymore.

Mark: Well, some Mormon groups do, as you have seen in the news.

LDS: Yes, but we don't consider them part of the LDS.

Mark: Doesn't your own Scripture state in Doctrine and Covenants section 132:34-65 that an LDS male can be involved in polygamy?

LDS: It does, but our president received a revelation in 1890 to stop polygamy.

Mark: Right, LDS President and Apostle Woodruff received this message from God soon after the US government gave him an ultimatum to stop the practice of polygamy or face closure. Do you think the timing was a coincidence?

LDS: I don't know much about it.

Mark: Okay, but since Doctrine and Covenants section 132 is your current Scripture and condones polygamy, aren't these other Mormon groups the ones being obedient to your Scripture?

LDS: *[Silence]*

Mark: Please consider who you are following. Joseph Smith was a false prophet who defied God's commands and opened the door for polygamy to enter your organization. You wouldn't want to follow someone like that, would you?

#10 LDS CONVERSATION

Strategy: Demonstrate the Jesus of Mormonism is different from the Jesus of the Bible. Because Mormons use the Bible, they have a dilemma. They both can't be right.

Mark: Your organization uses four books, including the Bible, correct?

LDS: That is true.

Mark: Okay. Do you believe, like the Bible teaches, that Jesus is the one, true God?

LDS: Absolutely.

Mark: Okay. Do you believe like the Bible teaches that Jesus is the one, true God?

LDS: Umm . . . yes.

Mark: Okay, that's interesting because I've read LDS doctrine teaches there are multiple gods.

LDS: Well, yes. We are all gods in a sense. I mean, we are made in His image.

Mark: But being made in God's image and likeness and actually being in very nature God are two very different things. The Bible clearly states there is only one, true God, like in Isaiah 45:5.

LDS: Yes, well that's where we would differ then.

Mark: Do you believe you are a spirit brother of Jesus and Lucifer (Satan)?

LDS: No.

Mark: So do you disagree with that LDS doctrine, even though your past Apostle Bruce McConkie and former President Spencer Kimball would agree with that teaching?

LDS: Well, yes, I suppose we are sprit brothers.

Mark: Then you believe differently than what the Bible teaches, as it says there is only one God who exists in three persons. It also tells us in John 1:3 and Colossians 1:16 that Jesus is the Creator of everything, including Lucifer.

LDS: I will research that more.

Mark: Do you know the earliest Christians believed and taught Jesus was Almighty God?

LDS: I am not sure what you mean.

Mark: Well, the earliest disciples believed He was the true God. Look at John 20:28, where Thomas saw the resurrected Jesus and called him "God." Of course, Thomas was Jewish, meaning He only believed in one, true God. So the fact He called Jesus "God" and Jesus accepted his statement as valid shows how He is the true God.

LDS: Interesting.

Mark: Yes—and besides, the eyewitness disciples directly taught their students that Jesus was God Almighty. For example, first century church fathers, such as Ignatius and Polycarp, were taught personally by the Apostle John. Also, Clement of Rome and Linus were directly taught by the Apostle Paul. Peter directly taught early church fathers as well. We have their writings that demonstrate this.

LDS: I have never heard that.

Mark: Yes, it's easy to find. I can help you find it if you'd like. I tell you this because the LDS organization has wrongly told you biblical Christianity is corrupt, when just the opposite is true. The Jesus of Mormonism is not the Jesus of history and the Bible. The eternal salvation of you and your family is at stake—please consider this.

#11 LDS/JW CONVERSATION

Strategy: Demonstrate the absurd idea that God would mislead people with false doctrine for one thousand eight hundred years.

Mark: How long has your organization been around?

LDS/JW: Since the 1800s.

Mark: Now your organization has stated all the Christian churches and leaders have become apostate and only your organization is God's true church or representative.

LDS/JW: True.

Mark: When you read the Bible, do you see how God is loving, honest, and desires everyone to know Him?

LDS/JW: Sure.

Mark: Okay, now does it seem logical or reasonable to you God would let people be misled for over one thousand eight hundred years until your organization showed up?

LDS/JW: I never really thought about that. I would have to think about it and ask some of our leaders what the proper answer would be.

Mark: Okay, that would be good. Let me know what you find out. And remember Jesus said just the opposite. In Matthew 16:18, He said the gates of Hades (hell) would not prevail against the church He just started. So the words of Jesus do not match up with your organization's teaching that all of Christendom would become corrupt. God would not allow everyone to believe falsehood for one thousand eight hundred years until Joseph Smith/ Charles Taze Russell came along. Think of it this way: The Bible was written by the eyewitnesses of Jesus. Jesus's miracles, claims, death, and Resurrection were all public, not private, events. Thus, they could have been easily disproved. However, your leaders receive private revelations that do not match up with the Bible. Do you see the problem here?

#12 LDS/JW CONVERSATION

Strategy: Refute the works-righteous system of both organizations.

Mark: Is it true we must do some works apart from repentance and faith in Christ to attain eternal life?

LDS/JW: Yes.

Mark: So Jesus's work on the cross was not all-sufficient to save us?

LDS/JW: Correct. We even read in the Bible that James says faith without works is dead.

Mark: Would you mind turning your Bible to Luke 23:39-43? Let's read the story of the criminal on the cross.

LDS/JW: *[Reads passage]*

Mark: See, the criminal on the cross did not perform any works, nor was he baptized. He simply repented and put his trust in Jesus.

LDS/JW: Well, this was before the New Covenant started, since Jesus hadn't died and risen.

Mark: That's irrelevant. From the Old to New Testament, salvation has been received by grace through faith. For example, Genesis 15:6 tells us Abraham was seen as righteous because he believed in God. John 3:16 says we must believe in God the Son to be saved. Even Jesus, according to Mark 1:15, said in the beginning of His ministry to "repent and believe in the Gospel."

LDS/JW: Then what about James? How could James 2 contradict the rest of the Bible?

Mark: Well, if you look at James 2:14 in context, he is talking about those who claim to be Christians but really aren't. So if you profess to have faith, you will show it by your works. The passage has nothing to do with how to be saved, but what a true Christian should act like.

CHAPTER 9
JESUS IS THE FINAL REVELATION

I t has been firmly established that the Christian faith has been *completely* revealed since the close of the Apostolic Age when the last apostle, John, died. We can read about God's plan for us in the Holy Bible, written by inspired men under the guidance of the Holy Spirit *(2 Tim. 3:16; 2 Pet. 1:21)*. But how else does God reveal Himself?

God reveals Himself through the Living Word, the Son of God, fully God and fully Man, Jesus Christ. Despite this, cultic leaders ignore the truth and instead prophesy and augment what God has spoken through fallen man. In short, these modern-day prophets and apostles are evil and unbiblical.

Biblically speaking, a prophet is someone who represents God to the people. He speaks on behalf of God and commands them to repent, obey God, and foretell the future. Because false prophets were prevalent even in biblical times, God gave us a test to determine whether a prophet was from Him or not. The test is found in Deuteronomy 18:20-22 and Jeremiah 28:9:

But the prophet who presumes to speak a word in My name, which I have not commanded him to speak, or who speaks in the name of other gods, that prophet shall die. And if you say in your heart, "How shall we know the word which the LORD has not spoken?"— when a prophet speaks in the name of the LORD, if the thing does not happen or come to pass, that *is* the thing which the LORD has not spoken; the prophet has spoken it presumptuously; you shall not be afraid of him.

As for the prophet who prophesies of peace, when the word of the prophet comes to pass, the prophet will be known *as* one whom the LORD has truly sent.

A true prophet of God will accurately predict the future 100 percent of the time. There is no margin for error since he/she is speaking on behalf of God, who is omniscient (knowing everything). Now let's examine what the JWs and Mormons believe about their organization's roles as prophets.

JW PROPHECIES

For nearly a century, JWs have held to the following: "Since the Bible was completed, and 'inspiration' is no longer necessary, a true prophet is one who is faithfully proclaiming what is written in the Bible."[304] Also, per the Watch Tower, the way to decide whether one is a true prophet is to see if his message comes to pass exactly as prophesied.[305] The Watch Tower obviously understood prophets of God foretell the future correctly 100 percent of the time (*Deut. 18:2; Jer. 28:9*).

Now that it has been established what constitutes a true and false prophet, let us see if the Watch Tower claims to be one. In a *Watchtower* article that blamed Christendom for approving the United Nations to be the "political expression of the Kingdom of God on earth," the magazine claimed that JWs are prophets:

---

304   The Watchtower, *"True and False Prophets,"* January 1, 1930, 154.
305   JW.org, "False Prophets," accessed March 7, 2017, http://wol.jw.org/en/wol/d/r1/lp-e/1101989228#h=25-33:0.

He[God] had a "prophet" to warn them. This "prophet" was not one man, but was a body of men and women. It was the small group of footstep followers of Jesus Christ, known at that time as International Bible Students. Today, they are known as Jehovah's Christian witnesses.[306]

The Watch Tower claimed in 1942 to be a mediator from God to his people (the Jehovah's Witnesses) and that those who believe it is from man should not waste time looking at it.[307] They even claim to be under "angelic direction and support."[308]

When their organization speaks on behalf of God, JWs have even compared themselves to the prophet Ezekiel. "From atop this celestial chariot like organization Jehovah commissioned this dedicated, baptized, anointed class of servants to speak to all the nations in His name. Thus, like Ezekiel, they became Jehovah's witnesses."[309] Clearly, the Watch Tower and JWs believe they are prophets of God who speak for Him.

Now we will look at some of their prophecies and see if they have come to pass. Two early and embarrassing prophecies by the organization took place in 1889 and 1894 when they said Armageddon would occur in 1914. The Watch Tower declared the following: "The battle of the great day of God Almighty (Rev. 16:14), which will end in A.D. 1914 with the complete overthrow of earth's present rulership, is already commenced."[310] [311] It was then suggested that 1915 would be the date of Armageddon; but when this did not come to pass, the date was moved again to approximately October 1917.[312]

---

306   The Watchtower, "*They Shall Know that a Prophet Was Among Them*," April 1, 1972.

307   The Watchtower, "*Announcing Jehovah's Kingdom,*" January 1, 1942, 5.

308   The Watchtower, "*They Shall Know that a Prophet Was Among Them,*" April 1, 1972, 200.

309   The Watchtower, "*The Nations Shall Know That I Am Jehovah,*" April 1, 1971, 66.

310   Zion's Watch Tower and Herald of Christ's Presence, *Millennial Dawn: The Time Is at Hand* (Allegheny, PA: Tower Publishing Company, 1889), 101.

311   Zion's Watch Tower and Herald of Christ's Presence, "Can *It Be Delayed Until 1914?*" July 15, 1894, 226.

312   The Watchtower, *Studies in the Scriptures Series VII—The Finished Mystery* (Brooklyn: Watch Tower and Bible Tract Society of New York, 1917), 268.

Furthermore, the Watch Tower declared that millions of Christians would be destroyed and Christendom would end. They wrote, "Also, in the year 1918, when God destroys the churches wholesale and the church members by the millions, it shall be that any that escape shall come to the works of Pastor Russell to learn the meaning of the downfall of Christianity."[313] Also, it was prophesied that, "In the year 1918 when Christendom shall go down as a system to oblivion, (Sheol) to be succeeded by revolutionary republics."[314] Obviously, Armageddon has not yet occurred, and Christendom is still alive and well.

Despite these false prophecies, the Watch Tower continued to attempt to predict the future. Obviously, they believed they had the ability to prophesy despite their past failings. In 1924 the Watch Tower confirmed their belief that Jesus would return in 1925 by stating, "The year 1925 is a date definitely and clearly marked in the Scriptures, even more clearly than that of 1914."[315]

The Watch Tower was a little wiser this time and gave themselves an escape by stating how one should not presume what the Lord would do, since several more years of witnessing to the nations may be required before "the body members shall be changed into glorious spirit beings."[316] Then, as one would expect, 1925 came around and the Watch Tower backtracked, stating the following about the prophesied event: "This may be accomplished. It may not be."[317]

Interestingly, the Watch Tower partially admits to these earlier false prophecies in their publication *Vindication 1* in 1931:

There was a measure of disappointment on the part of Jehovah's faithful ones on earth concerning the years 1914, 1918, and 1925, which disappointment lasted for a time. Later the faithful learned that these dates were definitely fixed in the Scriptures; and they also learned to quit fixing dates for the future and predicting what could come to pass on a

313   International Bible Students Association, *Studies in the Scriptures, The Finished Mystery* (Brooklyn: 1918: Peoples Pulpit Association), 485.
314   Ibid., 513.
315   The Watchtower, *"Our Present Duties"*, July 15, 1924, 211.
316   Ibid.
317   The Watchtower, *"Work for the Anointed,"* January 1, 1923, 3.

192 | **CULT SHOCK**

certain date, but to rely (and they do rely) upon the Word of God as to the events that must come to pass.[318]

Unfortunately, they did not learn their lesson. In 1968, the Watch Tower prophesied about the return of Jesus: "Just think, brothers, *there are only about ninety months left before 6000 years of man's existence on earth is completed* . . . the majority of people living today will probably be alive when Armageddon breaks out" (emphasis ours).[319]

Also, more recently, the Watch Tower prophesied the end of human history would occur in 1975 and Christ would set up his Millennial Kingdom on earth. In their 1967 publication, they wrote, "Interestingly, the autumn of the year 1975 marks the end of 6,000 years of human experience."[320]

Consequently, some JWs sold their homes and property before Armageddon in 1975. The Watch Tower approved their followers' faithfulness in a May 1974 publication:

Reports are heard of brothers selling their homes and property and planning to finish out the rest of their days in this old system in the pioneer service. Certainly this is a fine way to spend the short time remaining before the wicked world's end.[321]

When Armageddon did not occur, the Watch Tower did an incredible thing: it blamed the JW members for their blunder! In its July 15, 1976, issue, the Watch Tower stated:

It may be that some who have been serving God have planned their lives according to a mistaken view of just what was to happen on a certain date or in a certain year. They may have, for this reason, put off or neglected things that they otherwise would have cared for. But

---

318   The Watchtower, *Vindication 1* (Brooklyn, NY: Watch Tower and Bible Tract Society of New York, 1931), 339.

319   The Watchtower, *"Kingdom Ministry,"* March, 1968, 4.

320   The Watchtower, *"Where Are We According to God's Timetable,"* May 1, 1967, 262.

321   The Watchtower, *"How Are You Using Your Life,"* Kingdom Ministry, May 1974, 3.

they have missed the point of the Bible's warnings concerning the end of this system of things, thinking that Bible chronology reveals the specific date (emphasis ours).[322]

In the same article, the Watch Tower criticized members even more and advised them to not base their viewpoint of the end times on false premises. Ironically, JWs were just following what they had been told by the Watch Tower!

If anyone has been disappointed through not following this line of thought, he should *now concentrate on adjusting his viewpoint, seeing that it was not the word of God that failed or deceived him and brought disappointment, but that his own understanding was based on wrong premises* (emphasis ours).[323]

The Watch Tower tried to shift the blame onto its followers instead of accepting the fact that they are false prophets. However, by their own admission, the Watch Tower is a false prophet. Amazingly, a few years earlier they had this to say:

Jehovah, the God of the true prophets, will put all false prophets to shame either by not fulfilling the false prediction of such self-assuming prophets or by having His own prophecies fulfilled in a way opposite to that predicted by the false prophets. False prophets will try to hide their reason for feeling shame by denying who they really are.[324]

Often, JWs will attempt to cover the obvious errors by misapplying Proverbs 4:18, which reads, "But the path of the just *is* like the shining sun, that shines ever brighter unto the perfect day." This verse refers to the righteous choosing wisdom. The JWs have misapplied it to mean their organization is getting purer and purer.

---

322   The Watchtower, *"A Solid Basis for Confidence,"* July 15, 1976, 440.
323   Ibid., 441.
324   The Watchtower, *"Paradise Restored to Mankind-By Theocracy,"* 1974, 353-354.

In recent times, the Watch Tower seems to be backtracking on its role as a prophet. They state on their website, "Jehovah's Witnesses do not claim to be inspired prophets. They have made mistakes. Like the apostles of Jesus Christ, they have at times had some wrong expectations."[325] This is, of course, a contradiction of their previous claims.

LDS PROPHECIES

Let's now look at the Church of Jesus Christ of Latter-day Saints and see if they are true prophets. Like the Watch Tower, the Latter-day Saints organization has tried its luck at prophesying. Not only do the LDS consider their founder, Joseph Smith, a prophet, but they also have modern-day apostles and prophets. These apostles trace their priesthood authority back to Jesus Christ.[326] According to the LDS church, a prophet is defined as follows:

A person who has been called by and speaks for God. As a messenger of God, a prophet receives commandments, prophecies, and revelations from God. His responsibility is to make known God's will and true character to mankind and to show the meaning of his dealings with them. A prophet denounces sin and foretells its consequences. He is a preacher of righteousness. On occasion, prophets may be inspired to foretell the future for the benefit of mankind. His primary responsibility, however, is to bear witness of Christ. The President of the Church of Jesus Christ of Latter-day Saints is God's prophet on earth today. Members of the First Presidency and the Twelve Apostles are sustained as prophets, seers, and revelators. The prophet, "spake by the mouth of his holy prophets: Luke 1:70; (Acts 3:21;)" and, "By the Spirit are all things made known unto the prophets:1 Ne 22:1–2."[327]

---

325 Jw.org, "False Prophets," accessed March 19, 2017, http://wol.jw.org/en/wol/d/r1/lp-e/1101989228#h=25-33:0.

326 The Church of Jesus Christ of Latter-Day Saints, "Joseph Smith: A Prophet of God," accessed April 25, 2016, https://www.mormon.org/beliefs/joseph-smith.

327 The Church of Jesus Christ of Latter-Day Saints, "The Guide to the Scriptures," accessed April 25, 2016, https://www.lds.org/scriptures/gs/prophet.

The LDS organization ordains prophets they believe speak on behalf of God. Because Mormons consider the Bible as one of their Scriptures, they must also concede a false prophet is one whose prophecy does not come to pass.

Joseph Smith claimed to be ordained by God and made many prophecies, but he utterly failed. In his own personal diary (March 10, 1843-July 14, 1843), he prophesied Christ's return: "I prophecy in the name of the Lord God—& let it be written: that the Son of Man will not come in the heavens till I am 85 years old 48 years hence or about 1890."[328] As C. T. Russell did, Smith proved himself to be a false prophet because Jesus has not returned yet.

In 1832, Smith recorded in Doctrine and Covenants section 84 verses 2-5 that an LDS temple would be built in the western boundaries of the state of Missouri and he would dedicate it. The prophecy goes on to say this would occur with the current generation in 1832. This did not occur. Even later LDS apostles, such as Pratt and President Lorenzo Snow, were expecting this prophecy to be fulfilled. It never came to pass.[329] [330]

Furthermore, other members of the LDS have also falsely prophesied, including Heber C. Kimball. Kimball was one of the most prominent men in the early Mormon church, being ordained as an original member of the Quorum of the Twelve Apostles in 1835 and holding the position of First Counselor in the First Presidency of the Church from December 5, 1847, until he died in 1868.[331]

In the September 6, 1856 *Journal of Discourses* issue, volume 5, page 219, it is recorded that Kimball prophesied the following:

The Church and kingdom to which we belong will become the kingdom of our God and his Christ, and brother Brigham Young will become President of the United States . . . and I am Vice-President, and brother

328   utlm.org, *False Prophecy*, accessed April 25, 2016, http://utlm.org/onlinebooks/changech14.htm#418.

329   Orson Pratt, *Journal of Discourses*, Vol. 13, p. 138, accessed February 4, 2017, https://en.wikisource.org/wiki/Journal_of_Discourses/Volume_13/The_Latter-day_Kingdom_of_God,_etc.

330   *Dialogue: A Journal of Mormon Thought*, Autumn 1966, Vol, p. 1 Number 3, Autumn 1966, accessed February 4, 2017, http://cdmbuntu.lib.utah.edu/cdm/ref/collection/dialogue/id/3656.

331   eom.byu.edu, "Kimball, Heber," accessed May 1, 2016, http://eom.byu.edu/index.php/Kimball,_Heber_C.

Wells is the Secretary of the Interior—yes, and of all the armies in the flesh . . . You may think I am joking; but I am perfectly willing that brother Long should write every word of it; for I can see it just as naturally as I can see the earth and the productions thereof. [332]

Obviously, American history tells us none of this came to pass, which makes Kimball a false prophet. Even more startling is that one of the three principal witnesses to the writing of the Book of Mormon, David Whitmer, recounts in his *An Address to All Believers in Christ* that he and others witnessed one of Joseph Smith's false prophecies.[333]

The Book of Mormon was in the process of being printed; however, more funds were needed to see its completion. LDS leaders suggested they should go to Toronto, Canada, and sell the copyright of the Book of Mormon to attain a considerable amount of money. Joseph Smith told the LDS members who were going to Toronto, Hiram Page and Oliver Cowdery, he had received a revelation that they would successfully sell the copyright in Toronto. However, the mission failed miserably, as they were unable to sell the copyright and gain any funds.

When Joseph Smith was asked how he could have received a false prophecy from the Lord, he was greatly distressed. Thus, he decided to ask the Lord why this had occurred. Smith said the Lord told him, "Some revelations are of God: some revelations are of men: and some revelations are of the devil." Smith admitted this revelation he had received was not from God, but in fact was from the devil or from the heart of man.[334] Obviously, the LDS leadership and Joseph Smith are not true prophets.

TRUE REVELATION

Is there any new revelation from God? Or has He given us all the Scripture we need? Jude 1:3-4 provides a clear answer to this question:

---

332   watchman.org, "Beware of False Prophets," accessed May 1, 2016, http://www.watchman.org/articles/mormonism/beware-of-false-prophets/.

333   David Whitmer, *An Address to All Believers in Christ*, pages 30-31, accessed May 1, 2016, http://www.utlm.org/onlinebooks/address1.htm.

334   David Whitmer, *An Address to All Believers in Christ*, page 31, accessed May 4, 2016, http://www.utlm.org/onlinebooks/address1.htm.

Beloved, while I was very diligent to write to you concerning our common salvation, I found it necessary to write to you exhorting you to contend earnestly for the faith which was once for all delivered to the saints. For certain men have crept in unnoticed, who long ago were marked out for this condemnation, ungodly men, who turn the grace of our God into lewdness and deny the only Lord God and our Lord Jesus Christ.

The fact that the faith was once for all delivered (or "entrusted" in some translations) has a twofold meaning:

1. No new revelation can change the essence of this faith.
2. It is the faith that they have received (the word for "entrusted" indicates the passing on of a tradition) from their teachers, possibly including Jude.[335]

In Jude 1:4 we read, "For certain men have crept in unnoticed, who long ago were marked out for this condemnation, ungodly men, who turn the grace of our God into lewdness and deny the only Lord God and our Lord Jesus Christ." Jude wrote to the saints to combat the heresy of the false teachers who propagate new and erroneous doctrine—namely, that Jesus Christ is not Lord and God.

Furthermore, in Revelation 22:18-19, we are warned not to tamper with God's revelations:

For testify to everyone who hears the words of the prophecy of this book: If anyone adds to these things, God will add to him the plagues that are written in this book; and if anyone takes away from the words of the book of this prophecy, God shall take away his part from the Book of Life, from the holy city, and *from* the things which are written in this book.

---

335   Peter H. Davids, *The Pillar New Testament Commentary: The Letters of 2 Peter and Jude* (Grand Rapids, MI: William B. Eerdmans Pub. Co., 2006), 42.

The JWs and LDS leaders have falsely prophesied revelations that are not found in the Bible and are thus in danger of hellfire if they do not repent.

Before Jesus and the New Covenant, God used prophets as His mouthpiece. However, the Incarnation (*John 1:1-3,14,18*) was God condescending into the likeness of man to directly speak to us and save His creation. Hebrews 1:1-4 clearly teaches this:

> God, who at various times and in various ways spoke in time past to the fathers by the prophets, has in these last days spoken to us by *His* Son, whom He has appointed heir of all things, through whom also He made the worlds; who being the brightness of *His* glory and the express image of His person, and upholding all things by the word of His power, when He had by Himself purged our sins, sat down at the right hand of the Majesty on high, having become so much better than the angels, as He has by inheritance obtained a more excellent name than they.

When the writer of Hebrews indicates God speaks to us by His Son *in these last days*, "he intimates that there is no longer any reason to expect any new revelation; for it was not a word in part that Christ brought, but the final conclusion. It is in this sense that the apostles take "the last times" and "the last days." And the Apostle Paul means the same when he says, "Upon whom the ends of the world are come" *(1 Cor. 10:11)*. [336] Both the writer and his Messianic Jewish audience were fully aware that "the last days" are an expression used in Scripture to describe the final period of the world as we now know it.

In the Old Testament, the last days are anticipated as the age of messianic fulfillment *(Isa. 2:2; Mic.4:1)*. The NT writers regarded themselves as living in the last days, the era of the Gospel. Thus, for example, Peter explains the events of the day of Pentecost are the fulfillment of Joel 2:28: "This is what was spoken by the prophet Joel: 'And in the last days it shall be, God declares, that I will pour out my Spirit upon all flesh'" *(Acts 2:16, 17)*. [337]

---

336   John Calvin and John Owen, *Commentary on the Epistle of Paul the Apostle to the Hebrews* (Bellingham, WA: Logos Bible Software, 2010), 33.

337   Elwell and Beitzel, *Baker Encyclopedia*, 1,310.

Furthermore, it follows logically that the last days will also have a final day, the day of judgment. The use of the term "day" in the singular corresponds in the NT to the concept of the "day of the Lord," familiar in the OT, where it is generally presented as an awful day of final judgment against the unrepentant, but with the implication that it is also the day of the salvation and vindication of God's people (e.g., *Isa. 2:12–22; Ezek. 13:5; Joel 1:15; 2:1, 11; Amos 5:18–24; Zep. 1:7, 14).* The climax of these last days and, therefore, of all history, will be "the day of the Lord," which will overtake the world suddenly (*1 Thess. 5:2*) [338]

This concept of the last days is vital to the proper understanding of the text because God will no longer speak to His creation with new revelation. Thus, prophets, apostles, or any new revelators that seek to add to or take away from God's Word and what His Son has revealed are not from God.

God used His Son to speak to us because of the pervasiveness of false doctrine and teachers. The Apostle John warned his congregations about this only a few decades after Christ had come:

> Little children, it is the last hour; and as you have heard that the Antichrist is coming, even now many antichrists have come, by which we know that it is the last hour. They went out from us, but they were not of us; for if they had been of us, they would have continued with us; but *they went out* that they might be made manifest, that none of them were of us (*1 John 2:18-29*).

Even in the first century, cults and false doctrine spread like wildfire. Therefore, point out to the cultist that we follow the revelation that God has given to us through Jesus Christ because He is infallible and perfect, *unlike* sinful man.

Also, we must avoid the false teaching and prophecies of man. Because Jesus is the final and ultimate prophet, human prophets have been made obsolete. God no longer needs to use man as a communicator of new revelation if He Himself has come to speak to man and given us the Bible as his written Word.

---

338   Elwell and Beitzel, *Baker Encyclopedia,* 1,310.

(Note: We are not saying you cannot have the gift of prophecy, which would simply mean you proclaim biblical truth. Rather, we are saying prophets who speak extra-biblical teachings and doctrine are obsolete).

Furthermore, point out that Jude and Hebrews make it clear the faith has been delivered once and for all through Jesus Christ. Kindly show cultists the false prophecies and question their organization's credibility.

Finally, ask them if it is really in God's character to allow billions of people to be deceived from the first to nineteenth centuries because they did not receive the correct information from God. Also, ask, "Does it make sense that an omnibenevolent (all-loving) God would deceive His creation for nearly two thousand years and only in the last two centuries reveal the truth? Furthermore, is God's revelation not sufficient to save all who believe in Him?" These are important questions to ask to plant seeds of truth in the cultists' minds.

In conclusion, although God does reveal to us His plan through the Holy Spirit and the Bible, no new doctrinal or extra-biblical revelations exist. God became a man to speak to us, and we have all the sufficient revelation we need through God the Son and His Holy Bible.

The Jehovah's Witnesses and Mormons have tried prophesying but failed. The Bible warns us about such things—and, therefore, we should put our trust in the perfect and all-knowing Almighty God, who revealed Himself through Jesus Christ.

"THIS IS THE TRUE GOD AND ETERNAL LIFE" (1 JOHN 5:20).
The Gospel for the Cults

Romans 10:13 declares one must call upon the name of the one, true God to be saved. The Apostle Paul tell us in Romans 10:9-11 that Jesus is the one who saves us upon believing in Him as Lord. Therefore, no cult member can be saved since he has not called upon the true God.

Furthermore, only a perfect sacrifice could appease the wrath of God and pay for our sins. 2 Corinthians 5:21 states that God "made Him who knew no sin *to be* sin for us, that we might become the righteousness of God in Him."

Upon repentance and belief in Jesus, God transfers Jesus's righteousness to us so He no longer sees our sinful state but Jesus's perfect life. The only possible way this could happen is if Jesus is the Almighty God who is perfectly righteous and of infinite value. As the verse states, "that we might become the righteousness *of God* in Him" (emphasis ours).

The Lord Jesus wants to abolish the works-righteous system cults are captive to and take their (and all people's) burdens from them *(Matt. 11:28-30)*. Jesus desires to give abundant and eternal life *(John 3:16,10:10)*.

ABOUT THE AUTHORS

Mark Stengler Jr. is a student majoring in biblical studies with a minor in biblical languages at Liberty University. He is the founder and president of Please Tell Me the Truth Ministries (www.pleasetellmethetruth.org), a nonprofit organization that seeks to equip Christians with resources to defend their faith and to evangelize biblically and effectively.

Dr. Mark Stengler, NMD, is a naturopathic medical doctor and bestselling author/coauthor of more than thirty books. He holds a master of religious studies from Southern California Seminary. Dr. Stengler has been involved in apologetics and evangelism for more than a decade. He is a member of Calvary Chapel Oceanside, California, where he is a guest lecturer on apologetic and evangelism issues. Dr. Stengler is also an advisor to Please Tell Me the Truth Ministries.

GLOSSARY

Aaronic priesthood: The LDS term that refers to the priestly services of males who are at least twelve years old. LDS founder Joseph Smith claimed it was conferred to him by John the Baptist. It was originally a term in the Old Testament specific to the Israelite priests.

Alpha and Omega: The first and last letters of the Greek alphabet. This term is used in the book of Revelation to describe the eternality and, thus, divinity of Jesus Christ.

Apologetics: A defense or reason for the truth of the Christian faith.

Apologist: One who practices apologetics and defends the faith.

Apostle: Literally means, "One sent out." Strictly speaking, an apostle was one who saw the risen Lord.

Arianism: Named after Arius who had the heretical view that God the Father alone is eternal and that His Son (Jesus) was his first creation. The Jehovah's Witnesses hold to this false doctrine.

Arius: A priest in Alexandria, Egypt (AD 256-336), who promoted the heretical view that came to be known as Arianism.

Armageddon: The word in Hebrew means "Mount Megiddo," and it is thought to be an area between the western coastal area and Plain of Jezreel in northern Palestine. Generally, it is referred to as a future battle where

God destroys the demonic leadership of the kings of the earth and their armies at the end of history. The term is used in the New Testament in Revelation 16:16. Some Christians view this verse as figurative and referring to a final conflict between man and God.

Begotten: The English term means to generate offspring. The biblical definition derives from the Greek word monogenēs which means "only one of its kind," "unique." The term is used to describe Jesus Christ to show His uniqueness as the divine Son of God.

Blasphemy: A lack of reverence or a contempt for God.

Charles Taze Russell: The founder of the Jehovah's Witness organization. Originally, Russell (1852-1916) founded a sect known as Russellites or Millennial Dawnists, which later became known as the Jehovah's Witnesses. He wrote a series of books and was the first editor of *The Watchtower*. His denial of the deity of Jesus Christ, unbiblical doctrine of hell, and belief that Jesus came back to earth invisibly is still taught by Jehovah's Witnesses today. He falsely prophesied several times.

Church of Jesus Christ of Latter-day Saints: Also known as Mormonism, it's a religion that claims to be the restored church of Jesus Christ. It is based on the claim by Joseph Smith that God had revealed to him the true and restored gospel. The organization claims to be "Christian" but has several doctrines and Holy books that contradict historical biblical Christianity. Today, different sects have split off from the mainline church, which is headquartered in Salt Lake City, Utah.

Constantine: Also known as Constantine the Great, he was the first Roman emperor to profess and promote Christianity (AD 280-337). He ordered the Council of Nicea (in modern-day Turkey) in AD 325 for clergy and other leaders to deal with Arianism and the relationship between the Father and the Son.

Cult: Biblically speaking, any group that denies or deviates from the orthodox teachings of historic, biblical Christianity and essential Christian doctrine.

Deification: According to Mormonism, the doctrine that man becomes divine or god after death.

Doctrine: A set of beliefs or teachings. Essential Christian doctrine includes teachings such as monotheism (there is only one God), the deity of Jesus Christ, the reality of the Trinity, salvation is only received through repentance and faith alone in Jesus Christ, the existence of heaven and hell, the sinfulness of man requires a savior, and the church is the body of Christ.

Firstborn: Two main meanings exist. First, it can refer to the order of birth among siblings or animals. However, it can also mean having the highest rank or preeminence. In terms of Jesus, it always refers to his preeminence and sovereignty.

Grace: Favor or kindness. Biblically speaking, this means "unmerited favor" or God's blessing and favor for something an individual did not earn, such as salvation.

Heaven: Can refer to the physical expanse over the earth or location of stars. More commonly, it refers to the dwelling place of God.

Heavenly Father: For biblical Christians, this refers to the first person of the Triune God. For Mormons, it refers to the god they worship, who was once a man like humans but through a process of progression and exaltation has achieved Godhood. They believe Heavenly Father is the result of a celestial father and celestial mother having sex. LDS believe humans are the literal offspring between Heavenly Father and a celestial Heavenly Mother. LDS doctrine teaches that Jesus Christ is the product of sexual relations between Heavenly Father and Mary.

Hell: The place of eternal punishment where nonbelievers are separated from the love and grace of God.

Holy Spirit (or Holy Ghost): The third person of the Trinity who is fully God. According to the Jehovah's Witnesses, the Holy Spirit is an active force, not a person or God. Mormons identify the Holy Ghost as a god and member of their Trinity, which is composed of three gods.

Ignatius: The bishop of Antioch in Syria who was thought to be a disciple of the Apostle John (AD 35-107). He is best known for the seven letters he penned, which include his belief that Jesus was God, before his martyrdom at Rome.

Incarnation: This is when Jesus Christ took on human flesh (*John 1:14; Phi. 2:5-9*). Jesus came in human flesh to be the Savior and fulfill the law on humankind's behalf. He took the wrath of God as a substitution for sinful humans. In his incarnation, Jesus never ceased being God. He was fully God and fully man, yet did not display all of His divine attributes in his humanity. This is also referred to as the hypostatic union.

Israelites: A common biblical term used for the citizens of Israel. More specifically, it refers to the descendants of the patriarch Jacob, who God gave the name Israel.

Jaredites: This is a group recorded in the Book of Mormon who were descendants of Jared and lived at the time of the Tower of Babel. They came by boat to inhabit the Americas. Modern research has been unable to confirm this group existed.

Jehovah: A manmade term used for the name of God. In its original form, it is known as the Tetragrammaton. The English equivalent of it is spelled YHWH. The Jews regarded the name of God as being so holy that they were superstitious about even pronouncing it. Instead, they used the term Adonai, which means Lord. Eventually, Jewish scholars known as the Masoretes added vowels from the word "Adonai" to the Tetragrammaton and the term "Jehovah" or "Yahweh" was formed. Jehovah's Witnesses claim it is the only proper name for God and that the term is also synonymous with God the Father. Biblically speaking, though, "Jehovah" can be used as a term for the essence of God (although "Yahweh" would be more precise). The Bible refers to Jesus Christ as Jehovah, meaning He is the true God.

Jehovah's Witnesses: A religious organization that claims to be the sole mouthpiece of Jehovah God. Founder, Charles Taze Russell, believed Jesus Christ had returned to the earth invisibly. Russell had objections to historical Christianity's beliefs about hell and the person of Jesus Christ. The organization today is headquartered in Warwick, New York. It controls the production and distribution of evangelistic materials as well as doctrine.

Jesus Christ: The second person of the Trinity. He is also the Messiah, Savior, and head of the Christian church. He is the eternal, divine Son of God.

Jehovah's Witnesses view Him as a spirit creature who was created by Jehovah. They also believe He is Michael the Archangel. Mormons, on the other hand, believe Jesus Christ to be a god who resulted from the sexual union between Heavenly Father and Mary.

Jew: Originally referred to a person of the tribe of Judah, then, more broadly, someone living in the southern kingdom of Judah (Jew + Judean in Hebrew). After the Babylonian captivity, it referred to those living in the province of Judah, which by extension included remnants of all twelve tribes of Israel. In the centuries that followed, "Jew" came to describe all descendants of Israel.

Joseph Smith: The Mormon prophet and founder of the Church of Jesus Christ of Latter-day Saints (1805-1844). At a young age, he claimed to have a vision in which God the Father and Jesus Christ told him that all Christian churches were an abomination. Smith claimed a restoration of the lost gospel was needed and he was to be the instrument by which this would be accomplished.

Lamanites: The dark-skinned people of Jewish descent who descended through Laman, the son of Lehi. They were an evil nemesis of the Nephites. Modern research has been unable to confirm this group existed.

Last Days: Generally believed to be the days since Pentecost until the return of Jesus Christ.

Lord: Can refer to a master. When used in reference to Jesus Christ, it can mean "God" or "Master." The Greek term used for "Lord" is Kyrios, which can mean "Yahweh" or "God" when used in a religious sense.

Melchizedek priesthood: The LDS term for the priestly services of church leaders. They guide the church and preach the gospel worldwide. One must be at least eighteen years old to join. This term was originally used in the Old Testament and referred to in the New Testament.

Messiah: A term that means "anointed one." The New Testament equivalent word is "Christ." The Old Testament predicted the coming of a Savior Messiah, which was fulfilled by Jesus Christ in the New Testament.

Mormon: The followers of Mormonism (see **Church of Jesus Christ of Latter-day Saints** definition). It also can refer to an ancient Nephite prophet who compiled the records as recorded in the Book of Mormon.

Mormonism: Refers to the Mormon religion (see **Church of Jesus Christ of Latter-day Saints** definition).

Moroni: The last Nephite prophet in the Book Of Mormon. He delivered the plates of Mormon to his son, who was also named Moroni. He also added his own book to the Book of Mormon, known as Moroni. He sealed the gold plates and hid them in the hill Cumorah. Later in 1823, Moroni was sent as a resurrected being to reveal the Book of Mormon to Joseph Smith. He also instructed Joseph Smith for several years and delivered the plates to Smith in 1827. When Smith was done translating the plates, they were returned to Moroni.

Nephites: Recorded by the Book of Mormon to be a group of Jewish descent from Nephi, the son of Lehi. They inhabited the Americas and were destroyed in the fifth century AD by their nemeses, the Lamanites. Modern research has been unable to confirm this group existed.

New Testament: Also known as the New Covenant, it is the twenty-seven books of the Christian Bible that reveal the Messiah, who was predicted in the Old Testament. The New Testament provides God's plan of salvation through Jesus Christ.

New World Translation: The official Bible of the Jehovah's Witnesses. The translators have not been revealed by their organization. The newest translation was published in 2013. It contains numerous insertions of the manmade term "Jehovah" in the New Testament, even though no Greek manuscripts contain the term. It also alters numerous verses that clearly display the deity of Jesus Christ as the one, true God.

Nicene Creed: A summary of the Christian faith that emphasizes biblical Trinitarianism. It is also known as the Nicene-Constantinopolitan Creed because it was first adopted at the Council of Nicea in AD 325. It dealt with the deity of Jesus and the Trinity in opposition to Arianism. It was later expanded in AD 381 at the Council of Constantinople to clarify the concept of the Trinity.

Old Testament: The first thirty-nine books of the Christian Bible, which contain the identical contents of the Hebrew Scriptures. The books range from Genesis to Malachi and are followed by the twenty-seven books of the New Testament.

Polemics: The art of refuting false beliefs and arguments to defend Christian truth using an offensive challenge to false beliefs and worldviews.

Polycarp: Early church tradition holds he lived during the time of some of the twelve apostles (AD 70-156) and was taught by the Apostle John. He is considered an important early church father and bishop of Smyrna.

Polytheism: The belief in the existence of more than one god. Biblical Christianity, on the other hand, believes in one God.

Resurrection: For a physically dead person to be raised to life. The focal point of the Christian faith is the Resurrection of Jesus Christ.

Sabbath: The day of rest. In the Old Testament, it was a commanded day of rest from work.

Sabellianism: The heretical belief that God exists in three modes or manifestations and not three persons.

Salvation: Can mean the deliverance from evil or danger, such as the deliverance of the Israelites from the Egyptians. In the New Testament, it refers to the deliverance from sin and God's wrath by the substitutionary atonement of Jesus Christ.

Sin: The breaking or transgression of God's laws. This evil occurs by omission (neglect) or commission (knowingly).

Son of God: Used in the Old Testament in different ways, including the description of the nation of Israel, a title given to the monarch at the time of rulership, and angels. In the New Testament, it refers to Christ's divine nature and relationship with the Father.

Subordinationism: A term used to describe the false doctrine that the Son is not eternal or divine and not equal to the Father.

Tertullian: His full name is Quintus Septimius Florens Tertullian. He was born in the city of Carthage in North Africa and was an esteemed early church father and theologian (AD 160-225). He coined the Latin word *trinitas*, which means Trinity, to define the Godhead.

Tetragrammaton: Refers to one of the Old Testament names for God, which contains four consonants. The English equivalents are YHWH and, therefore, most scholars believe the closest English pronunciation is "Yahweh" (with vowels added in from the word "Adonai," meaning "Lord"). It refers to "the one who is, that is, the absolute and unchangeable one" or "the one who brings things to pass, causes things to happen."

Trinity: Refers to the biblical teaching that God is one and only one in His essence, but He is three in His persons. The three members include the Father, Son, and Holy Spirit.

Tritheism: The belief that the Trinity is comprised of three gods. This contradicts the Bible, which teaches that there is one God comprised of three persons. Mormons believe in tritheism.

The Watchtower: A publication of the Jehovah's Witnesses that deals with world events and Bible prophecies. It can also refer to a legal entity of the Jehovah's Witnesses known as the Watch Tower Bible and Tract Society, which publishes their New World Translation Bible and other literature.

Works: Can refer to man's attempt to achieve salvation through behavior, actions, or deeds. It can also be used in the sense of "good works," where one's thinking and conduct are obedient and pleasing to God because he has obtained salvation through faith in Jesus Christ.

Yahweh: The holy name of God in the Old Testament. Refers to the essence of God. Jesus Christ is referred to as "Yahweh" in the New Testament. See the definition of **Tetragrammaton**.

RECOMMENDED READING

The Holy Bible

41 Unique Teachings of The LDS Church by Sandra Tanner

Major Problems of Mormonism by Jerald and Sandra Tanner

Reasoning from the Scriptures with the Mormons by Ron Rhodes

Reasoning from the Scriptures with the Jehovah's Witnesses by Ron Rhodes

Mormonism 101 by Bill McKeever and Eric Johnson

Becoming Gods by Richard Abanes

The Forgotten Trinity by James R. White

Evidence for Christianity by Josh McDowell

To Everyone an Answer by Francis J. Beckwith, William Lane Craig, and J.P. Moreland

The Popular Encyclopedia of Apologetics by Ed Hindson and Ergun Cancer

The School of Biblical Evangelism by Kirk Cameron and Ray Comfort

BIBLIOGRAPHY

Abanes, Richard. *Becoming Gods*. Eugene, OR: Harvest House Publishers, 2004.

Achtemeier, Paul J. *Harper's Bible Dictionary*. San Francisco: Harper & Row, 1985.

Aland, K., M. Black, C. M. Martini, B. M. Metzger, M. A. Robinson, and A. Wikgren. *The Greek New Testament, Fourth Revised Edition (Interlinear with Morphology)*. Deutsche Bibelgesellschaft, 1993.

Ankerberg, John, and John Weldon. *Encyclopedia of Cults and New Religions: Jehovah's Witnesses, Mormonism, Mind Sciences, Baha'i, Zen, Unitarianism*. Eugene, OR: Harvest House Publishers, 1999.

Ankerberg, John, and John Weldon. *Fast Facts on Jehovah's Witnesses*. Eugene, OR: Harvest House Publishers, 2003.

"*Announcing Jehovah's Kingdom*." The Watchtower, January 1, 1942. Brooklyn, NY: Watch Tower Bible and Tract Society of New York.

A Solid Basis for Confidence. Brooklyn, NY: Watch Tower Bible and Tract Society of New York, July 15, 1976.

Avoidjw.org. "Bibles." Accessed March 16, 2017. http://avoidjw.org/bibles/.

Barry, John D. Long, *The Lexham Bible Dictionary*. Bellingham, WA: Lexham Press, 2016.

Beckwith, Francis J., William Lane Craig, and J. P. Moreland. *To Everyone an Answer: A Case for the Christian Worldview*. Downers Grove, IL: InterVarsity Press, 2004.

Belnap, Daniel. BYU Religious Studies Center. "The King James Bible and the Book of Mormon." Accessed February 5, 2017, https://rsc.byu.edu/archived/king-james-bible-and-restoration/10-king-james-bible-and-book-mormon.

Bible Hub. "Strong's Greek: 4396. προφήτης (prophétes)." Accessed August 15, 2016. http://biblehub.com/str/greek/4396.htm.

Blue Letter Bible. "Sects of Mormonism." Accessed July 26, 2016. https://www.blueletterbible.org/study/cults/ramd/ramd25.cfm.

Brown, Michael L. "Is Jehovah God's True Name." Accessed March 5,2017 at https://askdrbrown.org/library/jehovah-gods-true-name.

Bundy, Trey. "How Jehovah's Witnesses leaders hide child abuse secrets at all costs." The Center for Investigative Reporting. December 10, 2016. Accessed March 14, 2017, https://www.revealnews.org/article/how-jehovahs-witnesses-leaders-hide-child-abuse-secrets-at-all-costs/.

BYU. Harold B. Lee Library. "Blacks." Accessed March 16, 2017. http://eom.byu.edu/index.php/Blacks.

BYU. Harold B. Lee Library. "Council in Heaven." Accessed March 19, 2017, http://eom.byu.edu/index.php/Council_in_Heaven.

BYU. Harold B. Lee Library. "Book of Mormon Editions (1830-1981)." Accessed March 19, 2017, http://eom.byu.edu/index.php/Book_of_Mormon_Editions_(1830-1981).

BYU. Harold B. Lee Library. "Book of Mormon Editions (1830-1981)." Accessed March 19, 2017, http://eom.byu.edu/index.php/Book_of_Mormon_Editions_(1830-1981).

BYU. Harold B. Lee Library. "Missouri." Accessed March 19, 2017, http://eom.byu.edu/index.php/Missouri.

BYU. Harold B. Lee Library. "Nauvoo." Accessed March 19, 2017, http://eom.byu.edu/index.php/Nauvoo.

BYU. Harold B. Lee Library. "Nauvoo Expositor." Accessed March 19, 2017, http://eom.byu.edu/index.php/Nauvoo_Expositor.

BYU. Harold B. Lee Library. *Kimball, Heber C.* Accessed May 1, 2016. http://eom.byu.edu/index.php/Kimball,_Heber_C.

BYU Harold B. Lee Library. "Book of Mormon Geography." Accessed July 22, 2016. http://eom.byu.edu/index.php/Book_of_Mormon_Geography.

BYU Harold B. Lee Library. "Cumorah." Accessed July 30, 2016. http://eom.byu.edu/index.php/Cumorah.

BYU Harold B. Lee Library. "Premortal Life." Accessed June 28, 2016. http://eom.byu.edu/index.php/Premortal_Life.

BYUStudies. "History of the Church: Volume 6, Chapter 34." Accessed March 19, 2017. https://byustudies.byu.edu/content/volume-6-chapter-34, 618.

Carpenter, Eugene E., and Philip W. Comfort. *Holman Treasury of Key Bible Words: 200 Greek and 200 Hebrew Words Defined and Explained.* Nashville, TN: Holman Reference, 2000.

Calvin, J., and J. Owen. *Commentary on the Epistle of Paul the Apostle to the Romans.* Bellingham, WA: Logos Bible Software, 2010.

Carson, D. A. *The Gospel According to John.* Leicester, England: InterVarsity Press, 1991.Colson, Charles W., and Harold Fickett. *The Faith: What Christians Believe, Why They Believe It, and Why It Matters.* Grand Rapids, MI: Zondervan, 2008.

Comfort, Philip W., and J. D. Douglas. *Who's Who in Christian History.* Wheaton, IL: Tyndale House, 1992.

Craig, William Lane, and Shabir Ally. "The Concept of God in Islam and Christianity." ReasonableFaith.org. March 2002. Accessed October 16, 2016. https://www.youtube.com/watch?v=n52BzWKLn9g.

Daniels, Thomas. "Historical Idealism and Jehovah's Witnesses." Accessed July 4, 2016. https://archive.org/stream/HistoricalIdealismAndJehovahsWitnesses/Historical_Idealism_and_Jehovahs_Witnesses#page/n0/mode/2up.

Davids, P. H. *The Pillar New Testament Commentary: The Letters of 2 Peter and Jude.* Grand Rapids, MI: William B. Eerdmans Pub. Co., 2006.

Dockery, David S. *The New American Commentary.* Nashville, TN: Broadman & Holman, 1991.

Eckman, James P. *The Truth about Worldviews: A Biblical Understanding of Worldview Alternatives*. Wheaton, Ill.: Crossway Books, 2004.

Easton, M. G. *In Easton's Bible Dictionary*. New York: Harper & Brothers, 1893.

Edwards, J. R. *The Gospel According to Mark*. Grand Rapids, MI; Leicester, England: Eerdmans; Apollos, 2002.

Elwell, Walter A., and Barry J. Beitzel. *Baker Encyclopedia of the Bible*. Grand Rapids, MI: Baker Book House, 1988.

Elwell, Walter A., and Philip W. Comfort. *Tyndale Bible Dictionary*. Wheaton, IL: Tyndale House Publishers, 2001.

Encyclopedia Britannica Online. "Yahweh," Accessed June 20, 2016. http://www.britannica.com/topic/Yahweh.

Enns, Paul P. *The Moody Handbook of Theology*. Chicago, IL: Moody Press, 1989.

FairMormon.org. "Does the Church of Jesus Christ of Latter-day Saints Teach that God Had SEX with Mary?" Accessed May 1, 2016. http://www.fairmormon.org/.

Feinberg, John S. *No One Like Him: The Doctrine of God*. Wheaton, IL: Crossway Books, 2001.

Freedman, David Noel, Allen C. Myers, and Astrid B. Beck. *Eerdmans Dictionary of the Bible*. Grand Rapids, MI: W.B. Eerdmans, 2000.

Geisler, Norman L. *The Big Book of Christian Apologetics: An A to Z Guide*. Grand Rapids, MI: Baker Books, 2012.

Goodstein, Laurie. "It's Official: Mormon Founder Had Up to 40 Wives." NYTimes.com. November 10, 2014. Accessed July 26, 2016. http://www.nytimes.com/2014/11/11/us/its-official-mormon-founder-had-up-to-40-wives.html?_r=0.

Grudem, Wayne A. *Systematic Theology: An Introduction to Biblical Doctrine*. Grand Rapids, MI: Zondervan, 1994.

Hindson, Edward E., and Ergun Caner. *The Popular Encyclopedia of Apologetics*. Eugene, OR: Harvest House Publishers, 2008.

International Bible Students Association. *Studies in the Scriptures: The Finished Mystery*. Brooklyn, NY:1918.

"*Is Any Religion Good Enough?*" The Watchtower, December 1, 1991. Brooklyn, NY: Watch Tower Bible and Tract Society of New York.

Jackson, S. M., ed. *The New Schaff-Herzog Encyclopedia of Religious Knowledge: Embracing Biblical, Historical, Doctrinal, and Practical Theology and Biblical, Theological, and Ecclesiastical Biography from the Earliest Times to the Present Day (Vol. 8, p. 11)*. New York; London: Funk & Wagnalls, 1908-1914.

JewishEncyclopedia.com. "JEHOVAH." Accessed June 20, 2016. http://www.jewishencyclopedia.com/articles/8568-jehovah.

John Lund, "Council in Heaven," accessed March 19, 2017, http://eom.byu.edu/index.php/Council_in_Heaven.

Jw.org, "What is the Lake of Fire? Is It the Same as Hell or Gehenna?" Accessed March 16, 2017. https://www.jw.org/en/bible-teachings/questions/lake-of-fire/.

Jw.org. "Do You Have an Immortal Spirit." Accessed March 16, 2017. http://wol.jw.org/en/wol/d/r1/lp-e/1102001150.

Avoidjw.org, "Bibles." Accessed March 16, 2017. http://avoidjw.org/bibles/.

JW.org. "*Who Is Michael the Archangel?*" Accessed August 14, 2016. https://www.jw.org/en/publications/books/bible-teach/who-is-michael-the-archangel-jesus/.

JW.org. "Why Does God Have an Organization?" Accessed April 4, 2016. https://www.jw.org/en/publications/books/good-news-from-god/jehovahs-witnesses-organization/.

JW.org. "False Prophets." Accessed March 19, 2017, http://wol.jw.org/en/wol/d/r1/lp-e/1101989228#h=25-33:0.

JW.org. "Myth 4: God Is a Trinity." Accessed June 11, 2016. https://www.jw.org/en/publications/magazines/wp20091101/myth-god-is-a-trinity/.

JW.org. "Governing Body Announces World Headquarters Move | 2014 Yearbook." Accessed April 28. 2016. https://www.jw.org/en/publications/books/2014-yearbook/highlights/governing-body-news-world-headquarters-warwick/.

JW.org. "Why Is Jesus Called God's Son?" Accessed May 1, 2016. https://www.jw.org/en/bible-teachings/questions/jesus-gods-son/.

JW.org. "What Does the Bible Say About Salvation?" Accessed April 24, 2016. https://www.jw.org/en/bible-teachings/questions/what-is-salvation/.

Kingdom Ministry. The Watchtower, March, 1968. Brooklyn, NY: Watch Tower Bible and Tract Society of New York.

Kittel, Gerhard, Gerhard Friedrich, and Geoffrey W. Bromiley, eds. *Theological Dictionary of the New Testament.* Grand Rapids, MI: W.B. Eerdmans, 1985.

Knight, Kevin. "Against Heresies (Book I, Chapter 10)." Accessed October 14, 2016. http://www.newadvent.org/fathers/0103110.htm.

Kokul, Gregory. "Facts for Skeptics of the New Testament." Christian Research Institute. Accessed July 26, 2016. http://www.equip.org/article/facts-for-skeptics-of-the-new-testament/.

LaHaye, Tim. *Jesus, Who Is He?* Sisters, OR: Multnomah Books, 1996.

Lange, J. P., & Schaff, P. *A Commentary on the Holy Scriptures: John.* Bellingham, WA: Logos Bible Software, 2008.

Lewis, C.S. *Mere Christianity.* New York, NY: Harper Collins, 2001.

Lunceford, J. E. "Armageddon." *Eerdmans Dictionary of the Bible.* Grand Rapids, MI: W.B. Eerdmans, 2000.

MacArthur, John. *The MacArthur Study Bible: New King James Version.* Nashville: Word Bibles, 1997.

MacMahon, J.H. "Against Noetus." From Ante-Nicene Fathers, Vol. 5. Edited by Alexander Roberts, James Donaldson, and A. Cleveland Coxe. Accessed July 7, 2016. http://www.newadvent.org/fathers/0521.htm.

McDowell, Josh, and Don Stewart. *Handbook of Today's Religions.* San Bernardino, CA: Here's Life Publishers, 1983.

McKeever, Bill, and Eric Johnson. *Mormonism 101: Examining the Religion of the Latter-day Saints.* Grand Rapids, MI: Baker Books, 2000.

McKeever, Bill, and Eric Johnson. "Jeremiah 1:5." Mormonism Research Ministry. 2013, Accessed August 6, 2016. http://www.mrm.org/jeremiah-1-5.

Melick, R. R. *Philippians, Colossians, Philemon* (Vol. 32, p. 220). Nashville: Broadman & Holman Publishers, 1991.

Merriam-Webster. "Forever." Accessed May 7, 2016. http://www.merriam-webster.com/dictionary/eternal.

Morris, Leon. *The Gospel According to Matthew*. Grand Rapids, MI: William B. Eerdmans Publishing, 1992.

Orson Pratt. "The Holy Spirit and the Godhead." *Journal of Discourses*. Accessed October 15, 2016. https://www.journalofdiscourses.com/2/50.

"*Our Present Duties*." The Watchtower, July 15, 1924. Brooklyn, NY: Watch Tower Bible and Tract Society of New York.

Peterson, Daniel C., and Stephen D. Ricks. "Comparing LDS Beliefs with First-Century Christianity." Accessed May 15, 2016, https://www.lds.org/ensign/1988/03/comparing-lds-beliefs-with-first-century-christianity?lang=eng.

Quinn, D. Michael. *Early Mormonism and the Magic World View*. Salt Lake City, UT: Signature Books, 1987.

Qureshi, Nabeel. *No God but One: Allah or Jesus? A Former Muslim Investigates the Evidence for Islam and Christianity*. Grand Rapids, MI: Zondervan, 2016.

Religion Facts. "Branches of Mormonism—2015." Accessed July 26, 2016. http://www.religionfacts.com/mormonism/branches.

Rhodes, Ron. *5-minute Apologetics for Today: 365 Quick Answers to Key Questions*. Eugene, OR: Harvest House Publishers, 2010.

Rhodes, Ron. *Reasoning from the Scriptures with the Jehovah's Witnesses*. Eugene, OR: Harvest House, 1993.

Rhodes, Ron, and Marian Bodine. *Reasoning from the Scriptures with the Mormons*. Eugene, OR: Harvest House Publishers, 1995.

Rhodes, Ron. *The Challenge of the Cults and New Religions: The Essential Guide to Their History, Their Doctrine, and Our Response*. Grand Rapids, MI: Zondervan, 2001.

Roberts, Alexander, James Donaldson, A. Cleveland Coxe, Allan Menzies, Ernest Cushing Richardson, and Bernhard Pick. *The Ante-Nicene Fathers: Translations of the Writings of the Fathers Down to A.D. 325*. Bellingham, WA: Logos Bible Software, 2008.

Russell, Charles Taze. "1894 Zion's Watch Tower." Accessed October 15, 2016. https://archive.org/stream/1894ZionsWatchTower/1894_Watch_Tower.

"*Shepherds and Sheep in A Theocracy.*" The Watchtower, January 15, 1994. Brooklyn, NY: Watch Tower Bible and Tract Society of New York.

Slick, Matt. "If the Holy Spirit Is God, Why Didn't He Know the Time of Christ's Return?" CARM. Accessed October 15, 2016. https://carm.org/bible-difficulties/matthew-mark/if-holy-spirit-god-why-didnt-he-know-time-christs-return.

Smith, Joseph Fielding. *Doctrinal Answers: A Comparison of Religious Faiths with the Restored Gospel.* Salt Lake City, UT: Bookcraft, 1959.

Smith, Joseph, Joseph Fielding Smith, and Robert J. Matthews. *Teachings of the Prophet Joseph Smith Selected and Arranged.* Salt Lake City, UT: Deseret Book, 1977.

Smith, Joseph Fielding. *Religious Truths Defined: A Comparison of Religious Faiths with the Restored Gospel.* Salt Lake City, UT: Bookcraft, 1959.

Sproul, R. C., and Keith A. Mathison. *The Reformation Study Bible: English Standard Version, Containing the Old and New Testaments.* Orlando, FL: Ligonier Ministries, 2005.

Stewart, Don. "Who Were the New Testament Prophets?" *Blue Letter Bible.* Accessed August 15, 2016. https://www.blueletterbible.org/faq/don_stewart/don_stewart_389.cfm.

Story, Dan. *Defending Your Faith.* Grand Rapids, MI: Kregel Publications, 1997.

Strong, A. H. *Systematic Theology.* Philadelphia, PA: American Baptist Publication Society, 1907.

Strong, J. *Enhanced Strong's Lexicon.* Woodside Bible Fellowship, 1995.

Tanner, Jerald, and Sandra. *3,913 Changes in the Book of Mormon.* Salt Lake City, UT: Utah Lighthouse Ministry.

Tanner, Jerald, and Sandra. *Major Problems of Mormonism.* Salt Lake City, UT: Utah Lighthouse Ministry, 1989.

Tanner, Sandra. *41 Unique Teachings of the LDS Church.* Salt Lake City, UT: Utah Lighthouse Ministry, 2012.

The Church of Jesus Christ of Latter-day Saints. *The Book of Mormon.* Salt Lake City, Utah: 2013.

The Church of Jesus Christ of Latter-day Saints. "Doctrine and Covenants Section 130." Accessed June 12, 2016. https://www.lds.org/scriptures/dc-testament/dc/130?lang=eng.

The Church of Jesus Christ of Latter-day Saints. "Apostle." Accessed October 15, 2016. https://www.lds.org/topics/apostle?lang=eng.

The Church of Jesus Christ of Latter-day Saints. "Guide to the Scriptures." Accessed March 19, 2017, https://www.lds.org/scriptures/gs/moroni-son-of-mormon?lang=eng.

The Church of Jesus Christ of Latter-day Saints. "Guide to the Scriptures." Accessed March 19, 2017, https://www.lds.org/scriptures/gs/moroni-son-of-mormon?lang=eng.

The Church of Jesus Christ of Latter-day Saints. "Moroni, Son of Mormon." Accessed March 19, 2017, https://www.lds.org/scriptures/gs/moroni-son-of-mormon?lang=eng.

The Church of Jesus Christ of Latter-day Saints. "Moroni and His Captains: Men of Peace in a Time of War." Accessed March 19, 2017, https://www.lds.org/ensign/1977/09/moroni-and-his-captains-men-of-peace-in-a-time-of-war?lang=eng.

The Church of Jesus Christ of Latter-day Saints. "A Brief Explanation about the Book of Mormon." Accessed March 19, 2017. https://www.lds.org/scriptures/bofm/explanation?lang=eng.

The Church of Jesus Christ of Latter-day Saints. "The First Book of Nephi." Accessed March 19, 2017. https://www.lds.org/scriptures/bofm/1-ne/1?lang=eng.

The Church of Jesus Christ of Latter-day Saints. "Book of Mormon Historic Publication Site." Accessed March 19, 201., https://history.lds.org/article/historic-sites-new-york-book-of-mormon-publication-site-palmyra?lang=eng.

The Church of Jesus Christ of Latter-day Saints. "Chapter 6: The Mission of John the Baptist." Accessed March 19, 2017, https://www.lds.org/manual/teachings-joseph-smith/chapter-6?lang=eng.

The Church of Jesus Christ of Latter-day Saints. "The Restoration of the Aaronic and Melchizedek Priesthoods." Accessed March 19, 2017, https://www.lds.org/ensign/1996/12/the-restoration-of-the-aaronic-and-melchizedek-priesthoods?lang=eng.

The Church of Jesus Christ of Latter-day Saints. "Carthage Jail." Accessed March 19, 2017, https://history.lds.org/article/historic-sites-illinois-carthage-jail-carthage?lang=eng.

The Church of Jesus Christ of Latter-day Saints. "The Joseph Smith Translation: "Plain and Precious Things Restored." Accessed March 19, 2017, https://www.lds.org/ensign/1997/08/the-joseph-smith-translation-plain-and-precious-things-restored?lang=eng.

The Church of Jesus Christ of Latter-day Saints. "Mother in Heaven." Accessed January March 15, 2017, https://www.lds.org/topics/mother-in-heaven?lang=eng&old=true.

The Church of Jesus Christ of Latter-day Saints. "The Contributions of Martin Harris." Accessed March 19, 2017, https://history.lds.org/article/doctrine-and-covenants-martin-harris?lang=eng.

The Church of Jesus Christ of Latter-day Saints. "How We Got the Book of Moses," accessed January 29, 2017, https://www.lds.org/ensign/1986/01/how-we-got-the-book-of-moses?lang=eng.

The Church of Jesus Christ of Latter-day Saints. "Jaredites." Accessed March 19, 2017, http://eom.byu.edu/index.php/Jaredites.

The Church of Jesus Christ of Latter-day Saints. "Chapter 49: Mormon and His Teachings." Accessed March 19, 2017, https://www.lds.org/manual/book-of-mormon-stories/chapter-49-mormon-and-his-teachings?lang=eng.

The Church of Jesus Christ of Latter-day Saints. "Joseph Smith-History." Accessed January 29, 2017, https://www.lds.org/scriptures/pgp/js-h/1.5-20?lang=eng#4.

The Church of Jesus Christ of Latter-day Saints "Joseph the Seer." Accessed March 19, 2017, https://www.lds.org/ensign/2015/10/joseph-the-seer?lang=eng.

The Church of Jesus Christ of Latter-day Saints
"Significant Events." Accessed March 19, 2017. https://www.lds.org/churchhistory/presidents/controllers/potcController.jsp?leader=1&topic=events.

The Church of Jesus Christ of Latter-day Saints. "Book of Mormon Translation." Accessed March 19, 2017, https://www.lds.org/topics/book-of-mormon-translation?lang=eng&old=true.

The Church of Jesus Christ of Latter-day Saints. "Prophets." Accessed on August 15, 2016. https://www.lds.org/topics/prophets?lang=eng.

The Church of Jesus Christ of Latter-day Saints. "Baptisms for the Dead." Accessed August 19, 2016. https://www.lds.org/topics/baptisms-for-the-dead?lang=eng.

The Church of Jesus Christ of Latter-day Saints. "The Postmortal Spirit World." Accessed August 19, 2016. https://www.lds.org/manual/gospel-principles/chapter-41-the-postmortal-spirit-world?lang=eng.

The Church of Jesus Christ of Latter-Day Saints. "1 Nephi 13:30-31." Accessed July 23, 2016. https://www.lds.org/scriptures/bofm/1-ne/13.30-31?lang=eng.

The Church of Jesus Christ of Latter-day Saints. "Doctrines of the Gospel of the Student Manual, 2000, 9-10. Chapter 4: Jesus Christ, the Son of God." Accessed on June 27, 2016. https://www.lds.org/manual/doctrines-of-the-gospel-student-manual/chapter-4-jesus-christ-the-son-of-god?lang=eng.

The Church of Jesus Christ of Latter-day Saints. "Book of Mormon Translation." Accessed July 30, 2016. https://www.lds.org/topics/book-of-mormon-translation?lang=eng.

The Church of Jesus Christ of Latter-day Saints. "The Guide to the Scriptures." Accessed April 25, 2016. https://www.lds.org/scriptures/gs/prophet.

The Church of Jesus Christ of Latter-day Saints. "Articles of Faith 1:3." Accessed June 27, 2016. https://www.lds.org/scriptures/pgp/a-of-f/1.3?lang=eng.

The Church of Jesus Christ of Latter-day Saints. "Hell." Accessed June 27, 2016. https://www.lds.org/scriptures/gs/hell.

The Church of Jesus Christ of Latter-day Saints. "Introduction." Accessed July 22, 2016. https://www.lds.org/scriptures/dc-testament/introduction?lang=eng.

The Church of Jesus Christ of Latter-day Saints. "Introduction." Accessed March 19, 2017. https://www.lds.org/scriptures/pgp/introduction. html?lang=eng.

The Church of Jesus Christ of Latter-day Saints. "Doctrines of the Gospel Student Manual Chapter 6: Our Premortal Life." Doctrines of the Gospel Student Manual Chapter 6: Our Premortal Life." Accessed June 28, 2016. https://www.lds.org/manual/doctrines-of-the-gospel-student-manual/ chapter-6-our-premortal-life?lang=eng.

The Church of Jesus Christ of Latter-day Saints. "Becoming Like God." Accessed July 27, 2016. https://www.lds.org/topics/becoming-like- god?lang=eng.

The Church of Jesus Christ of Latter-day Saints. *Gospel Principles.* Salt Lake City, UT: Church of Jesus Christ of Latter-day Saints, 1992.

The Church of Jesus Christ of Latter-day Saints. "Plural Marriage in Kirtland and Nauvoo." Accessed July 26, 2016. https://www.lds.org/topics/plural- marriage-in-kirtland-and-nauvoo?lang=eng.

The Church of Jesus Christ of Latter-day Saints. "The Manifesto and the End of Plural Marriage." Accessed July 26, 2016. https://www.lds.org/topics/ the-manifesto-and-the-end-of-plural-marriage?lang=eng.

The Church of Jesus Christ of Latter-day Saints. "First Vision Accounts." Accessed July 30, 2016. https://www.lds.org/topics/first-vision- accounts?lang=eng.

The Church of Jesus Christ of Latter-day Saints. "Translation and Historicity of the Book of Abraham." Accessed July 26, 2016. https://www.lds.org/topics/ translation-and-historicity-of-the-book-of-abraham?lang=eng.

The Church of Jesus Christ of Latter-day Saints. "Prophets and Apostles. We need living prophets." Accessed June 28, 2016. https://www. lds.org/prophets-and-apostles/unto-all-the-world/we-need-living- prophets?lang=eng.

The Church of Jesus Christ of Latter-day Saints. "Race and the Priesthood." Accessed July 31, 2016. https://www.lds.org/topics/race-and-the- priesthood?lang=eng.

The Church of Jesus Christ of Latter-day Saints. "A Prophet of God." Accessed April 25, 2016. https://www.mormon.org/beliefs/joseph-smith.

The Church of Jesus Christ of Latter-day Saints. *The Plan of Salvation*. Salt Lake City, Utah: Intellectual Reserve, 2008.

The Church of Jesus Christ of Latter-day Saints. "Chapter 2: Who Am I." Accessed March 15, 2017. https://www.lds.org/topics/race-and-the-priesthood?lang=eng.

The Church of Jesus Christ of Latter-day Saints. "Doctrines of the Gospel Student Manual." Accessed May 1, 2016. https://www.lds.org/manual/doctrines-of-the-gospel-student-manual/chapter-4-jesus-christ-the-son-of-god?lang=eng.

The Joseph Smith Papers. "History, circa Summer 1832, Page 1." Accessed June 21, 2016. http://www.josephsmithpapers.org.

The Watchtower. *The Nations Shall Know That I Am Jehovah—How?* Brooklyn, NY: Watch Tower Bible and Tract Society of New York, 1971.

The Watchtower. *Studies in the Scriptures Series VII—The Finished Mystery*. Brooklyn, NY: Watch Tower Bible and Tract Society of New York, 1917.

The Watchtower. *Is This Life All There Is?* Brooklyn, NY: Watch Tower Bible and Tract Society of New York, 1994.

The Watchtower. *Vindication 1*. Brooklyn, NY: Watch Tower Bible and Tract Society of New York, 1931.

The Watchtower. *Paradise Restored to Mankind by Theocracy*. Brooklyn, NY: Watch Tower Bible and Tract Society of New York, 1974.

"They Shall Know that A Prophet Was Among Them." The Watchtower, April 1, 1972. Brooklyn, NY: Watch Tower Bible and Tract Society of New York, April 1, 1972.

"Top 10 Most Read Magazines in The World," Trendingtopmost.com, March 12, 2017, http://www.trendingtopmost.com/worlds-popular-list-top-10/2017-2018-2019-2020-2021/entertainment/most-read-magazines-world-best-selling-famous-newspapers-cheapest-expensive/.

"True and False Prophets." The Watchtower, January 30, 1930. Brooklyn, NY: Watch Tower Bible and Tract Society of New York.

Utah Lighthouse Ministry. "False Prophecy." Accessed April 25,2016. http://utlm.org/onlinebooks/changech14.htm#418.

Utah Lighthouse Ministry. "An Address to All Believers in Christ." Accessed May 1, 2016. http://www.utlm.org/onlinebooks/address1.htm.

Wallace, J. Warner. *Cold-case Christianity: A Homicide Detective Investigates the Claims of the Gospels.* Colorado Springs, CO: David C. Cook, 2013.

Wallace, J. Warner. "How the Book of Abraham Exposes the False Nature of Mormonism | Cold Case Christianity." Accessed July 27, 2016. http://coldcasechristianity.com/2014/how-the-book-of-abraham-exposes-the-false-nature-of-mormonism/.

Wallace, J. Warner. "What Was the Shape Of Jesus' Cross? | Cold Case Christianity." Accessed March 5, 2017 at http://coldcasechristianity.com/2014/what-was-the-shape-of-jesus-cross/.

Walvoord, John F., and Roy B. Zuck. *The Bible Knowledge Commentary: An Exposition of the Scriptures.* Wheaton, IL: Victor Books, 1983.

Walvoord, John F. *The Holy Spirit: A Comprehensive Study of the Person and Work of the Holy Spirit.* Grand Rapids, MI: Zondervan, 1991.

Watchman.org. "Beware of False Prophets." Accessed May 1, 2016. http://www.watchman.org/articles/mormonism/beware-of-false-prophets/.

Watch Tower Bible and Tract Society of New York, Inc. *The Kingdom Interlinear Translation of the Greek Scriptures.* Brooklyn, NY: Watch Tower Bible and Tract Society of New York, 1985.

Watch Tower Bible and Tract Society of New York, Inc. *What Does the Bible Really Teach?* Brooklyn, NY: Watch Tower Bible and Tract Society of New York, 2013.

"*Where Are We According to God's Timetable.*" The Watchtower, May 1, 1967. Brooklyn, NY: Watch Tower Bible and Tract Society of New York.

White, James. R. *Is the Mormon My Brother?* Birmingham, AL: Solid Ground Christian Books, 1997.

White, James R. *The Forgotten Trinity.* Minneapolis, MN: Bethany House Publishers, 1998.

White, James. "What Really Happened at Nicea?" Equip.org. Accessed June 15, 2016. http://www.equip.org/PDF/DN206.pdf.

"*Work For The Anointed.*" *The Watchtower, January 1, 1923.* Brooklyn, NY: Watch Tower Bible and Tract Society of New York.

"*Working Hard for the Reward of Eternal Life.*" The Watchtower, August 15, 1972. Brooklyn, NY: Watch Tower Bible and Tract Society of New York.

Wuest, K. S. *Wuest's Word Studies from the Greek New Testament.* Grand Rapids: Eerdmans, 1997.

"*You Can Live Forever in Paradise on Earth—But How?*" The Watchtower, February 15, 1983. Brooklyn, NY: Watch Tower Bible and Tract Society of New York.

Young Brigham. "Self-Government—Mysteries—Etc., by Brigham Young. *Journal of Discourses*, Vol. 1, Pp. 46-53. Accessed May 1, 2016. http://jod.mrm.org/1/46.

Zion's Watch Tower and Herald of Christ's Presence. A Living Christ. Allegheny, PA: Tower Publishing, 1880.

Zion's Watch Tower and Herald of Christ's Presence. *Can It Be Delayed Until 1914?* Allegheny, PA: Tower Publishing Company, 1989.

Zion's Watch Tower and Herald of Christ's Presence. *Millennial Dawn: The Time Is at Hand.* Allegheny, PA: Tower Publishing Company, 1989.

Zodhiates, S. *The Complete Word Study Dictionary: New Testament (electronic ed.).* Chattanooga, TN: AMG Publishers, 2000.

SUBJECT INDEX

SCRIPTURE INDEX

Morgan James
Speakers Group

↗ www.TheMorganJamesSpeakersGroup.com

We connect Morgan James published authors with live and online events and audiences whom will benefit from their expertise.

CPSIA information can be obtained
at www.ICGtesting.com
Printed in the USA
LVOW10s0308060517

533470LV00002B/2/P

9 781683 504849